The Feminine and the Sacred

◆ ◆ ◆ ◆ ◆ ◆ ◆ ◆ ◆ ◆ ◆

EUROPEAN PERSPECTIVES

EUROPEAN PERSPECTIVES

A Series in Social Thought and Cultural Criticism

Lawrence D. Kritzman, Editor

European Perspectives presents outstanding books by leading European thinkers. With both classic and contemporary works, the series aims to shape the major intellectual controversies of our day and to facilitate the tasks of historical understanding.

For a complete list of books in the series, see page 191.

THE FEMININE
AND THE SACRED

Catherine Clément and Julia Kristeva

Translated by Jane Marie Todd

COLUMBIA UNIVERSITY PRESS
New York

COLUMBIA UNIVERSITY PRESS

Publishers Since 1893

New York   Chichester, West Sussex

Columbia University Press wishes to express its appreciation for
assistance given by the government of France through the Ministère de
la Culture in the preparation of this translation.

Le féminin et le sacré © 1998 Éditions Stock
Translation copyright © 2001 Columbia University Press
All rights reserved
Library of Congress Cataloging-in-Publication Data

Clément, Catherine
[Le féminin et le sacré. English]
The feminine and the sacred / Catherine Clément, Julia Kristeva;
translated by Jane Marie Todd.
p.   cm. — (European perspectives)
ISBN 0-231-11578-4 (cloth: alk. paper) —
ISBN 0-231-11579-2 (pbk.: alk. paper)
1. Clément, Catherine, 1939—Correspondence. 2. Kristeva, Julia, 1941—
Correspondence. 3. Women philosophers—Senegal—Correspondence.
4. Women novelists, French—Senegal—Correspondence. 5. Women
philosophers—France—Correspondence. 6. Women novelists, French—
France—Correspondence. 7. Women. 8. Holy, The. 9. Women and religion.
I. Kristeva, Julia, 1941– II. Title. III. Series.

B2430.C634 A4 2001
200'.82—dc21
00-052307

Casebound editions of Columbia University Press books
are printed on permanent and durable acid-free paper.
Designed by Lisa Hamm
Printed in the United States of America
c 10 9 8 7 6 5 4 3 2 1
p 10 9 8 7 6 5 4 3 2 1

Translator's Note

ALL QUOTED MATERIAL is my own translation, with the exception of biblical verses, which are from the King James Version, and the passage from Marina Warner's *Alone of All Her Sex,* which is taken from the original English-language edition.

The Feminine and the Sacred

✦ ✦ ✦ ✦ ✦

W̲E HAD KNOWN each other since the late 1960s, had shared similar interests in the human sciences, in philosophy, and in psychoanalysis as well as in politics. The experience of motherhood, of writing novels, and of nomadism had brought us even closer together, but the chance events of life always kept us apart: a mutual respect persisted, punctuated by brief encounters, warm or suspicious, and acquaintances in common. Very recently, Catherine wrote a sensitive response to my view of women's lives as a detective novel, an unfulfilled revolt, a latent atheism. For myself, I had liked her travels among Charcot's hysterics or through the religions of India, her passionate female characters, the way she was tuned in to cultural and social events.

As for me, I liked Julia's rigor, her precision, the vast store of knowledge judiciously dispensed; I also liked her imagination, her black humor, the musicality of her language, the savagery of her novels. A day came when the long association revealed its friendly face, a day when the collaborative work gently took hold. Like this.

IN A PERSONAL and professional trajectory, there comes a time when you want to pursue the essential thing, within the shelter of solitude and without the strictures of the group. Sometimes, for a woman, it also happens that the essential thing appears to be what is shared with other women. Why, then, not try to do that jointly, between the two of us?

For myself, "that" could only be what had always preoccupied us, visible in our trajectories as intellectuals and novelists, on the edge of the unconscious and of the social tie, which the imminent end of the second millennium charged with burning relevance: the sacred. Not religion or its opposite, atheistic negation, but the experience that beliefs both shelter and exploit, at the crossroads of sexuality and thought, body and meaning, which women feel intensely but without being preoccupied by it and about which there remains much for them—for us—to say. Does a specifically feminine sacred exist? What place is there for women in that history dating from the birth of Jesus, what chance for them two thousand years after him? What about the feminine in Judaism, in Buddhism, in Confucianism, in Taoism, in Islam, in the animist religions of Africa and elsewhere? How is it understood or misunderstood, but also, what future, what prospects does it have? If, as we believe, it is true that women will awaken in the coming millennium, what can the profound meaning of that awakening, of that civilization, be?

It was Julia who proposed the "subject" to me, as one normally says in the case of a book. What a surprise! For many long years, I believed myself in the clutches of a lonely song that, from my essays to my novels, did not let me go, an obsessive personal little tune. And who turned out to be on the same path? Kristeva in person. I had not expected it. But as soon as it was proposed, I knew we would get along well, like violin and piano, soprano and mezzo. The choice of a book in two voices stems from chamber music; between us, the tacit agreement needed only a line of melody to exist.

"The awakening of women in the coming millennium." On this last point, I hesitated. But Julia was like that, a visionary. She convinced me. It was not easy. As a matter of fact, in eleven years of living abroad, I have seen women everywhere more advanced than they are in France. And everywhere I have seen them use the sacred with more intelligence than we do: in India, in Africa, and even in Austria, the beginning of the East. Other women have explained very well the causes of the French delay, the misogynous tradition of the French Revolution, the restrictions placed on girls' education, a false notion of republican equality: that's all well known by now. As for the sacred, that was another matter, to be handled with kid gloves. Feminine—for women only? What about men in all that? We were not about to start up the war between the sexes again! That wasn't my style or hers. So that was it, then—awakening civilization, the future.

THAT WAS A vast plan, as engaging as it was impossible to deal with. Unless we limited ourselves to raising questions rather than giving answers, to giving a rough sketch of the fields rather than fencing them in within definitions—beginning with the very themes of the debate, the "feminine" and the "sacred." Because we were living thousands of miles away from each other, working out this puzzle "live" was out of the question. We were left with correspondence. Nobody writes letters anymore, I said, taken aback. Oh yes, some people do,

Catherine maintained. An archaic genre? No, a space for precision. An artifice? Perhaps, but a place for sincerity as well. Why not try?

That's right. At first, Julia wanted nothing to do with correspondence. And yet, nothing is more up to date, since faxes and "e-mail" on the Internet are restoring the true essence of that ancient genre: writing to the other. And is not the fake interview the worst artifice—spoken, recorded into a tape recorder, transcribed right down to the "um, ums," duly erased, its style polished after the fact? No such escape routes. We thus corresponded in the very classical way, taking our time. It is not correct that time plays no part in the matter: in passing through space, it does its work.

FROM THE BEGINNING, our correspondence was true: everyday life occupied a place in it, and both women and the sacred had to submit to our very profane concerns. More than that, our correspondence helped us face them.

In a letter written to a woman friend, one cannot avoid telling of one's problems, great or small. We might have erased them upon rereading, but they allowed us to advance in our ideas, and that is why they have remained in their place, naturally. That is how we came to understand that real worries, though profane, have something to do with the sacred. We were no longer "outside," but "inside." That's life—in effect.

AND SO A book came into being, as happens with any writing that collects questions in order to shed light on them. But it is a book in two voices, on two themes, which ask only to find a particular resonance within every woman, within everyone. We would like it to be read in the spirit of trust and polemics that animated us throughout this journey.

Julia Kristeva
Catherine Clément

Dear Julia,

EVER SINCE YOU told me about the strange link between women and the sacred, I run into it at every turn, right here in Africa. Nothing surprising about that, you'll say, on the "dark continent" to which Freud compared femininity in general. But let me describe to you what I saw yesterday, since, as surprises go, it was really something . . .

There was a Catholic pilgrimage in honor of the black Virgin of a large town called Popenguine, about twenty miles from Dakar. Imagine a huge crowd on a raised strip of ground, barely shaded by a few spindly trees, facing a platform where the bishops of Senegal are celebrating a solemn mass together, under the authority of the cardinal of Dakar. It's noon, the sun is at its zenith, 104 degrees in the shade, indigo sky. We dignitaries are sheltered next to the altar. By my rough estimate, there are at least eighty thousand men, women, and children in the congregation.

The mass begins. All of a sudden, there's a shrieking from the crowd—a woman's voice. The medics rush in immediately, stretcher in hand, discover the source of the voice, firmly strap down the woman who's screaming, and disappear. "A nervous attack," I tell myself. But it happens all over again ten minutes later. And for the two hours of the ceremony, at regular intervals, there'd be a woman's screams, medics, stretcher, evacuation. Again and again. A strange, sacred phenomenon was breaking out at a religious ceremony. Is the mass sacred? No doubt. Nothing is lacking, not chasubles, or censers, or church choir. Why, then, do I have the impression that the screams of these women were introducing a form of the sacred that is different from that of a Catholic mass?

Nevertheless, the first aid workers knew the drill. They were obviously used to these screaming women, whom you could still hear in the distance, like a plaintive opera chorus; they were strapped down but they didn't stop screaming, one after the other, in canon. What exactly were they saying in the middle of the mass? What were these bound women expressing with their screaming?

The word came to me: *trance.* All the fallen screamers were black. In the assembly, I noticed many white-skinned nuns, who did not budge. But the African nuns did not budge either. The "stricken" ones were young African laywomen, often with children at their sides. No men, not even an adolescent boy. The cries were absolutely identical: same tessitura, same modulations. But what stunned me most was what the African man beside me—buttoned up tight in his suit and tie, a dignitary, since he was there with me—whispered in my ear.

"Hysterical fits," he declared. "It's not uncommon."

Damn, and I hadn't even asked him anything! So here was a member of the African elite giving the name *hysteria* to what I called a trance. He was thinking like a *toubab*, a word used to designate the white man in Africa. Perhaps because he was speaking to a European, he put himself in the skin of a black *toubab*, that is, a Westernized African. (Thus, in Senegal, some of President Senghor's adversaries called him the "black Toubab.") And that too is not uncommon in Africa, especially when the receiver of the message belongs to the nation that colonized the country. What name to choose? Trance or hysteria? After all, the word *trance* is no less Western than the other. . . . He's upset me, that man standing next to me. Now I'm completely lost.

The women are black and Catholic, they throw fits during a solemn mass in the sun. They were born on the coast of West Africa, the place where the first Portuguese colonizers and the first Muslim preachers arrived at the same time, in the fifteenth century. The introduction of Islam and African Catholicism dates from that era. But since Senegal is now 90 percent Muslim, Catholicism represents only a tiny portion of the population: the women who cried out belong to a religious minority. And what about animism from before the fifteenth century? Quite simply, it has remained everywhere.

All the monotheistic religions introduced into Africa have kept their animist past almost intact. Muslims worship both Allah and their spiritual leader, whether caliph or marabout; they invoke genies by chanting "Bismillah"; initiates are sprinkled with blood after a Christian baptism. None of that bothers anyone, and the jinns get along quite well with the one and only god. But, for the piercing cries stirred up by a mass, the word uttered by the officials refers to a Western pathology! Hysteria, don't you see, just like in Vienna at the end of the nineteenth century. . . . It seems clear to me that this is an ancient phenomenon, rebaptized in the language of the toubabs; and, in a country where the elites speak French perfectly, they can't possibly be unfamiliar with the word *trance* to designate such attacks. No, it's something else that my dignitary friend was expressing: denial, embarrassment. Hysteria would seem to be less disturbing than the trance, that great secret of Africa.

In Senegal, it's difficult to analyze what exactly connects these trances to animism, which has been repressed since the fifteenth century. The Serer in the coastal regions knew Marranos, Portuguese Jews, and Protestants; then Catholicism glazed everything over with a deep faith, but with hybrid modes of expression. Under the glaze, the African trance emerges. The trance, African? What am I saying? The trance is universal: it is found everywhere in the world! And yet, I cannot let go of the idea: African trance. Probably because I imagine a particular porousness in black women, I think I can make out a fulminating access to the sacred, similar to that of their African-Brazilian cousins during the candomblé ceremonies in Bahia: their bodies are totally uninhibited, their eyes rolled back, and, as in Popenguine, they have shaking fits.

Yet, once you get past appearances, it's a very different thing in Brazil. The trances of the candomblé are anticipated, expected. Under the influence of African gods duly named by the saints' calendar— Shango, Saint Jerome; Yemanja, the Virgin Mary; Ogun, Saint Antony—the possessed are guided by the "Father," the officiating voodoo priest. In Brazil, because of slavery, African rites have once more assumed the upper hand and the women in trances do little screaming, or it's the normal state of affairs. Here, in Popenguine, they are not "guided," they are strapped down. Those who break loose must be put in chains, whereas, in the candomblé, the "breaking loose" is contained in advance. A strange reversal of the chains of slavery. . . . In Bahia, the bond between the "Father" and the possessed is purely spiritual; in Popenguine, the bonds between the clergy and the screaming women are material, they're straps. Over there, in Bahia, Catholicism has bowed under the weight of Africa in exile; here, in Popenguine it doesn't quite know what to do with this sacred disorder from the past mounting a resistance on native soil. For lack of anything better, first aid workers limit the damage. With straps.

Let's move on. When I was living in India, I did not see any sacred disorder in the religious practices of middle-class Indian women, thoroughly "bound" by a century of British Puritan occupation, and also by their caste of origin. In the high castes of the Hindu social system, in fact, the body's porousness is not part of the code of good manners. Letting oneself go is out of the question. But, having seen the mass pilgrimages of Indian peasant women, who also break loose, I suspect that the trance and its porousness probably have something to do with the caste of origin. The caste of origin? Careful . . . Let's take a closer look.

A caste is a kind of file drawer into which the newborn individual is classified at birth and from which it cannot escape. The caste has nothing to do with "social class," that's certain. But it maintains a very close relationship with the old Marxist concept of "class origin," that mental file drawer that determines the drives and thoughts from birth. For Marx, you can obviously change your social class, but you cannot rid yourself of your "class origin" any more than, according to Sigmund Freud, you can rid yourself of the unconscious. That being the case, the "caste" of origin plays the same role as the return of the repressed: the slightest opening and it comes out. Impossible to get rid of it. A little emotion and it reappears. It takes a very disciplined setting to be able to contain the return of your origins. . . . That's why, in India, the high castes, bound by the strict manners of Hinduism, are capable of resisting the trance; and that's why, in Popenguine, the African nuns, "bound" by the training of their order, did not yield to it, any more than the wives of the dignitaries on the podium. The women who screamed were Serer women, villagers or servants.

They are minorities and servants, and they fall into a trance. Well, no need to go to Africa to observe that phenomenon. I remember seeing, in Paris in the 1960s, a true "hysterical" fit at Sainte-Anne Hospital, unintentionally set off by Dr. André Green, chief physician at the time. That day, the young woman, who was from Brittany, pulled out all the stops: a stunning feat of hysterical acrobatics, perfectly executed, her head and feet holding up her stiff body, curved into an arc, her mind gone, her eyes far away, without a care, uninhibited. The good doctor's comment: "You don't see this archaic phenomenon anymore, except in illiterate Breton women when they come to town via the Gare Montparnasse." There was no need to explain why illiterate Breton women were arriving in Paris: it was well known at the time that they came to be "placed" as domestic servants.

In the nineteenth century, during Charcot's and Freud's time, middle-class European women still had acrobatics in their hysterical repertoire. Partly because of education, the opisthotonos—that's the scientific term for the arced figure—retreated to the countryside; it has probably disappeared by now. But, in the 1960s, illiterate Breton women still possessed that archaic art of the acrobatic trance: the culture shock of the city made them lose consciousness and caused that brutal somatization. Such was precisely the case of that young woman in 1964. But we were at the psychiatric hospital, where the sacred has no place. When she came to, the Breton woman was said to have had a hysterical fit, and neither she nor the doctors knew exactly what to do about it. In psychiatry, no one knows how to deal with a "secular" trance; and, since the sacred is not among the classifications, it is declared an opisthotonos. That's a technical term, and a bluff. A lot of good it did her, that Breton women arriving at the Gare Montparnasse. Elsewhere, she might have used her gift for the trance to religious ends; perhaps she might have attained the status of a visionary. But she was a patient in the emergency ward of a psychiatric hospital in Paris. There you have it.

To tell the truth, I'm more certain about class origins than about the porousness of the body, your field. Not that I'm all that knowledgeable about social class! But through travels and extended stays all over the world, everywhere I have seen women in the grip of the sacred. The fact is, I've rarely seen it when they knew how to read and write, except as a kind of trendiness, like the European women so taken with the primal scream American style. Even today, in Senegal, women rarely venture far from the traditional family, and national education is deteriorating. Is it for that reason that Senegalese women display a kind of "porousness"? In this country, which has become largely illiterate, majestic African women saunter through the streets with an ostentatiously sexual gait, their *boubous* slipping off their shoulders. The porousness of these six-foot-four-inch goddesses literally leaves something to be desired.

That is not really the case for my screamers in Popenguine. There is nothing majestic about them; on the contrary, their appearance is insignificant. I told you they were villagers or servants. That's not insignificant. In Africa, what is so easily called an "ethnic group" also depends on the caste system—very concealed but still extremely present—as well as on social roles. Serer women from the Popenguine region are often placed as "maids" in the capital, in middle-class homes in the big city. In Dakar, a "maid" (*sic*)[1] is Serer, just as a maid was Breton in Paris in the early part of this century. There is even a union of

---

1. *Bonne,* the French term for "maid," can also mean "good woman"—Trans.

Serer maids. In plain language, they are some of the most exploited women in the Senegal metropolis.

From that I infer, perhaps a bit hastily, that they achieve a trance state more easily than their mistresses. Yes, I think that the capacity to accede violently to the sacred truly depends on one's minority status or on economic exploitation. "Id"[2] must find an out somewhere, and, in the absence of education, that place of expulsion is the sacred. Or crime. Or both—that's been known to happen. Do you remember the violent fit observed in Le Mans in the 1930s, when the two Papin sisters, excellent servants, fine in every respect, knocked off their employers, a mother and a daughter, one stormy night? They dismembered them in a raptus, or, in other words, in a trance. They were exhausted after the crime and showed no remorse, like the murderous heroines of Greek tragedy overcome by passion. Supposedly, as they carefully cleaned their carving knives, they simply said, "What a fine mess this is." The Papin sisters were also good maids.

But, after all, to be a "good maid" in other people's homes gives rise to revolt, and the trance is one form of that. There's good reason to turn nasty when you're enslaved. There's good reason to take advantage of a mass to scream at the top of your lungs if you're a peasant or servant woman, a Catholic and a Serer in Senegal. You don't belong to the Muslim majority, you're not one of the powerful. And then, too, you're not the sex that rules the nation. In short, you're right to rebel, and the setting of a solemn mass does the trick. Through the sacredness of a monotheistic rite, another form of the sacred, the ancient form, slips in. Choirs, incense, gold on the chasubles, glitter, the sun at its zenith, a little black Virgin placed at the base of the altar, and, all of a sudden, the breach . . . It's come out. Who will stand in its way? Not the straps or the clergy. The cry is irresistible, and that's what it's made for.

Let me propose a first pathway to you, one effaced by the centuries. The sacred among women may express an instantaneous revolt that passes through the body and cries out. Now it's your turn to shed some light on porousness.

Catherine

---

2. When placed in quotations marks in the original French, *ça*, both "that" and the psychoanalytic "id," is translated as "id."—Trans.

Dear Catherine,

YOUR LETTER WAS waiting for me in Paris for over two weeks, while I was rediscovering the hustle and bustle, and the brutality, of New York. I always have trouble landing in France, the unpleasantness of the time change is combined with the increasingly painful impression that the French are *sulking*: sulking over history, which, to be sure, is no bed of roses, but which is actually unfolding elsewhere. . . . In fact, what remains of a nation in the "United States of the World"? That's an extremely grave question, but it is not the subject of our correspondence. . . .

You mention the black women who scream in a crowd of eighty thousand people in Senegal, around a statue of the Virgin; joyful libertines transformed by screams into possessed women; the porousness of their bodies; the efficient indifference of the nuns and medics, who are blasé about that ostentatious sensuality transformed into a hysterical fit, and the "psychiatric" diagnosis of a distinguished Senegalese.

As for me, I still have a vision of American "Africanness" before me. With every trip, New York seems more black and more ethnically mixed. But, curiously, it's the female bodies—often so heavy and awkward—that give that mutant humanity its most reassuring—appeased, even—aspect of indelible serenity. They are not in a trance at all, these black ladies who manage the store racks, the department offices of universities, the branch offices of banks, and even, sometimes, the panels at symposiums and other televised or cultural events. Whereas their husbands and sons always seem about to get worked up, when they do not openly manifest their violence in the guise of personal or political demands—and we both know there is plenty to be done in America, especially when you are black—these dark matrons display professional competence and unfailingly solid nerves. That has nothing to do with the feverish agitation of emancipated women who, even a few years ago, believed they were liberating themselves by becoming more like men. The ones I saw this time behave like ordinary mothers, and proud to be so, women who quite simply speak up, and, just as simply, conduct the affairs of the city. Whether it is professionalism or indifference, they indicate to us that they have the time—that they have their whole lives ahead of them.

That is another dimension of the sacred: self-assurance here and now, which comes from the assurance that one has time. Not the fear of castration, in which man dresses up his fear of death, to the point of making the latter the sleepless lookout and ultimate support of the sacred; not the catastrophe of mourning, which women know in the flesh and which makes them eternal hired mourners, with or without dead bodies—I'll tell you another time about the sources of that uncontrollable female melancholia. No. That attitude, so serene that one hesitates to link it to the sacred—the word *sacred* has a melodramatic or "hysterical" resonance, as the learned man standing next to you on the platform of dignitaries would say—is rooted in a certainty about life. There is life and women can give it: *we* can give it. Hence time is transformed into an eternity of miraculous instants. Some women do it with more or less desire, pain, joy, or suffering, and even manage to communicate its meaning. The meaning of the most modest, the most nondescript life. With a gesture of humility, a smile, the feeling of effectiveness, of patience, of tomorrow is transmitted. Those bodies have the opaque charm of terra cotta, the warm resistance of bronze, the wherewithal to sing Negro spirituals, but also to lead a country—gently.

I began with American Africanness and I hasten to reassure you: I despise the "politically correct," I do not preach the future of the black woman, as opposed to the impasse of the black man, nor even woman's superiority to man, and even less the black goddess's superiority to the hysterical white woman—on that last point, the "soap operas" produced in the U.S., now consumed by everyone who's tuned in, do not spare either of the sexes, or any ethnic group, even though the middle-class white woman seems to be a good length ahead of her black sister in acting out nervous attacks and using emotional blackmail as a means of financial manipulation. . . . No, I will cling to life as the ultimate visage of the sacred. First, because that was one of the purposes of my trip: to present "Hannah Arendt and the Concept of 'Life' " to the New School; and, second, because, no doubt haunted by my subject, I saw my intuitions confirmed in the theater of everyday life. These black, Hispanic, and Chinese women who give the American metropolis the cosmopolitan face of the third millennium, impose, in counterpoint to the anxious and hectic poverty, the image of an imperturbable and even sensual verticality.

Since "life" has become the safety valve in our advanced democracies—Christian or post-Christian, as you like—we forget that this sacredness of life has a history; and that this history depends on the place that religions and societies have granted to women. I would like us to return to the Virgin some day—she is deeroticized, it is said, perhaps too hastily, but surely she is not without a body—and to that extraordinary balancing act between, on the one hand, the cult of birth that Mary, the mother of God, set in place, and, on the other, the "control of the birth rate" (as it is now called), which she may have allowed to be set in place!

But let us stay within the modern age: it is also too quickly forgotten that the two forms of totalitarianism, Nazi and Stalinist, have in common the monstrosity of the camps, that is, nothing other than the destruction of life. Moreover, the technological progress of our advanced democracies, which has the ambition simply to "manage" life in complete innocence, is laden with the same totalitarian threat: the threat of destroying life after having devalued the question of its meaning.

What about women in all that? The freedoms we acquired thanks to contraception and artificial insemination do not keep the desire for motherhood from being and continuing to be the wave bearing aloft the female experience. Nor do they keep the future of the species from depending and continuing to depend on that desire, if we do not wish technology to be the only one to "manage" our destinies. Love between the sexes and the tenderness of both parents, male and female, will continue to be a shelter to the child's psychic life—its life period—to the life of the eternal child we all are. That life, desired and governed by a loving mother, is not a biological process pure and simple: I am speaking of the meaning of life—of a life that has meaning. We stand here at the "zero degree" of meaning, to borrow the expression of Barthes, whose irony and love philosophy I have not forgotten. What if what we call the "sacred" were the celebration of a mystery, the mystery of the emergence of meaning?

Along with the Greeks, Hannah Arendt distinguished between *zōō* (biological life) and *bios* (the life to be told, capable of being written). Since, thanks to technology, women are more likely than ever to decide about life, they are also more ready than ever not to be simply genitors (supposing that being a "genitor" is something "simple"), but to *give meaning* to the *act of giving* that is life.

That does not go without saying. It is very possible that a society dominated by technology and profit may reduce women to being merely the possessors of "zoological" life and will not in any way favor the inquiry or spiritual restlessness that constitutes a "destiny," a "biography." When I proposed this exchange regarding "women and the sacred," I particularly had that danger in mind: the new version of "soft" totalitarianism that, after the famous "loss of values," erects life as the "supreme value," but life for itself, life without questions, with wives-and-mothers supposed to be the natural executors of that "zoology."

Nevertheless, the penetration of the feminine into every continent, of which I gave you an everyday picture in New York, leaves the question open. What if the ancestral division between "those who give life" (women) and "those who give meaning" (men) were in the process of disappearing? What do you think? It would be a radical upheaval, never before seen. Sufficient to herald a new era of the sacred, in fact, which might well be the surprise of this third millennium. After two thousand years of world history dominated by the sacredness of the Baby Jesus, might women be in a position to give a different coloration to the ultimate sacred, the miracle of human life: not life for itself, but life bearing meaning, for the formulation of which women are called upon to offer their desire and their words?

I am not forgetting the porousness of the body in a trance. Even the placid madonnas I ran across in the cosmopolitan streets of New York, even the most sensible mothers, who know how to speak of their womanly desires and of their maternal tenderness, are not safe from "possession." I let myself be dazzled by the delicious language of the oyster women on my Ile de Ré, where you know I have now set down roots—as if one could set down roots in a land of salt marshes or fjords—but I know that language goes hand in hand with an irritable melancholia. So many meaty bits of language with which they saturate their children, abruptly interrupted by cries of rage, when not by suicide or murder! Where is the sacred? I propose no definition to you; you know more than I do about anthropology, philosophy, psychoanalysis, and all the rest. Simply put, given the waters we are in now, between the Virgin and her "stricken," the time of absence, serenity, and the loss of self, I claim that what comes back to us as "sacred" in the experience of a woman is the impossible and nevertheless sustained connection between life and meaning.

The human body, and, even more dramatically, the body of a woman, is a strange intersection between *zōō* and *bios,* physiology and narration, genetics and biography. Freud drew the map of that cleavage, adding the stages of the unconscious, the preconscious, and the conscious to the biological reservoir. Language moves about in those stages but cannot be reduced to them: a borderline separates it from biological excitation.

The prohibition sets in place and reinforces that borderline: "Thou shalt not kill [thy father]," "Thou shalt not commit adultery [with thy mother]." A prohibition on murder and incest, it is experienced by the soma as an act of violence. The Jewish God said it just right, as it had never been said before, something for which he continues to be criticized. The prohibition "cuts": *bereshit* is the first word of the Bible. All religions, using the trenchant effects of language in various and less conscious ways, celebrate the sacred as a sacrifice: that of a plant, an animal, or a man. Judaism, and then Christianity, admit that this sacrifice is the one that inscribes language in the body, meaning in life. And it does so through a prohibition that does not need to kill to cut, but confines itself to setting out a moral system. A *sacré* moral system, laden with revolts and passions.[3]

The devotees of the sacred are careful not to emphasize the violence that this sacredness or sacrifice or prohibition conceals and imposes. Only the "divine marquis" de Sade drew the hyperbolic consequences—now called sadomasochistic—of our condition as biological-and-speaking beings; but his bald truths are bothersome when they are not frightening.

And yet, since woman speaks, she is subject to the same sacrifice: her excitability falls under the prohibition; the *jouissance* of her reproductive body is expressed in the representation of a word, an image, or a statue.[4] Nevertheless, the sacrifice does not manage to impose itself as an absolute, capable of subduing all passion and of leaving nothing behind. In addition, the representations themselves—hymns, words, sculptures—do not remain in their place of representation but plunge back into the flesh, which is not quite so sacrificed after all, allowing it to resonate, in jouissance. The sadomasochism of the sacred connection (body/meaning) seems more obvious to a woman, more operative in a woman. She is there, she is "in step," she manifests it. In a trance. Woman, a being on the borderline, biology *and* meaning, is likely to participate in both sides of the sacred: in calm appeasement, where na-

---

3. *Sacré,* which normally means "sacred," can also be used as an expletive equivalent to "damned," "blasted," or "bloody," especially when it precedes the noun. I have retained the French term in such cases to indicate the dual reading possible. The adverbial form, *sacrément,* is similarly ambivalent.—Trans.

4. *Jouissance,* a term with a very weighty past in French psychoanalytic and feminist theory, signifies extreme pleasure, including sexual pleasure and even orgasm, to the point of losing control or consciousness.—Trans.

tivity finds assurance in eternity (my New York women who run the city) but also in the rending of the sacred cloth, where language and all representation are lost in a spasm or delirium (your Senegalese women in trances). Whether she is serene or breaking loose, a women is, by reason of that dual nature, on equal footing with the sacred, and, at the same time, she is its most relentless adversary—a potential atheist.

"The horizon of Being is porous," wrote Husserl, as quoted by Merleau-Ponty: he was suggesting the oozing of sensations irreducible to language itself. A woman—with or without the trance—is the daily demonstration of that more or less catastrophic or delicious distillation of flesh within the mind, and vice versa. The psychoanalysts will say that woman, who is capable of giving life, is a subject, to be sure, but a subject whose repression remains very problematic. Rather, she is subject to generalized vapors. In *The Flowers of Evil,* Baudelaire speaks, in more elegant terms, of perfumes: "The tyrannical Circe with dangerous perfumes"; and "There are strong perfumes for which all matter is porous. It is as if they penetrate glass."

There you are. I propose *perfume* as a figure for that problematic repression, that troubling porousness of women. The "glass" of repression does not withstand the pressure of an internal reality: the female ego (like the Baudelairean ego?) is "vaporous." As you can see, I link the fate of female eroticism to the fate of motherhood: even though they are two perfectly distinct sides of the female experience; in any case, the vaginal body, that dwelling place of the species, imposes on woman an experience of the "interior," of "internal reality," that does not allow itself be easily *sacrificed* by the prohibition, or represented by the codes resulting from the prohibition (language, images, thought, and so on). Whether mistress or mother, a woman remains a stranger to the sacrifice: she participates in it, she assumes it, but she disrupts it, she can also threaten it. It is therefore understandable how that vital *depth* also constitutes a *social* danger: in fact, what moral system, what ethics, could exist if the sacred had to face the assaults of screaming women with their endogenous animism?

But there is woman, and then there is woman, and since I would no more want to give you a picture of the universe in black and white dominoes than one in psychiatric structures (hysterical, psychotic, and so on), I will speak to you later about particular case histories, on the sacred as my women patients—and my novel characters—encounter it, or not.

I know you are perfectly well acquainted with all these things I write about in the rough, thrown-together form of the letter. I wonder whether this genre suits the fast pace of our lives and the complexity of the subject. Still, for the moment I want to continue these epistolary exchanges, which also sometimes give me the feeling that I am situating myself before and after an effort. Before and after the emergence of an impression or a thought, even as I give its innocence back to it, in a mood of relaxation and almost of joy, with the sole concern to make my moments coincide with your expectations, but without the requirement of exactitude. A hesitation, in short, that wagers on what is to come. Which, after all, is perhaps the essential thing in friendship.

Julia

◆ ◆

Dakar
JANUARY 7, 1997

Dear Julia,

YOUR LETTER UPON your return from New York fell down on me like the rain from a monsoon. I opened my umbrella and began to sort out the seeds.

The African American women whose calm solidity you admired in New York are, in fact, the worthy sisters of the Senegalese women. But what a difference in their situation! Clearly, your peaceful American women are not living in poverty. Moreover, in North America, there is no matriarchy on the horizon, whereas, in Sahelian Africa, societies live in family groups under the sole authority of the father. Worse, despite the legal choice possible between monogamy and polygamy, polygamy is gaining ground among the young, for all social backgrounds combined. In addition, certain marabouts are allowed to practice unlimited polygamy, with thirty or forty wives, a harem, so to speak. The prescriptions of Muhammad have been shattered, and these marabouts, as enterprising in capitalist businesses as in the capitalization of legitimate wives, adopt the pre-Islamic traditions without encountering any resistance. It's a long way from New York, and yet . . .

How is it, then, that the Senegalese women resemble the New York black women to such a degree? Obviously, one must dig deeper into what is "of Africa." Why? Because women possess particular functions there, which stem from the sacred above all. For example, the city of Dakar is surrounded by a tiny people, the Lébou fishermen. Now, since the dawn of time, when the fisherman returns to the pier, he must give the fish to his wife, the only one entitled to sell it; along the way, she will take her tithe, her own money, which is called "sacred." It is also the Lébous who practice a spectacular therapeutic rite, the N'Doeup, which is very much in force in the outlying regions.

The ceremony, designed to expel a vengeful genie from the body into which it has "descended," lasts seven days and seven nights. It includes infinitely sophisticated rituals for measuring the body, seances of public possession in the streets, and the sacrifice of a bull onto which the spirit of the genie has been transferred. Then, finally, the worship of the spirit is celebrated in a generalized trance. I attended the day of the preparation of the sacrifice—seven hours! I came away from it exhausted by the psychic tension of the group, which was led by the healer women. Yes, the N'Doeup therapy is reserved for women, brought together village by village into colleges of official healers. There is only one male healer today: and, to officiate, he must dress in women's clothing.

A man dressed as a woman in order to heal. This bald fact would require a flood of commentary on the bisexuality of therapists in general, but we will return to that later. For the moment, I prefer to point out the role of African women in the treatment of mental illnesses. As always in Africa, the operation consists of delicately transferring the "jinni"—genie—of a suffering body to a sacrificed animal, then to public worship, with a millet pestle planted into the ground, a statufied ancestor. Who "fixes" the roving genie? The healer. Who transfers? The healer. Who repairs the group damaged by the madness of one of its own? The healer. And how does one become a healer? A sole condition: one has to have been oneself possessed, and then to have recovered. The transformation is de rigueur. A woman healed by the N'Doeup has no right to sidestep her status as a healer; otherwise, she falls back into the clutches of her genie.

Imagine that all the women who have done time on the analyst's couch were obliged to become psychoanalysts: such is the situation among the Lébou women on the outskirts of Dakar. And the Lébou rite, far from disappearing, is gaining ground. Similarly, the Ethiopian ceremony of the *zar*, which functions in a similar way, with trances, and is also practiced by women, has now reached even the outskirts of Cairo! It's clear: when poverty invades the slums, the healers deal with it. The N'Doeup in Dakar, the candomblé in the poor neighborhoods of Bahia, the macumba in the favelas of Rio, the zar in Egypt, and, if we open the compass as wide as possible, Mother Teresa in Calcutta, Sister Emmanuelle in Cairo. . . . Others will be upset, but not I. I see that phenomenon as a good antidote to fundamentalism of every stripe. Modernist, masculine, and extremely technological, fundamentalism excludes women. It strikes me as an amusing ruse of reason that they should recover the power to heal by resorting to the archaism of the rite, and I like the fact that historical regression might stand in the way of the most well-spoken modernity.

Let's get back to New York. Whereas, in South America, Catholicism had no trouble integrating the African polytheism of the former deported slaves, in North America, Protestant upbringing has confined the expressiveness of bodies within the pigeonhole of slavery. Tom-toms, allowed relatively early by the masters in Brazil, were long prohibited in the United States, in favor of Christian hymns. The African Americans found sanctuary only by inventing the Negro spiritual, then the blues, and finally jazz. Choirs broke loose in Baptist and Pentecostal churches, which leaned more toward the spontaneous expression of faith than toward rigid supervision. Yet the Protestant trademark gives me an insight into the enterprising aspect of the African Americans you saw in New York: it is still true, in fact, that the Protestant countries do better at business than the Catholic ones.

And the African origin of these beautiful entrepreneurs gives me an insight into their calm. You are right: they look like givers of life, givers of time. All the same, is the difference between "those who give life" and "those who give meaning" really in the process of disappearing? I think you are an optimist. Look at the current epidemic of philosophy in France. The brilliant and charming "philosophers of the third kind" are all men, just like the *nouveaux philosophes* in 1978. The very celebrated "return to philosophy" cuts both ways: when the philosophers return, women are not among them. The French philosophical cafés have nothing in common with the salons of the Encyclopédistes, where women were true discussion partners in debates where morality played only a small role. . . . We do not stand in the open space of the Enlightenment, we are sinking back into the obscurantism of Balzac's aristocratic circles, to which the young duchesses of the Faubourg

Saint-Germain did not have access. At the time, the world of meaning was that of secret societies for men only. As for women, in Balzac they were old by the time they were thirty. Women did not "last." What was their role? To go off to passion as they go "off to the kitchen." Are you really sure they are now allowed to progress toward the giving of meaning? In politics, yes. But in the matter of thought, no.

You propose perfume as a metaphor for the porousness of women, as a symbol for their easy access to the trance. While you're at it, you remark that women assist in the sacrifice but do not make sacrifices. That's right. Such is the case of the N'Doeup: it is always a man who cuts the bull's throat; and, in fact, that is the only masculine gesture in the ceremony. In contrast, the very active women healers use their own secretions. The "baptism" of the genie, once it has been identified, is made official by the healer's saliva: she spits the name of the invader onto the possessed, through a wooden tube. She spits on the body of the bull when the genie agrees to be transferred to it. You will not be surprised that the ethnologists call that sacred operation the "vaporization" of the saliva. Now we are truly in the realm of perfume, even if it is spittle. Where, then, is the sacred? In the healer's mouth, doing duty as a vaporizer. Materialized by the stream of saliva, it becomes sacred through the rattle of the larynx, which forces it out the open lips of a priestess. It is up to her to sanctify what comes out of her body.

Perfume, a poetic word, too polite to be honest. In any case, the manufacture of perfume does not entail flower extracts alone, and musk is an animal secretion of genital origin; it all hangs together. Instead of "perfume," I propose secretion, humors, odors. I am thinking of what Freud said about them, in *Civilization and Its Discontents,* regarding the animal that goes from walking on all fours to standing up: when he stands erect, the ape-turned-man loses his sense of smell. Clearly, his sex organs have moved away from his nostrils. Only coitus, says Freud, gives the human being back the sense and taste of the sexual humors. For that, a "letting go" is needed, something not unrelated to the trance; and, as Professor Charcot would say, regarding the hysterical fits he called forth before the young Freud's eyes in Paris, "There is something genital in all that." Is that to say that sex is sacred? Not a sure thing. But let's reverse the terms: because it authorizes the brutal insurrection of the forbidden humors during ceremonies, the sacred is sexual.

Catherine

Dear Catherine,

WHETHER CHANCE OR necessity, I don't know—your stay in Dakar on the one hand, the fascination that Africa has exerted on ethnologists and writers for centuries on the other—but here we find ourselves fixed on a "sacred" that is increasingly "black"! Black women, black religions: our journey continues to link the three enigmas—the *feminine,* the *sacred,* and the various fates of *Africanness*—in a metaphor that becomes more substantial as we write, and which further complicates, if need be, what Freud in his time called the "dark"—that is, the black—continent. I envy you for being able to take part in those seven-hour rites, the N'Doeup therapies reserved for women who emerge from them as . . . healers. As for me, I got no further than . . . Raymond Roussel's *Impressions of Africa,* strange not ethnologically but in a personal way, *sacrément* demoniacal, unless it makes you die laughing. And, of course, the "possessions" described by Leiris, given that Marcel Griaule recruited him as his secretary-archivist and researcher, and given that, with the consent of his psychoanalyst, Adrien Borel, the author of *Manhood* spent two years, 1931–1933, in Dakar-Djibouti, and came back with *Afrique fantôme, Message d'Afrique,* and *La possession et ses aspects théâtraux* [Ghost Africa, Message from Africa, and Possession and its theatrical aspects]. Among the Ethiopians he describes, as in the ceremonies you observed, bisexuality and transvestism seem to dominate the possessions, and, apparently, wondrously feed the imaginary . . . African as well as European. Hence, Leiris relates a sacrifice of chickens—white, black, and red—during which a man, possessed by a feminine zar and rendered impotent, is made to eat the animal. In that way, the maleficent zar is transferred onto his sister, who, as a result, becomes a "horse" capable of bearing the evil spell better than her brother could have done, not to mention the fact that she can in turn practice sacrifices; all of which unfolds in a language reserved for ritual use within various confraternities. It seems that participation in these rites of totemic metamorphosis and transsexuality, and above all, in the art of recounting them, had a more cathartic effect on the subtle writer Leiris than did psychoanalysis. And he admits he is "sexually abnormal" because affected by "an enormous capacity for boredom." By the yardstick of boredom, which I find to be an absolute criterion, there would be a plethora of sexual anomalies throughout the world; but very few perspicacious travelers who allow themselves to be possessed and dispossessed of them.

Knowing nothing about the N'Doeup, I am nevertheless attracted to "possession," as you know, and have even devoted a meditation in the form of a novel to it—*Possessions*. A woman this time, but one who has absorbed, body and soul, a dead and adored brother, allows herself to be possessed by this double male, and by an unthinkable desire for revenge against their mother, against the Mother. In that case, the possession gives way to a depression, of which my heroine manages to dispossess herself only through a crime: the decapitation of the body of another woman. That was a sacré femininity I was allowed to see, on the analyst's couch but also in myself, and one that is not unaware of the trenchant aspect of sacrifice. On the contrary. As a matter of fact, perfume, or vapor/odor if you like, permeates the relation of women to the sacred—Mary Magdalene, who anoints the feet of Jesus with perfumed oil, is the consecrated figure for that—but it is nevertheless charged with a great deal of violence, and also attests to a sacré sense of unease.

To approach sacrificial and feminine things in a less serious vein, think of the fearsome Françoise, the servant of the narrator in Proust's *Remembrance of Things Past*: one of her favorite occupations (is it a reflection of her perception of the art of the writer, whom she adores with boundless devotion?) consisted of . . . cutting the throat of a chicken in the yard and crying ecstatically: "You nasty thing! You nasty thing!" Like my own grandmother. Now there's some voodoo close to home! As a more noble replica of that butchering cook, was not the lovely Oriane de Guermantes a cruel little girl who "kicked cats around, gouged out the eyes of rabbits"?

All that just to tell you that I am not avoiding Africanness, that I am very much interested in the things you have witnessed. Even though they come to me from far away, I am trying to understand them from the inside. A long time ago already, I chose my ethnological "field" by changing languages, choosing to reside in French and in France. I do not regret meeting that tribe, which has repaid me fairly well in curiosity and in kindness. All things considered. I even set about moving deeper into the inquiry, first on the analyst's couch, then by listening to people who do me the honor of confiding to me in the same situation. In short, it seems to me that psychoanalysis is a micro-anthropology of the depths, where ethnic and national boundaries become permeable (am I Bulgarian or French? Both? Neither?) and give way to our irremediable strangeness, so many singular possessions to be shifted about ad infinitum . . .

Those who undertake an analytical experience—in any case, with me—are rarely believers. Some have been, most are not at all, or, almost not at all. So I rarely hear people talk about God, and, when it happens, as you can imagine, my "free-floating attention" momentarily fastens, even crystallizes, on that word. I experience a hint of shame at the idea of that curiosity; might it prove that God has not completely abandoned me, as I have a tendency to believe ordinarily? That's the way it is.

Marianne, a dramatic young woman who has suffered from anorexia-bulimia, and who, after three years in analysis, is emerging from it more and more—though she has replaced the old alimentary suicide with passionately erotic and "killing" relations with two men—described her relations with her partners as follows: "A force beyond my power flattens me against the ground, it's God, there's no other word. He asks me for an implacable, relentless, unforgiving offering. An obligation to suffer. To go suffer everywhere, elsewhere, without love, always-botched love." I repeat: "God, botched love." Marianne: "I say 'God' because it is a force outside of me, impersonal, neither feminine nor masculine, a merciless firmness that makes the feminine and the masculine impossible. You see what I mean? [She always questions me—a complete waste of breath—when she knows perfectly well that I see what she means, and especially, that she doesn't know what sex she is.] But when you say 'botched love,' that makes me think of my mother: of the suffering I endured with her because she was sad after my father dumped her, and because she favored my brother. When I say God, I think of an absolute suffering, close to my mother, an ineluctable sorrow, to the point that, in the end, you become persuaded that it's normal, and even that it's sweet."

I am not quoting Marianne's words to tell you that, in women, the "divine" corresponds to their masochism: that side of things is not insignificant, but I prefer to come back to it later. I quote Marianne's words as a way of saying that what is experienced as "sacred" is a translation of eroticism into more noble terms. It is when she does not find the word for jouissance—strictly speaking, exorbitant, a sadomasochistic jouissance with partners who humiliate her or hurt her, but which she is the first to ask for, a jouissance that negates her, that "flattens her on the ground"—that Marianne uses the word *God,* which, however, has been no more than a very bland reference point from her Catholic upbringing, commonplace, all in all. It is the jouissance of sacrifice, desired and submitted to, that she calls "God." Georges Bataille wrote key pages on this subject: the internal experience is a transgression of sexual prohibitions in jouissance, on the threshold of self-annihilation, of consciousness, and often on the threshold of death. Paradoxically, in evoking the divine—the absolute of spirituality—we evoke journeys to the opposite limit, where the human sinks into animality and nothingness.

But I mention Marianne here for another reason. It is often believed, with Freud, that the benefit of religion consists of consoling man (and woman) by proposing, against narcissistic anxiety, an omnipotence: the omnipotence of the thaumaturgic gods, and of the One and Only God, who is, finally, a condensation of the father's powers. That view of things has its pertinence, and I do not in any way dispute it. Still, there would be a great deal to say about the need a woman can have for a father, but also of the distrust, the disbelief, the feeling of strangeness itself that a woman feels toward paternal "potency." That is another sacré subject to which we will have to return. Marianne, therefore, leads us farther: her "God" is . . . her dependence on her mother. A mother whom we are never sure loves us. There is nothing more powerful, more "divine" if you like, than *a love that does not give itself,* since that is what we depend on, absolutely. If you understand that a daughter is in osmosis with her mother, that daughter and mother do not have *secrets* from each other, that the depressed mother *transfuses* herself entirely into her daughter, while, all the same, forcing herself to *seduce* her son, well then, it's a good bet that Marianne has it right. That is, that an implacable maternal force, a "divine" omnipotence, very often dominates the female psyche. And that the strategies that help one to protect oneself against that "God" are not absolutely safe. In fact, how is one to go about it: avoid femininity? repudiate the maternal in oneself? immolate oneself using every means to satisfy that specter of omnipotence?

An analyst spoke to us recently about one of her patients, Clara, who, in her sessions, proclaims her early choice of atheism, thus opposing the Catholic religion, which was primarily that of her father. And yet, since the death of her mother, Clara again feels confused and needs to forge an ideal for herself. Whereas, previously, she criticized her mother, who "continued to oppress the whole family and to lay claim to the truth," Clara is suddenly beginning to idealize her, to the point that no one else is tolerable or lovable in her eyes, especially not . . . her husband. As a result, the sessions unfold in accordance with two contradictory discourses: an atheistic profession of faith on the one hand, a "religious" justification of the mother on the other. A cleavage has come about in Clara: on the one hand, she rejects (the father's) religion; on the other, she shelters her mourning in a far-from-dead idealization . . . of the dead woman, by means of which she tries to redeem herself for not loving her enough, and to restore to herself the "not sure at all" love she thinks her mother had for her.

Question: if the need for idealization is undying, since it consoles us of our frustrations, of our hardships, of our sacrifices, if it can concern the father, and, even more secretly, more slyly, the mother, does that mean that religion cannot be transcended?

Clara allows us to evoke a few figures—no longer private but very public—of contemporary atheism. Hence, when our debt toward our father and mother is not recognized or transcended, we can choose to deny it. As a result, we deny the religious ideal that replaces it and we celebrate in its place the omnipotence of thought; for example, that is the case for the intellectual Clara. It is not God who protects me, a suffering and impotent child, it is My Thought. Who could fail to recognize the benefit of such a choice, the roads of intellectual and professional success it opens? It remains true that the nonrecognition of that debt toward our parental ideals can fall back on us like a weight crushing our shoulders, and can place our intellectual successes, always provisional and fragile, in danger. Religious consolation does not resolve the question but conserves the utility—illusory, of course, but no less healing—of allowing us to "rely on someone."

In another way, many of us, still within that same tribe of Europeans, and more specifically of French people, which is my own tribe at present, have chosen, against the religion of our fathers, another "religion": that of communist atheism, as a counterweight to their childhood debts and ideals. No, I am not oversimplifying, I am not unaware that a host of reasons—and often very good reasons—have led men to subscribe to an ideology; I am speaking of the personal, of the microcosm. One need only read the critical writings of some of the old communists, including some of the most lucid of them, to observe that their atheism is described in religious terms: at issue is nothing less than the construction of an antireligion to take the place of the previous religion (often that of the parents), and which alienates the individual even more brutally than does the classic dogma. Edgar Morin,

Emmanuel Leroy Ladurie, Jean-Toussaint Desanti, and François Furet have noted these new beliefs, which they call "strange," "sacrifices of the intelligence," "blind submission" to the demands of the Party, which makes you "eat worms," that is, swallow anything. These are all metaphors with fundamentally sadomasochistic connotations, as my colleague Martine Bucchini has noted in a brief and clear study, which reveals that it is the shadow of a feared but idealized mother that lies concealed in a number of dissident beliefs, so long as they remain beliefs. Cf. Marianne, Clara.

Let us distinguish between belief and religion, on the one hand, and the sacred, on the other. I would like to propose the following schema to you, succinct, as is only right and proper. Belief and religion, as constructions, may be imaginary (as in Marianne or Clara), ideological (as in the atheistic communist believers), scientific (where one believes in the omnipotence of science): all these constructions deny sexual jouissance and the immature child's narcissistic dependency on its parents, but also our dependence on nature, biology, genetics. They propose figures of consolation and of healing omnipotence. In that sense, Freud is right in *The Future of an Illusion*: these illusory constructions—beliefs and religions—can gradually be transcended by science, but they always have a bright future in front of them; and it is only a certain modesty, a certain humility that, in time, can rid us of these illusions: "The critics persist in calling 'profoundly religious' any man who confesses the feeling of the insignificance of man and of human powerlessness in the face of the universe, even though it is not that feeling that constitutes the essence of religiosity, but rather the behavior that results, the reaction against that feeling, a reaction that seeks help to fight it. Anyone who does not take that step, who humbly acquiesces to the minimal role that man plays in the vast universe, is, in contrast, irreligious in the truest sense of the word."

I think, but I will tell you why another time, that a woman is more apt to agree "humbly" to play a "minimal role" in the vast universe: that a woman, finally, is less narcissistic than people say, and hence more . . . irreligious, in the Freudian sense to which I have just alluded.

Even so, the sacred may not be the same as the religious. Relax, I'm not going to launch into a definition of the sacred: theology, philosophy, anthropology, and all the rest have taken on that task. I shall give an approximate sketch so that I can continue with you to worry over the question of women and meaning. What if the sacred were the

unconscious perception the human being has of its untenable eroticism: always on the borderline between nature and culture, the ani-
malistic and the verbal, the sensible and the nameable? What if the sacred were not the religious *need* for protection and omnipotence that
institutions exploit but the jouissance of that *cleavage*—of that power/
powerlessness—of that exquisite lapse? This incompleteness is explored in metaphorical ceremonies, it is celebrated in sacrifices, it is
enjoyed while revisiting, in one's mind, childhood, dependence, or a
more or less strange, more or less "telling" word. Women might therefore be otherwise placed, even, I daresay, better placed, to stand on
that "roof" . . .

But why don't they talk about it? Never enough, and even less
today than a short time ago, you write. As a matter of fact, "they" do
not seem to want to rush to the philosophical cafés, or to the televised
debates, "they" do not really aspire to give meaning, "they" are content to give life. Even political life, "parity," and so on, interest only a
few of them passionately, you and I, the most "evolved," the most
masculine. . . . So, is that a regression in relation to the eighteenth
century? In relation to post-'68 feminism? In a sense, yes. But also,
perhaps, a difference that continues to carve out a place for itself and
which we ought to try to measure: what if "id" (that "roof") were not
absolutely demonstrable, visible, expressible? What if "id" could simply be felt, done, understood? "Id," the sacred. Of course, what I am
suggesting cannot fail to worry me as well, "rational" and "active" as
I am, and as you know me to be. In fact, does "id" exist if "id" does
not show itself, if "id" is not said? Not a sure thing. Personally, I en-
trust "id" to psychoanalysis, or to the novel. But that is surely not the
only path. Unless, when consciousness become conscious of that reserve, when the consciousness of women themselves becomes conscious of that reserve, we might be able to discover, in that "id," something like a resistance. A resistance to the Spectacle in which the
religion of the Word culminates. But how to let the Spectacle and the
Word know? In fact, is it worth the trouble of letting them know?
That is what leads me to open the dossier on the Christian female
mystics, for next time.

Love,
Julia

Dear Julia,

I'LL START AT the end of your last letter: with the "roof" of the sacred that you designate with the word *id,* like a drive. In reading those lines, I had an irresistible impulse; I thought, not "ox on the roof," but, instead, "cow on the roof." . . . And India, the land of sacred cows, fell on my head with its usual crash. It must be said that, between the sacrifice of the "ox" in Africa and Indian cows, I've been stewing among the cattle for nearly a decade.

Get along then, now! . . . Like the goddess Hathor in Egypt, the sacred cow in India is the envelope of the universe, since it is within the sewn skin of a cow that the first man was born. Male, that goes without saying. The cow is thus maternal and enveloping, granted. The Hindus draw the consequence: everything that falls from the cow is not only sacred but useful. They drink the milk, make butter for everyday, the same as that used to moisten the corpse during cremation; they eat the leftover curds, use the urine as an antiseptic floor cleanser, and the dung, compacted into briquettes and dried on the walls, as fuel. In Hinduism, the coherence goes so far as to compose the sacred drink par excellence from these five elements, dung included. . . . I have often been offered a taste, but I chickened out, I admit it. The curds and butter, the milk, fine, but as for the rest, no thanks, no, really. The Hindus, however, are perfectly logical, since, in the mother, everything is good. As you can see, the maternal component cannot exempt itself from secretions, however fetid they may be.

In that case, why the devil couldn't that "roof" of the world be expressed? Do not women in rebellion try to raise that roof, lift that lid? Did not Judith, the biblical heroine, perform the same act of decapitation as the character in your last novel? Are not war heroines constrained to raise the sacred "roof" of the world? It seems to me that the resistance to generalized communication can accommodate itself to a sort of public spectacle in the epic style, as Judith, Joan of Arc, Golda Meir, and Indira Gandhi have shown. "Strong" women, they say. "Masculine women"? No, despite breastplate, sword, dagger, terrorist bombs, or silk sari. Joan of Arc was judged, and burned, in a chemise. Not in breeches. When things get serious, the artifice that leads you to believe there is something of a man there disappears.

Do you really believe that women are capable of accepting more "humbly" the human race's modest role in the universe? Give a little thought to the founders of religious sects in India, where women are legion, and even to the founders of the monastic orders in Europe. In general, whether men or women, religious founders are "modest" only in appearance; or rather, the narcissism proper to saintliness confers on them a propensity for the immodesty of the sublime. What did Mother Teresa require of her nuns? The most total humility was combined with personal macerations, the freely chosen humiliation of the person before God, in which I perceive a formidable pride, far from the modesty you mention. Any reformist will is suspect; and I still have in my head a few admirable lines from Lacan on the unconscious sadism of philanthropists, educators, reformists, and altruists. . . . Yes, anyone who wishes, whatever the cost, to effect a profound change relies on the unconscious resources of sadism, the nature of which is force. To impose a new order, in fact, one must permit a fierce resistance, an extreme anger, a revolt of pride, to come into oneself.

But if, as you say, it is no longer God who protects, but "My Thought," then I don't see why women should escape that pridefulness. The humility of women? What about the two of us, what have we undertaken together? Granted, neither of us is in an antireligious, anticlerical, or antireformist tradition—that's true. All the same, in striving to conceive of the relation between the feminine and the sacred, I do not find us either humble or modest. And, in fact, why should we be, in a world where the sham, the bluff, the unverified, dominate? Thought has always appeared healing to me. It is not omnipotent, far from it; it rapidly reaches its limit. But, provided that it does not transform itself into an implacable logical system, it is a rather good plumber, capable of plugging up the holes and venting the leaks of being. Still, the exact site of the leak must be detected.

When the sacred, a leaky being par excellence, is at issue, it is in our interest not to get the wrong pipe. So as not to mistake one for another in some impossible way, let us distinguish, please, between the religious and the sacred. We are already confusing them, we are mixing up ceremony and daily life, the exceptional and the common. So let's be precise. It seems to me that the sacred predates the religious. Let me explain.

Beyond the cleavages between Good and Evil, pure and impure, permitted and forbidden, intellectual and sensible, the sacred is "sublime" in the sense Kant understands that term in the *Critique of Judgment*: a short circuit between sensibility and reason at the expense of understanding and knowledge. A strike by sensibility against the intelligence. It is the enveloping sensation of the absolute when one stands before a mountain landscape, the sea, a sunset, a nocturnal storm in Africa. So, yes, the sacred authorizes the lapse, the disappearance of the Subject, the syncope, vertigo, the trance, ecstasy, the "above-the-roof" so blue.

As for the religious, I can hardly imagine it without organization. With a clergy under papal authority as in Catholicism, or with the question of community as in Islam, the function of the religious always comes back to the organization of worship: one enters here, goes through there, here one prays, there one bows, one begins and ends; in short, time and space are well managed. The sacred does exactly the opposite: it eclipses time and space. It *passes* in a boundlessness without rule or reservation, which is the trait of the divine. In short, the sacred is an immediate access to the divine, while the religious installs a marked access road, with mediations provided for the difficult cases. It goes without saying that the sacred does not vanish with the appearance of religious codes: it erupts in its time, or rather, in its instant, since its nature is to turn the order upside down. But the religious can exist without the sacred; in fact, when it is practiced without an inner conviction, that is its most common status.

Now, of all the bolts along the cleavages that the sacred gleefully blasts off, the distinction between the sexes is undoubtedly the most important. It is at this point that I shall introduce into the record the frequent bisexuality of mystics, which I mentioned in reference to the man who must dress as a woman to exercise the duties of the N'Doeup. Examples of sacred transvestism are part of the classics of ethnology, and even in the realm of the Holy Catholic Church. Michel de Certeau, a Jesuit scholar outside the law of his order, noted that Teresa of Avila's nickname was . . . *il padrecito*. Not "the mother" but, because of her authority, the "little father." In India, the most extravagant character I have ever met is an adult male of about fifty, married with children and not effeminate in any way. But when he is in a trance and renders the oracle of his temple (on Tuesdays and Fridays), he is no longer called by his legal name, he is called the "Mother." You cannot imagine the effect pro-

duced when, in an enormous temple in the south of India, you are po-
litely introduced to "the wife of the Mother." The elementary structures
of kinship, duly learned from Lévi-Strauss, implode. It's done on purpose. Here, they unsettle you.

And yet, since, in this country, bisexuality is part of the elementary
symbolic tool kit, no one pays any attention to it. The intellectual who
knows Lévi-Strauss is unsettled by it, which is not a bad thing. My cherished structures of kinship are imploded. You therefore have to rack
your brains a little and change the plumbing to understand. Where is
the leak?

Shiva, the great god of life and death, is sometimes represented in
a strange form: half woman, half man. Divided from the top of his
chignon to his cute little toes, flat chest on one side, a pretty round
breast bulging on the other, the god of ascetic virility is endowed with
a pinup's left hip. That is because sacred bisexuality is not something
one can move beyond, it is the movement itself. I am thinking of Ramakrishna, the nineteenth-century Bengali mystic who dressed as a
woman for many years to seduce the "Mother" (the eternal mother in
India), the goddess Kali. The goal of that seductive disguise was illumination, which flooded over Ramakrishna at the precise moment
when he rushed at the beloved Mother, saber in hand. . . . Then, miracle of miracles, ecstasy spurted out in tiny drops of seawater. At that
moment, the transvestite wanted . . . what exactly? To die, or to strike
the mother goddess? He himself did not know. With sword in hand,
he hurled himself onto the Mother, and said, "Behold!" That "behold!"
is a fine headlong rush. Better to vanish from oneself and dissolve into
the infinite.

Moving from one sex to the other is common currency in the history of mysticism, but the mystic does not stop at that difference: he
passes, that is his act. He passes beyond. Woe to those who complete
that passage beyond the division of the sexes by pronouncing, like the
Iraqi Sufi al-Hāllaj, the sacrilegious statement: "I AM GOD." Neither
man nor woman but God. Because he pushed the profound logic of
the mystic contact with God to its extreme, al-Hāllaj was crucified,
flayed, decapitated, tarred, burned. Yet he had done nothing but pro-
nounce publicly the essence of the sacred. He had confined himself to
saying it. But, in saying it, he brought the sacred out of its wild preserve. And, although one has the right to scream, to stammer, or to
sing, it is forbidden to articulate. To fix the sacred outside the instant

is sacrilege. As a result, al-Hāllaj was not only punished, he was materially soiled. As it happens, in the register of the sacred, the "dirty" is ambivalent: sometimes it exalts, sometimes it punishes.

It is a commonplace of universal history that a condemned man walking to meet his fate has garbage thrown on him. What is stranger is the glorification of filth in the sacred. For example, the mysticism of the Himalayas commonly has dealings with the unclean. What is called Tantrism "of the left hand" has long resorted to the use of urine and excrement: if one is to be God, it is prescribed that one do everything backward. One must submit to the foul smelling. There are countless initiation rituals in Africa in which the hands of initiates are tied behind their backs and they are forced to eat on the ground from a bowl that has never been washed, using only their mouths, like an animal. Saint Antony, as Flaubert dreamed him up in *The Temptation,* escapes his demons by sinking into an animal nature, and it is there he has an illumination confusingly similar to God.

That fantasy is not rare. In "The Apotheosis of Augustus," an outline for a tragedy written by the young Claude Lévi-Strauss on his way home from Brazil in the 1930s, the author presents "Cinna" as an ethnologist, who boils ethnology down to "id": the act of becoming an animal. It is a superb fable of an ethnologist exhausted by field work. . . . When, on the eve of his apotheosis, the future Emperor Augustus discovers that his deification will require him to let insects mate on the back of his neck and birds cover him with their droppings, he runs off at top speed. Often, in fact, the sacred is animal and God combined. For Ramakrishna, who attached an ape's tail to his backside, God is an ape, a woman or mother, head and ass. Curiously, when certain feminists in the 1970s began to write about women's menses and secretions, the vox populi—ladies included—was shocked. It is true they did a bit too much of it, but why so much generally agreed upon repulsion? Might "id" be the unspeakable, the roof? Might thought not have access to the scent of sex?

Of course the mama is wanted, but only her breast, please. Indians do not stand on such ceremony; the maternal sacred cow of India provides milk, but also dung and urine. . . . But, careful. I recognize that animal worship can threaten humanism. I have not forgotten the Nazi law protecting animals, which explicitly placed them in a better position than the Jews in the train cars; Luc Ferry has demonstrated that very well in a wonderful book. In France, look at Brigitte Bardot: everything for the animal, but nothing for her son, nothing for the immigrants. The protection of animals and its unconscious reformist sadism directly attacks the human race. Where did the generosity of mother's milk go? To the dogs. *La vache!* [5]

Love anyway,
Catherine

* *

Paris
JANUARY 22, 1997

Dear Catherine,

I TELL YOU about atheistic communism, a religious atheism that will swallow anything, even worms, and you reply: *"La vache."* Brava! There's the proof that an exchange of letters, just as much as the automatic writing of the surrealists or the patient's "free association" on the couch, can cause sparks to fly that say more about the body and the mother of the protagonists than mountains of laborious arguments. You're very good at flashes of temper, I knew that, but really— I got the message. Things are heating up, so much the better! *Cherchez la femme,* look for the woman, look for the cow—a sacré nourishing mother, but also an obstinate producer of dung, and perhaps never one without the other.

Let me return to humility and the unspeakable. No, I do not want women to remain humbly at home or in the antechambers of the political parties; I even think—always in the vanguard!—that we have the right to "parity" in the National Assembly, in the government, and in everything imaginable in terms of national, international, and any other political power. And far be it from me to insinuate that women revel in their "status" as passive subjects, when not in that of the sorrowful martyrs of religions.

---

5. *La vache!* literally "the cow!" is used as an expletive, roughly equivalent to "Damn!" or "Drat!"—Trans.

It seems, for example, that the ecstasies of Saint Teresa of Avila (1515–1582) went hand in hand with the forcefulness of a leader, and that her *Way of Perfection* did not prevent her—any more than her *Interior Castle*—from distinguishing herself as the founder of some fifteen reformed Carmelite convents throughout Spain. On the contrary. Granted, she was the granddaughter of a Jewish merchant from Toledo who had converted to Christianity. Let's admit that she benefited from the fervent and effective support of Saint Peter of Alacantra. And, above all, that of Saint John of the Cross and Gratian, that goes without saying. But it was she and she alone who imposed her authority on her sisters, it was she and she alone who took the risk of exposing herself to the Inquisition, before Gregory XIII sanctified the autonomy of the Discalced Carmelites; it was she and she alone whom her charges called "very holy Mother, our Protectress and Sovereign" (and not only *il padrecito,* as you remind me, and which gently caricatures her). Then, when I read her recommendations for the humility indispensable for entering into a state of prayer ("Well then, there is no lady like humility to oblige the divine King to surrender"), I do not think this is a case of simple conformity to Christian obedience or to the ancestral ruses of the feminine. I also do not think she exhibits a penchant for irrational passivity: as a matter of fact, she also knows perfectly well how to exhort her girls not to be satisfied with "praying vocally" but also to "meditate"—since it is through "contemplation" in "meditation," Teresa recommends, that her girls can and must "stay close to the Master."

The apprenticeship in concentration, meditative mastery, and self-contemplation through the power of thought does not strike her as a male virtue in any way, but rather as a state perfectly accessible to women. Nevertheless, and quite particularly when she describes the soul as a diamond in *The Interior Castle,* Teresa warns us: "In truth, our intelligence, as clear-sighted as it may be, *cannot understand* [the soul], just as it could not *represent* God. . . . Yet if the thing is true, and it is, there is no reason for us to tire ourselves trying to understand the beauty of the castle." All the same, Teresa corrects herself. She fears that clinging, to that extent, to the "very secret things" might be a "folly." Then she bravely tries to penetrate that impenetrable diamond—beginning at the very bottom, in the company of "reptiles," if necessary. . . . And so on, always guided by love, and knowing that the journey is possible but that "comprehension" or "representation" remain forever imperfect. I am convinced that, with that diamond—impenetrable, and nevertheless to be known—she holds a *reserve* that confers flexibility and energy on her. A subtle conqueror, she is so because she feels and communicates *her limits*. The limits of what we call "the unconscious"? The limits of an "other logic"? Or of no logic at all? A journey to the end of the night, a scansion of the unknowable unknown that Freud nicely calls the "navel of the dream"? Teresa's diamond is her most intimate being, as lovable or desirable as it is dazzling and inaccessible.

The Middle Ages lent themselves even better to that confession of unrepresentable experiences. Hildegard of Bingen, Angela of Foligno, to mention them alone at this point, say nothing less: our lives are blazing with *sense,* but that fire has no direct *meaning* and is not directly communicable. So they create poetry, they submerge us in metaphors, images, plastic words, they paint and embroider in the very substance of the words. They do not know they are "authors," they simply auscultate what is not said from the outset. Much later, Marcel Proust would write: "Style is a vision."

Like the Beguine nuns you mention, whose exhibit I admired and for which I wrote a preface a few years ago, there are no written works this time, but especially—and that is what takes hold of me as I write to you—woven and embroidered works, assemblages of stones, dolls, flowers, bark, grass. "Installations," as one would say today, where these women were celebrating their resonances with . . . the Heart. Hearts of every ilk in that exhibition: hearts that were painted, sculpted, sewn, and knitted. . . . Hearts of love and of pain, hearts of Christ, naturally—a sublime and impossible child, with a father just as sublime and just as impossible, whom the Beguine nuns nevertheless managed to reach in the silence of their works, whom they were persuaded to incorporate into their own hearts and bodies. Bisexuality, no doubt. Fantasized motherhood of eternal daughters in love with the father, that's glaringly obvious. And, along with that, something more complex, which supports all creative experience, which is in league with the experience of love. It entails passing through the nothingness of oneself as well as the nothingness of language, to obtain a bouquet of traces and sounds that challenge intellection, in favor of what they call the "paradise of love." It seems to me that that ambitious expression designates an act of giving a form to sensible flesh, a delicious act always to be begun again, but one that requires a certain annihilation of self, of self-consciousness.

"In the middle of the chest of the figure I had contemplated within the airy spaces of midday, a wheel of marvelous appearance appeared. It contained signs that connected it to the vision in the form of an egg that

I had had twenty-eight years ago." So writes Hildegard (1098–1179), a dynamic abbess who was able to separate herself from the male community of Disibodenberg and to found a model cloister on the banks of the Rhine, near the city of Bingen. These extravagant "visions," which are filled with wolf's heads, leopard, bears, and lions, have not prevented posterity from seeing her as one of the most enterprising personalities of the Middle Ages. Among the most beautiful of her visions, I still see before me her gluttonous and lucid canvases of viscera and humors. Hildegard of Bingen, as if equipped with a movie camera, descends into the folds and cavities of the body, not sparing the blood and the brains, and succeeds in capturing a precise impression of the swarms that inhabit it, never appeased, always to be remade, decidedly unnamable—and for that very reason to be named endlessly. "The vessels of the brain, the heart, the lungs, the liver, and other things give the kidneys their strength, the veins of the kidneys descend to the ankles, which they strengthen." Hildegard is in the process of visualizing the circulation of blood, she discovers it before our eyes! It is as if she also has an inkling of the flow of hormones: Listen to this: "Phlegm becomes dryer and more virulent, it rises to the brain, it brings on headaches and pain in the eyes; the bone marrow shrivels up, and sometimes there is an outbreak of epilepsy in the last quarter of the moon. When thoughts are overtaken by savagery, harshness, and tyranny . . . they push knowledge to the point of despair, as in epilepsy, because the light of truth that illuminated it has already grown weak. As for the humidity found in the navel of man, chased there by his own humors, it is driven to dryness, to hardness." And so on. This is at a time when the first crusaders were heading toward Jerusalem, and Hildegard undertakes her microscopic crusade to deliver the tomb of the suffering body from its bonds, by naming it. She becomes the precursor of modern medicine and of the various "psychiatric" techniques; her experience of the sacred is a battle against the invisible and the unspeakable. This is an extraordinary reflection on epilepsy, a sacred malady as you know, which Hildegard compares to a science "pushed to the point of despair, since the light of thought has grown weak"! Yes, she balances on the "roof" of words, but perched above an ocean of suffering mucous membranes and convulsive humors.

The more melancholic Angela of Foligno (1248–1309) sincerely confesses the gap, the distance, the *nothing* that separates the pounding of her desires or anxiety from a potential and always imperfect grasp. "The body relaxes and sleeps, the tongue is cut off and motionless," she writes in *The Book of Visions*. "Neither laughter nor ardor nor devotion nor love, nothing on the face, nothing in the heart, not a tremor, not a movement." Negative and nihilistic, Angela describes herself as "composed of nonlove."

The divine (a diamond palace for one, a palpitating heart or mucous membrane for the other) is, for Angela of Foligno, an "abyss," "a *thing that has no name* . . . and defies the desire to ask beyond it." At this point, "nothing can even be stammered any longer. . . . *Do not approach, human word.*"

Let me say that this sacred, this "thing without a name" may betray, beyond the depressive silences of our mystic, a suggestion of disbelief. In fact, if the divine has no name, does it truly exist? One may believe in it, one may also doubt it. The latencies of a mystic atheism (perhaps the only one, which has nothing to do with the atheistic religion of the so-called materialist intellectuals I told you about last time), and, I think, of a subtle, specifically feminine atheism, take root, it seems to me, in that suspicion borne aloft on the powers of the Word, in that retreat to the unfathomable continent, concealed from the sensible body. "Cow body," said . . . Saint Bernard. Yes, him too! But, precisely, it is not a matter of saying that this body does not exist, or that it is identical to the Word. But of approaching it in its difference, in its resistance. Otherwise, woe to the religion of atheists, they are not done "eating worms" and committing other acts of abjection . . .

Until modern times, women's familiarity with their intense and evasive body made their religious experience a confrontation with *abjection* precisely, and with *nothingness*. The most spectacular, and perhaps the most pathological, of these explorers of nothingness is undoubtedly Louisa of the Nothingness, for that is what Mlle. de Bellière du Tronchay, in the seventeenth century, asked to be called. In abandoning her prestigious "name-of-the-father" to nullify herself, while at the same time nullifying paternal authority, that maiden of Anjou became "a hospital tramp" out of pure love for an abject Jesus Christ. She identified with the humiliation of Christ, allowed herself to be confined to Salpêtrière in 1677—well before Pinel's madwomen and Charcot's hysterics—where everyone was delighted, and considered it a duty, to go see the figure of Nothingness. With boundless suffering in a theater of madness and of cruelty, which she endured and where she performed—something Artaud does not fail to recall—Louisa changed her pseudonym in mid-life: in the end, she asked to be called Louisa-the-poor, Louisa-servant-of-the-poor. She adopted the attitude not of a nihilist but of a child, and died serene in Loudun.

So, could that unnameable secret/sacred be simply the overexcited body of the hysteric? We're making a mountain out of a molehill! Some might congratulate themselves, saying: Psychiatry gets to the bottom of it, brutally perhaps, but effectively. And psychoanalysis does the same with kid gloves, others might murmur. I know you do not agree with those hasty people. I read your book, *The Madwoman and the Saint,* with Sudhir Kakar, and I like the way you show that one cannot bypass desire by confining it within pathology. That is why we get along so well, you and I, all things considered, and why we have tried to travel this road together for awhile.

Indeed, that unspeakable jouissance is at once *provoked* in me by the other—by "my neighbor," by language—and *irreducible* to their transparency. The indomitable excitability of the hysterical body attests to that paradox, and the sacred was the space where woman could give free rein to that abjection and to that pleasure, to nothingness and its glory. That does not mean that the sacred experience can swing entirely into (psychiatric) pathology or (psychoanalytical) symptoms. What remains—the irreducible thing—is the *very dynamic of splitting in two,* which makes my being an irreconciled being, a being of desire. Psychoanalysis as I understand it attempts to leave open that freedom— the freedom of the "navel of the dream"; it seeks to restore *illusion's* rights—which must truly be said to be salubrious. Winnicott, even more firmly than Freud (who is accused a bit hastily of "rationalism," even though he predicted—however much a man of science he may have been—a beautiful "future" for our "illusions," which proves his clear-sightedness rather than a scientistic bias), bases creativity on the "transitional space," which is none other than the space of reverie or illusion that the mother leaves open to her young child . . .

In leafing through my old books in order to quote you a few sentences I underlined when I read them long ago—for I must say that it has been a long time since I have returned to these archaeologists of faith, to which the love of my father once propelled me (but that's another story, for another time), I happened to lay my hand on an art catalogue by Georgia O'Keeffe (1887–1986), which seems to me to have turned up at just the right moment. I adore that sober and sensual painter, her fleshy flowers, her visions of eggs (her too!), of wet bones and of skulls picked clean. Yet another modest explorer of the unnameable, whom I would like to add to the list of prestigious ancestors, from whom I have just copied a few fragments for you. She does not miss a chance to trace mysteries, but of what? Her body, a flower/

sex organ, life, death, the cosmos, being? Secretly, modestly, she moves about—she does not name but keeps quiet. And she draws. She does not draw what she draws, but something else in the thing itself; an insignificant thing, almost nothing, God knows what, but which is everything, or rather a "roof" from which I see and sense what cannot be seen or interpreted, and which seduces me. I try to say something about it, I cannot, I would have to write a poem, a novel. . . . In the meantime, I am making you two photocopies, which I hope you will like: *Series I, No. 1* (a title that means nothing, but the spiraling color of that obscene bud thrills the eyes and the flesh) and *Cow's Skull with Calico Roses* (here we are again, at another stop, and a very beautiful one, along the infinite metaphors of the *cow*).

Finally, a very down-to-earth question: how to square all that—that fervor and that doubt, that intensity and that nothingness, that enthusiasm and "god knows what" . . . with the issue of "parity"? Impossible? Undesirable? Perhaps. And yet, what if so-called parity allowed a slight breath of all that "id" to quiver in so-called political life? . . . But I'm dreaming, naturally, necessarily, along with those sacré women . . .

Julia

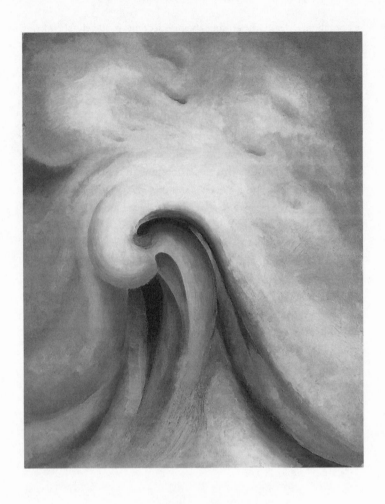

Georgia O'Keeffe, *Series I, No. 1* (1918)
oil on board, 50.6 × 40.4 cm
Amon Carter Museum, Fort Worth, Texas
Purchase with assistance from the Anne Burnett Tandy Accessions Fund

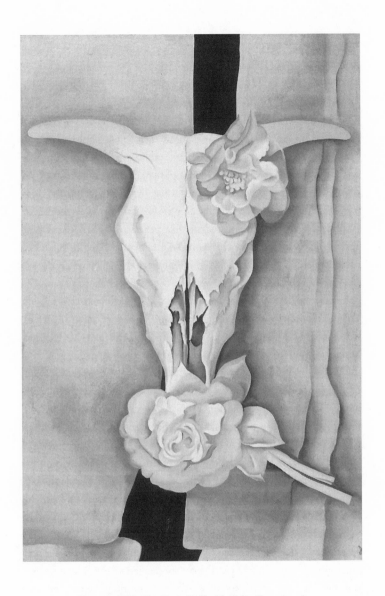

Georgia O'Keeffe, *Cow's Skull with Calico Roses* (1932)
oil on canvas, 92.2 × 61.3 cm

Oxford
TUESDAY,
FEBRUARY 4, 1997

Dear Catherine,

I HAVE NOT yet received your letter, it seems to me you are trav-
eling, and, in any case, nothing requires us to pursue this correspondence as call and response, question and reply, stimulus and reflex. . . .
Night has fallen over Oxford, a very English rain is pouring down on the
lawn under my windows, and I do not feel like sleeping. That is often
how it is after a lecture, especially after a "successful" one, as they say: a
lot of people, an audience of students and professors, heterogeneous and
attentive, perfect silence—who would not be flattered by that? No discussion, naturally—the ritual of these prestigious Zaharoff Lectures is
too ceremonious for that; the wine, in contrast, loosened tongues and
revealed lucid and cordial listeners, sharp, faithful, unexpected friends.
Then dinner finally, in a half-religious, half-studious elegance, succulent,
with plenty to drink besides. . . . How could I sleep after that? Especially since I don't know who had the perfidious idea of putting me up at
the French House—a hospitable place, to be sure, but so ugly! So de-
pressing! A sort of seedy motel on the outskirts of the city, which makes
me yearn desperately for the old Gothic or Renaissance stones I just left,
the splendors of the Bodleian Library, the sumptuous guest room at
New College where I stayed on my first visit here, and the "Voltaire
Room" in which I just gave my paper, escorted, as is only fitting, by
what they call the "beadle," and with the indispensable and august authorization, as is only fitting as well, of the vice-chancellor, both of them,
as you may imagine, in period gowns.

So here we are in the heart of another form of the "sacred," don't
you think? I like the academic rituals of the English, I like them very
much now, though a few years ago they seemed to me ridiculous in a
sinister way. I remember my first visits to Cambridge before and after
May 1968: the fact that the great sinologist Joseph Needham, the object of my admiration and the reason for my visit, could sing in a
church choir seemed to me a most extravagant whim. And I burst out
laughing when I was invited to lead the prayer procession before dinner with those gentlemen, when my shoes with platform heels—as dic-
tated by the fashions of the time—echoed terribly on the old waxed
parquet floor, as my friend, Marian Hobson, the only woman in that
learned assembly, blushed with embarrassment or pleasure, I don't

know which. For both of us and for the infamous "sacred" . . . Since then, I've been exposed to other cases, and I know how to behave myself. Not so long ago, in Canada, I myself had to put on a violet archbishop's robe, at the University of Western Ontario, where I was voted *doctor honoris causa*. While the orchestra and all the people present— more than a thousand graduates assembled with their families—sang "God Save the Queen" in my honor (and in their honor, let's be fair!), well, I had tears in my eyes thinking of my parents. Of them and nothing but them, that goes without saying. They would have been so proud! A sacré debt, the debt to one's parents, of which one is never finished paying the sacré dividends.

And, on my return to Paris, I became convinced that the hideous poverty of Jussieu was not really a requirement for carrying out the work of science and the pursuit of secularism. I even attempted to persuade our president that the university needs money, of course, to develop and acquire prestige, but it may also need to return to it its symbolic values, its celebrations, its rites, its ceremonies—medieval, Renaissance, Encyclopédiste, why not? Per Diderot, since he is now our patron saint! He looked at me as if I thought I was the Joan of Arc of an a intra- or infra-academic spiritual renewal, and that was the end of the matter.

In short, these English get on my nerves a little with their obsolete formality, but they intrigue me. Granted, they're in no rush to have women move into the university, and many of my English friends are champing at the bit in inferior positions. True, the realm has a queen at its head, but her graceful crowned head cannot hide the misogynous forest any better than Mrs. Thatcher's iron grip could: the Anglicans and the Protestants allow their ministers to marry, they even have women deacons and priests, but they continue to eject women from the realm of the spirit, and nothing prevents women from being excluded from the highest positions. I have my own idea about that: what if it were because they have forgotten . . . the Virgin Mary?—who was not her son's slave as Simone de Beauvoir believed. Didn't Mary make it possible for women to hold up their heads? It seems to me that her absence is secretly and even cruelly felt in the male chauvinism and its exclusive clubs on the other side of the Channel. This is a question that deserves to be raised, but I will speak to you about that dear Virgin Mary another time; as a matter of fact, an Englishwoman, Marina Warner, has written the finest and most complete of modern books on her, *Alone of All Her Sex: The Myth and Cult of the Virgin Mary* (1976).

What impresses me this evening is the ceremonial: I had the physical sensation that, when everything is collapsing, their ancient ballets confer a certain dignity on the poor bodies we are, and draw our words upward. Which words? Neither obvious nor very clear, but isn't it better that way, in the chiaroscuro of a high church or a more or less Gothic hall? Just now, it was a cross between the medieval rite and . . . the memory of Voltaire. As you know, thanks to Besterman, the Voltaire archives ended up in Oxford, precisely, and not in one of the temples of our republican university. And the Voltaire Room where I did the honors is a center that welcomes everyone who thinks throughout the world at the present time, or is supposed to do so.

By chance, the nondescript "French House" motel is nevertheless endowed with a sumptuous edition of the complete works of—you guessed it—Voltaire, in forty-two volumes, dating from 1829, thanks to M. Dupont, the publisher and bookseller in Paris. Can you imagine! A treat on this sleepless night, and I am thinking of you, of us. I go directly to the words *sacred* and *women*. Nothing on the sacred in the *Dictionnaire philosophique,* but a few nasty things about women all the same, which this great friend of Emilie did not fail to set out in black and white—humor requires it, with humor the noble face of hatred, by virtue of which we (men and women) separate ourselves from our mothers and become what we call "ourselves." I'll pass them on to you. For example:

"It is not surprising that, in every country, man has made himself the master of woman, since everything is based on force. Ordinarily, he is very much superior in body, and even in mind."

"There have been very scholarly women just as there were women warriors; but there have never been any women inventors."

All the same, he acknowledges women's right to love—taking a few swipes at the "Greek" smugness of his dear Montesquieu—going so far as to maintain that the "divine" is nothing other than "the love of women." That is a subject we must take up again!

"Montesquieu, in his *Spirit of Laws,* in promising to speak of the condition of women under the various governments, maintains that 'among the Greeks, women were not considered worthy of sharing true love, and that, for them, the only form love took is one that dares not speak its name.' He cites Plutarch as his authority."

"It is a mistake, hardly forgivable except of a mind such as Montesquieu's, who is always swept along by the speed of his ideas, which are often incoherent."

Pow!

"Plutarch, in his chapter 'On Love,' introduces several interlocutors; and, under the name of Daphneus, he himself refutes with the greatest force the argument made by Protogenes in favor of the debauchery of boys.

"It is in this same dialogue that he goes so far as to say that there is something divine about the love of women; he compares that love to the sun, which animates nature; he attributes the greatest happiness to conjugal love and concludes with magnificent praise for the virtue of Eponine."

I admire that man, who, even two centuries ago, was able to write as follows on "faith." Pope Alexander VI, a voluptuous and incestuous man, not knowing if the newborn of his daughter Lucretia was his own child, that of his son, or perhaps that of his son-in-law who passed for impotent, called on Pico della Mirandola and received this response:

"'I believe it's your son-in-law,' replied Pico. 'Oh! How can you believe that foolishness?' 'I believe it by faith.' 'But don't you know that an impotent man can't produce children?' 'Faith,' replied Pico, 'consists of believing things because they are impossible; and, in addition, the honor of your house requires that the son of Lucretia not appear to be the fruit of incest. You have me believe more incomprehensible mysteries. Must I not be persuaded that a serpent spoke, that, since that time, all men are damned, that the ass of Balaam also spoke very eloquently, and that the walls of Jericho fell at the sound of the trumpets?' [The pope replies to his teasing:] 'Tell me, what merit can there be in telling God one is persuaded of things of which, in fact, one cannot be persuaded? What pleasure can that give God? Between you and me, to say that one believes what is impossible to believe is a lie.'

"Pico della Mirandola made a large sign of the cross. 'Oh, God our Father,' he cried, 'may your holiness forgive me, you are not Christian.' 'No, by my faith,' said the pope. 'I suspected it,' said Pico della Mirandola."

And Voltaire says of "sects":

"Every sect, of whatever kind it may be, is the rallying of doubt and error. Scotists, Thomists, Realists, Nominalists, Papists, Calvinists, Molinists, Jansenists, are only assumed names.

"There is no sect in geometry; one does not speak of a Euclidean or an Archimedean."

"When the truth is obvious, it is impossible for parties and factions to rise up. No one has ever argued whether there is daylight at noon . . .

"You are a Muhammadan, hence there are people who are not so, hence you might actually be wrong.

"What would the true religion be, if Christianity did not exist? That in which there are no sects; that in which all minds necessarily agree. . . .

" 'What my sect teaches is obscure, I admit it,' said a fanatic; 'and it is by virtue of that obscurity that one must believe it; for it says itself that it is full of obscurities. My sect is extravagant, hence it is divine; for could what appears so mad be embraced by so many peoples, if there were no divine?' . . .

"But who will judge that trial? . . . The reasonable, impartial man, knowledgeable in a knowledge that is not that of words, the man freed from prejudices and the lover of truth and justice; the man, finally, who is not a beast, and who does not believe he is an angel."

It is not only thanks to Besterman that the Voltaire archives ended up in Oxford, along with Montesquieu's, in fact. The ritualism of the English may also confer a lightness on the way they experience the sacred—constantly performed—a lightness that frees the sacred even in the management of profane life, of social space. And that allows minds as insubordinate as Voltaire's to live as exiles among them, to express themselves among and before them, to reach the point of disbelief, almost atheism. Is that possible anywhere other than in this English cultural context, where the "sacred" (and hence the gravity and weight of the "sacrifice") both comes into being and is toned down through gesture, custom, example?

This sarcastic, tonic Voltaire, causing upheaval with his disobedience, echoes in my rainy night as I copy these sentences for you, as if he were an extraterrestrial, as if he were not of our world. In fact, we have become so used to worshiping idols, ideals, or simply "differences," that his laughter, which mocks the pious, looks like a sacrilege to many. It is because I am in strong agreement with his sarcasm—even though I am incapable of articulating it—that I proposed this book on the sacred to you. Religious souls will find that paradoxical, but not you. In fact, it is only when one "does not belong" that, it seems to me, one can appreciate both the strengths and the impasses of an allegiance. And yet, I do not feel the Voltairean need to thrash the "evildoer." Times have changed, religious wars, still fundamental and fierce, have taken on new faces. It is up to us to root out the reason they appeal to men and to women.

Even before reading the salutary texts by the sage of Ferney, I felt I had no capacity for God. Is it the company of Voltaire? Moments from my childhood and adolescence, never clearly recalled before today, have suddenly come back to me tonight.

Under an icon representing my namesake, Saint Juliana, which my father had hung above my bed, and of which I retain no precise image—a mark of how much the tale of her ordeals must have terrified me in the past—I remember that, one night, I was trying to *feel* the faith whose prayers my family had taught me to recite. The Communist school disapproved of it, and I was wavering between the desire to please my parents by sharing their faith, on the one hand, and revolt on the other, which impelled me to displease them by aligning myself with the school's orders, per Oedipus. I had reached the age when I needed to discover what I myself believed, sincerely, personally. A friend had confided to me that she had found faith because of death, since, she said, only God is capable of giving us immortality, ergo . . . I struggled to think of my own death—in the hope of getting closer to Him. What was my surprise when I observed that the eventuality was, properly speaking, unthinkable to me! If I try to restore the components of that "flash" of insight, I remember that the idea of my body, which I had set about to imagine lifeless, filled me with terror, since I imagined it devoid not so much of heat or desire but, fundamentally, of thought. Was I already an "intellectual"? Perhaps, in a country where thought was the only resistance possible to evil and poverty. . . . I thus assimilated thought to the freest part of life and its charms, and I was petrified with horror at the idea of one day being deprived of it. But that glaciation did not last. I had the physical sensation that thought was not my own in any way, that, on the contrary, it went beyond or transcended me, and that it was indestructible. Not "my" thought: no, an apperception had permeated me with the discontinuous thought of the species, if I can formulate that inclusion of the finite within the infinite in that way. Eternity was quite simply that infinite discontinuity beyond individual death, that is, the thought of the species—so long as men survive—clashing on the border of every body or thought of one's own. The idea that someone or something can claim to take the place of that infinity of thought, marked off by the unthinkableness of death, and, even more, that one can claim to remedy one's improbable, unthinkable extinction—that idea, which my friend had expressed to me, seemed illogical, pointless, incongruous. What need or desire was there for such a supreme being, since thought endured without me?

That state suddenly made me serene, with a troubling calm whose silence and peace I still understand today. It had nothing to do with an exaltation of the omnipotence-of-thought-denying-the-fear-of-death kind. On the contrary, in the face of the limitlessness of thought *outside myself,* I was confronted with the limits of my mind, beholden to my flesh. It seemed natural to me that they were perishable, and, logically speaking, natural and regrettable, but in no way frightening that they should be so. I had the feeling, in the confusion of that train of thought, of a strange humility, a version of what is called in learned terms "castration": I had only my thought, it was limited, and there was nothing without it or beyond it. Nothing but the indestructible discontinuity of limited thoughts, ad infinitum. It was a feeling of poverty combined with pride that made me feel ashamed. I wanted to reawaken the fear, the fear of death, to call for help as my friend had done, but I was not afraid. I was quite simply alone with my limited thought, without fear, within the silence of the thinking species. Undoubtedly, one had to be a pubescent girl, a woman, to transfuse the passing from one generation to the next for which my sex prepared me into the fragile destiny of a given thinking body. To imagine thought as a life beyond life proper, and life as a thought more powerful than death or one's personal destiny.

Years later, while I was in charge of a group of children during summer vacation, I made another discovery. These children caused me a great deal of worry: I wanted them to be better than they were, I wanted to be the best counselor: you see the adolescent neurosis, the anxiety of competition, and the phallic ambition to improve the world at every turn? I was crying from rage, powerlessness, failure, up to that very clear and naked instant, which I see again today on this torrid evening. The children were making an infernal racket instead of napping, and I was supposed to discipline them. All of a sudden, I had the certainty that there was nothing to be done. Not with them, and not in any other case: *there was nothing.* Of course, one had to "do," and I was doing, and I would do. But it was because there is absolutely nothing to be done that one did the best one could. Otherwise—if there were something absolute and not nothing—it was a race toward martyrdom, toward war. And I did not love either of them, my adolescent body was barely awakened to other pleasures.

These two moments became telescoped that day: the absence of a fear of death, under my quilt in front of the icon of Saint Juliana, and the conviction that there was nothing to be done at summer camp. . . . But it is only now that I can make out their shape: humility and the endurance of thought, apart from which there is nothing—to the point that death itself naturally retreats into the unthinkable and the nothing. That's not all. I am convinced that that conjunction of thought and of the nothing can and ought to be celebrated as "sacred." But it could in no way lay itself open to the sort of faith Voltaire makes fun of, a faith that is potentially fanatical.

Later, I read this in Dostoyevsky, which might sum up my illuminations of the moment: "Every man will know he is entirely mortal, without resurrection, and he will welcome death proudly and calmly, like a god." I could take that sentence for an epitaph, if it had not been pronounced by the devil addressing Ivan Karamazov, but instead in positive terms, by a clear mind—which would mean that the pride it contains would not need the word *god* to make itself understood.

You will perhaps find this version of my atheism too sober, unappealing, drab. Perhaps I allowed myself to be permeated by the restraint of the Anglican sacred, by the banality of the lawns at Oxford, soaked by a winter rain, and by my childhood, which, come what may, obstinately resisted Communist enthusiasm and Orthodox antienthusiasm. Even so, it is true that I still seek variants of that conjunction between the power of thought and the nothing. . . . You who are familiar with every religion, might you know of one that would celebrate my own simple sacredness, which I imagine to be the turf from which the sparkling Voltaire was able to extract his burning-hot embers? Unless it is not a religion I was invoking there, under the icon of Saint Juliana or in the neurosis of the Girl Scouts, but, quite simply, something like literature. I have not yet told you that, this evening in the Voltaire Room, I was speaking on Proust, that ironist, that blasphemer.

Julia

✦ ✦

FEBRUARY 20, 1997

Dear Julia,

I AM BACK from a film shoot in India; my sacred cows are present and accounted for in the urban landscape. But there is no dearth ei-

ther of Indian women behind the wheel and women on the streets
equipped with portable phones. In contrast, in the villages and on
roads, where women break stones on road crews, nothing has
changed. They are not lacking in the calm self-assurance of the American black women you ran into in the streets of New York, but their impoverished condition has not yet been affected by the so-called trickle-
down theory, namely, that the middle class is getting richer and that
the wealth will "trickle down" to the poor. . . . Oh, really?

There, as everywhere else in these times of accelerated moderniza-
tion, temples proliferate. The increasingly rich middle class is becoming computerized and is returning to its Hindu identity. And it takes
its pick of deities. Shiva, the great bisexual of the old pantheon, is
being set aside in favor of cute gods shaped like big babies or like
apes, faithful servants of their masters. Wealth, air conditioners, tele-
visions, computers, obedience, and kids. The sacred is losing ground
in favor of family life. All of a sudden, the move into bisexuality is becoming rarer.

Let us therefore speak again of that bisexuality, which we have been
dragging from one epistle to the next. As a matter of fact, what strikes
me in your last letter is the strange power of the saints you describe. If
only by virtue of their profoundly rebellious heads, creative impeni-
tents from religious orders or with the internal methods of mystical
anatomy. It's a curious act, the revolt that impels Sister Louisa to nullify the father's name in favor of Nothingness. "I am unbegotten"—another way of saying "I am God": remember that, in Islam, nothing is
more sacrilegious than to identify with the unbegotten. Like al-Hallāj,
Sister Louisa resorts to the declaration of the absolute: apart from
dying from love, there is none stronger than that.

Are these saints feminine or masculine? The response require a digression, which leads us back to the Englishman Winnicott. Yes, he's
the only one to detect the zone of creativity, of freedom even, which he
calls "transitional," that space of formidable potential that is established
between the baby and the mother the moment she withdraws from the
child. Until then, the child has no body of his own. Then comes the
precise moment when the mother's body separates itself from his. He
is no longer "her," he becomes a little bit "him." Then, in the absence
of the breast, the child catches hold of a piece of anything at all with
his fingers, provided "id" is soft and gentle, can be sucked as much as
one likes, masticated at will. It is that object, subjected to all the baby's
destructive aggression, that Winnicott calls the "transitional object."

And yet, the object will not disappear. Damaged, enucleated, torn, attacked, the object remains indestructible. A teddy bear, a scrap of underwear, a cuddly toy, or a pair of tights belonging to the mother, the object in question allows the baby to occupy the space of play abruptly opened between the mother's body and himself before he has had the experience of his own sack of skin. He is going to acquire it with the first object, the "not-me," the seed of the future "me."

It is forgotten in a corner. It is not thrown away. It is no longer thought of, but it is there. My own transitional object was a rubber Snow White that I clutched under the screaming sirens as Paris was being bombed. My father told me every time: "Take what you love most in the world." If I have any relation at all to the sacred, its secret source lies in that threatening memory. I do not have the capacity to believe in a god, but the day-to-day sacred returns to me from the war. A lamp being lit (signal), dawn through the window (the milkman's hour, or the Gestapo's), dusk (will there be bombs tonight?), my family leaving on a one-way train trip, no return ticket, the end of a text. Absence and nonreturn are commonplace in child psychoanalysis.

Here's something more interesting: after describing the object of the transitional zone, Winnicott takes on the task of explaining how that potential space is also that of bisexuality. He begins by getting rid of any confusion between homosexuality and the bisexuality of the transitional zone. Much more is at issue as well. Every man has a pure feminine principle within him, every woman, a pure masculine principle within her. Everyone has an enclave containing the principle of the opposite sex. This cannot be demonstrated, but it conforms to so many mythologies that one must attend to it. Winnicott is quite capable of reinventing the most archaic myths regarding the birth of humanity. . . .

I am thinking of the African myths of twinship, of which the Dogon myth is the most famous. Let me give a summary of its major features. Because of the sin of an ambitious traitor, the clever Fox, humanity has lost its initial twinship, inherited from a god who was betrayed. Tainted by the traitor, it now belongs to God alone: except for unusual births, there are no more twins on earth. For men, it is a cruel loss. But traces remain in each of us of the lost male twin and the disappeared female twin: out there in the pond dwells the boy's secret girl twin, who guides him, and, as for the girl, her male twin is concealed in the water. Let us add that God, the imperfect creator, does not succeed at his job and leaves to humanity the task of repairing the damage: the pure masculine and pure feminine principles encysted in each of the two sexes are the amends made for God's shortcomings. And he, weary, withdraws without saying a word. Work it out yourselves! It is done, Lord. We humans invented the zone of play.

In the margins of the game defined by Winnicott, the pure feminine is being itself: it is primal, up to the time of weaning. Then, when the child leaves the place of fusion, the first true act of the pure masculine principle makes its appearance, with the fingers clutching the manipulable object: "doing." The feminine principle stems from being in the pure state, while the masculine principle takes charge of doing—and the acceptance that comes with it. I like the way Winnicott sums up his thinking: "After being, doing and being done, but first, being." Being is the feminine. Doing and being done is the masculine.

What relation does that have with our cogitations? Well, Winnicott characterizes the transitional zone very well: it is sacred. The bisexual transvestism in shamanistic ceremonies, the porous fluidity of a free space that is not closed off by any sexual norm, the pure masculine force that animates your favorite female saints and, last but not least, their fabulous capacity for creation, are all explained thereby. Thus their ecstatic passivity is set in place, since "doing" and "being done," acting and being acted upon, are part of the same pure masculine principle: to reduce oneself to nothingness is not to return to the being of the feminine. On the contrary. Angela of Foligno is not in pure being when she lies writhing with her tongue cut off: no wailing, no screaming, active silence. We are truly located in the split—the problem is that man is located there as well.

As a matter of fact, I do not see any reason to leave the privilege of reactivating the transitional zone, and of thereby acceding to the sacred, to women alone. If you want to be rigorous, we have the obligation to imagine that man might accede to the sacred by rediscovering his feminine principle, being. Could that be Heidegger's philosophical solution? Perhaps. In terms of the philosophers, I observe that the Supreme Sweeper of Thought in Progress, as I call G. W. Hegel, posits woman along the dialectical path on the side of stone, the immediate: she is there, and it is her function to be there. As for man, he provokes the act and mediation. War, then negotiation. Family, that is, contract and exchange. The social, then the state. Religion, then ecstasy. And, during all that time of thought on its way, woman was there, is there, will have been there.

As for bisexuality in the narrow sense, it's not an issue. But Hegel does not fail to analyze a feminine character with a masculine soul, dear Antigone. The symbol of the contradiction between sacred laws and the laws of men, Antigone, the ideal young woman in the philosopher's mind, is the one who dares bury her brother despite the prohibition by the commonwealth. Of course, there is an act of Antigone. She comes out at night, she scratches at the ground, she covers her brother's dead body. But, when she is discovered, "she is there," stubborn, motionless, made of stone. When the guards approach Antigone to arrest her, she does not run off. It seems to me that a new path is opening: society governs by the pure masculine principle, whereas the sacred resists by the pure feminine principle. "Resist" would be the word befitting the sacred.

But Hegel hardly insists on this. At the very most, in *The Phenomenology of Spirit*, he lets it slip in passing that woman is "the irony of the community." He does not explain himself, and yet, what an intuition! The feminine is a troublemaker, truly situated on the margins of play, in the sense that assembled pieces of joinery always leave a space to accommodate the "play" in the wood. Not that women are eternal rebels, out-and-out anarchists. The irony of the community does not require a radical commitment. On the contrary. Just, at the right moment, a shift. A flick of the finger, or the *fin mot,* the heart of the matter. Never the *mot de la fin,* the final word.

What could the feminine spring of that secret mechanism be? There's little to choose from. We can only observe that, whether or not a woman is a mother, her body does not entirely obey the norms of society. Its natural cycle does not correspond to the months of the year; it is not synchronized with the calendars of the modern city. For a long time, feminist litanies on the menses and the moon set my teeth on edge—as if it were a matter of founding a new cult of Artemis, or a new witchcraft, American style—but it is undeniable that, side by side with social time, you can't get around the cyclical time of women and its relation to the lunar system.

That question of the differences between the Copernican astronomical system regulated by the sun and the Ptolemaic system regulated by the moon bothers me. In India, the sum total of life commitments is regulated by the lunar system: the sun plays no role. The astrologers, masters of the moon, decide the date of weddings, of contracts, of elections, of business affairs, of relocations, and so on.

No one complains about it, so the astrologer plays the role of a notary of time. And it is not for no reason that, in English, India calls itself "Mother India"; the title of a famous populist film of the fifties, or the nickname of Indira Gandhi in the electoral campaign, Mother India is evoked constantly. In Varanasi, there is even a temple of "Mother India," whose deity is the map of India, in white marble. Refrain: "But in India" . . . In short, on this continent, the transitional zone occupies almost the entire terrain: one slips fluidly from one god to another, from one sex to the other, from one life to another; time is cyclical and astronomy necessarily lunar. As a result, the sacred is everywhere.

It appears to be established that Aditi, the first deity of India, was female. Only later did the male gods install themselves. It is as if that distant feminine memory were endlessly returning, for better—fluidity—and for worse—the incredible violence of the vindictive goddesses. It is as if the masculine polytheistic universe had not succeeded in suppressing its maternal source and its potential horrors, except by invoking the feminine energy, Shakti, equally shared between man and woman, between male gods and female deities: for lack of anything better, nobody's jealous. Everyone has his or her "shakti" within. Decidedly, it's the relation between the masculine and the sacred that intrigues me. There is no doubt that a relation between man and God exists. But what about between man and the sacred? What if, by chance, in other regions of the world, including our own, the worship of the only god barred the masculine from acceding to the sacred?

I may be raving. Examples: however dominant the masculine may be in Hindu polytheism, the presence of divine spouses makes it possible for any male individual to identify easily with the "woman" in the godly couple. That is the claim of one of my male Indian friends, who experienced ecstasy by identifying with the beautiful Radha, mistress of Krishna. In contrast, on the side of Christian monotheism, I do not see how a male saint could identify with any female figure whatever, especially not the Virgin. As for Islamic monotheism, it is implacable: no quarter. Except for the moment when Ramadan begins, there is not even a quarter moon on the horizon. In the Koran, it's clear, woman is weak, dangerous, confused, fit for service. Unless she dies in childbirth: then she's a saint and a martyr.

Until the fall of the Jerusalem temple, Jewish monotheism also brooked no quarter. After that, there was a female double of God, whom the Jews call the Shechinah. But that beautiful and plaintive figure, who resembles Rachel grieving the death of her children, makes her appearance only to count the tears of Israel in exile. It's the same thing in Buddhism, which, in its Tibetan version, allowed a twin deity of the bodhisattva to be instituted: Tara, the Tibetan twin deity, represents only the tears of the bodhisattva, that is, the secretion of his compassion. In many regions of the world, the feminine share of the sacred is tears.

Only the men and women of the mystic branch of Islam, the Sufis, truly let identification with the feminine, bisexuality, and "the whole lot" get by. They reach ecstasy by panting, shaking, spinning, screaming if necessary. Rabhia, the first woman Sufi, was Iranian; people came from afar to venerate her. It is known that male Sufi saints often fancied men: in Turkey, the master and founder of the brotherhood of the whirling dervishes was desperately in love with a certain Shams, who vanished. The loss of the young man he loved led the lover to the deity: although homosexuality is forbidden by the Koran, in Muslim Sufism it is a matter of indifference. Only "love plain and simple" counts, whatever its object. The Sufis, victors of the transitional zone, grab hold of any human being whatever to practice divine love. As it happens, the Sufis, as if by chance, champion tolerance in the matter of religion: everything that is divine is equivalent, man and woman, temple, church, mosque, fetish. I see that as additional proof of the freedom proper to the sacred transitional zone: it knows it is amoral. I believe that is its function.

I realize I have not given you an answer about parity. As it is promoted, it seems to me that it is governed by the universe of separate but equal sexes, which is very masculine in its conception. For myself, I know it is necessary, but I put up with it only as a stopgap solution. I'm afraid that, via parity, the cleaving machine will reduce the "slight breath" you mentioned to a monkey's fart. Women's predisposition for the sacred better accommodates itself to naked rebellion, insurrectional heroism, the enthusiasm of the moment, in short, to the gaps in social time. To have it move legally into parliamentary representation is a disagreeable—but good—detour from the ideal. We would need a breath of public discourse, a period of eloquence. But right now, eloquence, you know . . . It's celebrated, but who applies it? The socialist left, sometimes . . .

Catherine

Dear Catherine,

I HAVE RECEIVED your letter just as I am preparing to accompany David to the hospital for an operation, and only one thought occupies my mind as I read it: "Nothing is more sacred, for a woman, than the life of her child." That is one of those commonplaces of popular wisdom that has been fixed for all eternity, and which could lead to denigration: what a shame that women stick to children, don't you find? The proof, if any were needed, that they lack a relation to the sacred. . . . Allow me to fasten on that sentence, which both eats away at me and sustains me. Hospital ordeals cause me anxiety as they do everyone, and, since I'm not sleeping and can't do anything else, writing you this evening forces me to wait, and in some way comforts me. This correspondence may thus be in the process of becoming vital. Naturally, I'm exaggerating, I always exaggerate when I'm anxious.

That great, subtle pediatrician, the English psychoanalyst Winnicott, has a curious idea I like, namely, that the mother's primordial connection to her child stems from "being," and is distinguished from "doing," which will occur only later, with the drive, desire, and acts. Like you, it occurred to me that the "serenity of Being" imagined by Heidegger may be rooted in these zones of experience, if one chooses to see such things with an anthropologist's eye. *She is* simply *there,* the mother, with a part of her that is already an *other. Being there with:* the dawn of difference. Peace, recognition, devotion. It is not that she "does" nothing, but the eagerness for action is suspended in a capable tenderness. Seduction, affect, drive, desire—the assets of the lover she was, barely nine months earlier, are not destroyed but deferred, "inhibited regarding the goal" (as my colleagues, the female psychoanalysts who have read their Freud, would say). I distrust that suggestion of inhibition; I prefer to speak of waiting. The serenity of maternal love is a deferred eros, desire in waiting. By deferring and waiting, that love opens the time of life, of the psyche, of language—the time of the unknown, about which one cannot or does not wish to know anything, for better and for worse. It is truly at the dawn of the mother's connection to the child that a miraculous alchemy occurs: the "object" of erotic satisfaction, the father (or some relationship, profession, or gratification) is slowly resorbed into a loved, and only loved, "other."

Love-tenderness takes the place of erotic love: the "object" of satisfaction is transformed into an "other"—to care for, to nourish. Care, culture, civilization. Outside motherhood, no situations exist in human experience that so radically and so simply bring us face to face with that emergence of the other. The father, in his own, less immediate way, is led to the same alchemy; but, to get there, he must identify with the process of delivery and birth, hence with the maternal experience, must himself become maternal and feminine; before adding his own role as indispensable and radical distance. I like to think that, in our human adventure, we can encounter "the other"—sometimes, rarely—if, and only if, we, men and women, are capable of that maternal experience, which defers eroticism into tenderness and makes an "object" an "other me."

Do you follow me? What I am telling you may be insolent, presumptuous, scandalous, and yet it seems obvious to me—this evening, more than ever, because of my worries, no doubt, and everything that connects us to our children, and which certain circumstances suddenly bring to light. If all love of the other is rooted in that archaic and fundamental, unique and universal, experience of maternal love, if maternal love is the least ambivalent kind (for a son, according to Freud; in any case, since it is in "Being," insists Winnicott), then, the *caritas* of Christians and the human rights of secular people . . . are built on maternal love. Another heresy? I'm still exaggerating, granted! In any case, is not the ethics of love always a "herethics"? I had fun writing it that way, precisely at David's birth . . . in my *Tales of Love*.

Nevertheless, it is here that I take my distance somewhat from the kindly Winnicott. Even though I find that serenity of the mother-baby being seductive, I only half-believe in it. Per female narcissism, that "other me" of the child is a "me-me" all the same: the mother is never short on the tendency to annex the cherished other, to project herself onto it, to monopolize it, to dominate it, to suffocate it. Everyone is familiar with the tragic games of mirrors and settlings of accounts that surreptitiously transform fairies into witches, beneficent mothers into dead mothers or horrible stepmothers. . . . Moreover, the mother also remains a woman, with her desires and her erotic or professional "doing," and that tension of existence (that bisexuality, if you prefer) is continually interfering with her serenity and her connection to the child. A warm, conflictual connection, laden with all the noise of the world. And fortunately so! Without that pulsating, active, phallic share of maternal love, where would the call of language come from, the thrill of breaking free, that erection (yes, I say the word and insist upon it), which allow the mother and baby to stand up, to move beyond each other toward third parties?

In short, the woman and the Phallus: here we are again, with the scandal our feminist friends have condemned so, leaving old Freud behind! In the meantime, there has been talk, based on the discoveries of the genetic code, of the early feminine nature of every human being, with the male chromosome appearing only at a later stage—it is said to take more time, in short, to become a man, which exposes you to the risk of catching a little genius . . . and a few malformations. As a result, there has been a desire to speculate on "the universality of the feminine nature" of every man and woman, and so on, forgetting that human beings are speaking beings, psychosomatic, and that the bisexuality one speaks of, that you speak of, is shaped by connections to others; that it is, therefore, in the last instance, a psychic bisexuality. Which means that, if psychic bisexuality exists, it is not because men have an X and a Y chromosome: which chromosome would women's bisexuality be based on, then, since our sex is defined by two X's and we do not have the Y marker of the male?

In fact, if psychic bisexuality exists, it is truly because women, like men but differently, are not unfamiliar with the Phallus—yes, I've said the dirty word, what a fuss! Many sects attest to the fact that the Phallus is fundamentally sacred, perhaps even the sacred par excellence, from the Greek Dionysus to the Hindus' lingam. The veiling and unveiling of mysteries were often, if not in the first place, an unveiling and veiling of the Phallus, especially among the Romans, and that rite has been resilient, as had to be expected. Recently, in Naples, I was able to observe that, in Pompeii, the cult of the . . . veiled Christ in the form of a Baroque marble in the church of San Severo was celebrated on the same site, seventeen centuries later, as the mystery of the veiled Phallus with Elagabalus. From the organ to the body as a whole, the passion of the Phallus seduces, still and forever. Why does the male organ lend itself to that troubling ceremony of hide-and-seek? Because it is visible, apparent proof of jouissance and fertility? No doubt. But also because it detaches itself, no mistake about it. It is detachable, likely to appear/disappear, to be present/absent, and, as a result, to inscribe opposition, the minimal condition for meaning, on the surface of the body itself: yes/no, one/zero, being/nonbeing. It is as if the male organ "incarnates" logical potentialities, which make it our corporeal . . . computer: the condensation of the 0/1 binary system, which lies at the foundation of all systems of meaning (beginning with language and ending with . . . computers). An extraordinary encounter between sexuality and thought, that phallic experience, where physiology intersects symbolization. Indeed, what is called a Phallus is precisely that co-presence of sexuality and thought that defines our human condition—we are neither pure biological or animal body nor pure mind, but the conjunction of drives and meaning, their mutual tension: sacré tension!

The little girl, who loves her father and compares herself to her brother, does not escape that phallic encounter. She observes it, confronted with the male body, father or brother, and with her own, but with her clitoris as the sole equivalent of the penis—at once disadvantaged because lesser and mysteriously intimate because invisible. The phallic phase is structural, therefore, for both sexes, but it is so in a different way for the girl and for the boy. Each confronts (phallic) power and (paternal) meaning (removed from the sensible connection to the mother), a power and a meaning both erotic and symbolic; but the boy tries out that confrontation with the conviction of "belonging to it," and the girl with the impression of a *strangeness*. Because she will acquire and strengthen her capacity to speak, her capacity to assess herself in terms of the law of the other, to enter the order (of thought and of society), the girl will be part of the phallic order. But since she will remain a stranger there, she will preserve a sense of inferiority, of exclusion, or, at best, of irony: "I belong to it, but not really, I play the game, I act as if."

In his study *On Female Sexuality* (1931), Freud perceives that strangeness when he asserts that bisexuality is more prominent in woman than in man. By that, he means particularly that the girl must tear herself away from her osmosis with the mother and choose the father—and the Phallus—as an erotic object, whom she will ask, indefinitely, to give her a child, to try to satisfy (without ever succeeding) the desire for the missing penis. That osmosis with the primal mother, which Freud compares to the Minoan-Mycenaean civilization at the foundation of ancient Greece, might be the source of woman's splitting in two. I also see it as the reason why women cling more firmly to the sensible, to prelanguage, to "perfumed paradises"—so many imponderables that make women seem a little absent, not really in their place in the phallic order, not at ease in its stilted language. . . . There is, in fact, nothing reassuring about that strangeness. That sense of being the pariah of the phallic sacred, in fact, can lead just as well to depression ("I am nil, I'll never get there") as to the relentless competition of the phallic virago, which produces the well-known figures of the stuck-up, argumentative woman, the mannish lesbian, or the scoutmistress. . . . But it is also that sense of strangeness that confers on certain women the appearance of a disabused and benevolent maturity, a serene detachment that, it seems to me, is the true sense of what Hegel so enigmatically calls the "eternal irony of the community." In fact, women do not remain on the near side of phallic power, but they accede to it only to better learn their way around its omnipotence. That *detachment,* which is the very mark of femininity, stems from our immersion in Being and sensible timelessness. Which gives some of us (most of us? the best of us?) the chance to realize asocial sociability, which the world receives as intimacy or tenderness. Of course, the child is a *real presence,* which no Phallus in the world could replace. But he also is not "id"; nothing is "id." "It is not id": that, in substance, is what the irony of the eternal stranger to the sacred phallic order says, an order in which she nevertheless takes part. What if that distance, that disabused withdrawal, were the guard rail that, precisely, prevents the sacred from being transformed into fanaticism?

Let us venture another step. I claim that that distance, that irony, that placing in doubt of the Phallus-Word via the Minoan-Mycenaean intimacy of the sensible, is the true path of atheism. I am not speaking of secularism, understood as a battle against religion, but of atheism as the resorption of the sacred into the tenderness of the connection to the other. And that sober and modest atheism relies on the maternal. You will say that is not self-evident. On the one hand, the churches are filled with women; on the other, feminism has dispersed iron ladies, who are not tender at all, nearly everywhere. But do they believe? Surely, but how? Always inside and outside, being and nothingness, neither one nor the other, both at once, sorrow and delight.

Does not feminine faith identify more with the crucible of mysticism than with a dogma, whatever it may be? It is the path open to doubt—to skepticism—to pragmatism: always along the edge of the most essential connection, that between the mother and her other, looking down toward our children, when we have them; and up toward our mothers, whose shadow we carry with us in all our relationships with women. . . .

The figure of Mary, for two thousand years already, has diffused throughout Christianity and the rest of the world, always under her spell, that combination of power and sorrow, sovereignty and the unnameable. I already told you, I never understood Simone de Beauvoir, who rebels against what she believes to be the humiliation of the Virgin before her son: the kneeling Mary is supposedly the passive servant of a male power. I have looked at the Nativity of Piero della Francesca to which the philosopher refers; but to no avail, Mary appears delighted and trusting, in no way defeated in her gentleness. There is no doubt that, in effacing the body and female sexuality in favor of the ear and virginity, Christianity dangerously censors female fertility, battles paganism and its mother goddesses, and imposes a Mary, pure priestess of asceticism, in opposition to Eve the sinner. Nevertheless, if women have found recognition beyond that denigration, it is because Mary points to the "deferred affects" of motherhood that I mentioned to you earlier, and that are essential to feminine jouissance. Moreover, the *mater dolorosa* is not simply an encouragement to female masochism: the *pietà* recognizes the participation of the stranger in the uncanniness of her son, in man as "man of sorrow," in castration, in his mortality—an inseparable stand-in for his "power." Mary, Mother of God (*theotokos*), and finally, quite simply, Mary the queen (*regina*), also sends all women a very flattering picture of their own phallicism. Those Maries confirm our participation in the order of the powerful, and encourage our latent paranoia. Who would deny herself that?

It is not pointed out often enough that, in reality, the Gospels are very discreet about Mary. The story of her own miraculous, so-called immaculate conception by Anne and Joachim after a long and sterile marriage, and her life as a devout young girl, appear only in apocryphal sources from the late first century. The book of James, the Gospel according to Pseudo-Matthew: these "particulars" were cited by Clement of Alexandria and Origen, but were not officially recognized; and, even though the Eastern Church willingly tolerated them, they were not translated into Latin until the sixteenth century. Yet the West, for its part, was not long in glorifying her in its own way, always finding inspiration from the Orthodox Church: the first Latin poem, "Maria," on the birth of Mary was, as you know, written by the nun Hroswitha of Gandersheim, a playwright and poet, who died in 1002. How many logical debates on causality and temporality—for example, to reconcile Christ God and Christ Man—elect as their privileged terrain the body and biography of Mary! A true treat for the mind, and I sometimes reread these texts, which I discovered while writing my book on the history of the feeling of love. No one reads them today, it's really a shame, you ought to take a look at them if you have not already done so: a treat, I assure you. After Saint John Chrysostom and Saint Augustine, it's Saint Bernard and Duns Scotus who distinguish themselves. One would have to salute in passing, very particularly, the artists, painters, and musicians who did not wait for the Vatican's green light to celebrate the maternal: perhaps because they secretly share its ambiguities. *Vergine Madre, figlia de tuo figlio,* exclaims Dante, in *The Divine Comedy,* condensing the three female functions (daughter-wife-mother). Monteverdi exalts the Blessed Virgin Mary in his *Vespers,* a true sacred opera; you know it better than anyone. But it was the Jesuit counterreformation that prevailed: from then on, Catholics venerated Mary for herself. And all the churches blossomed with her pictorial beauty and reverberated with her orchestrated rapture. I admit my weakness for the *Stabat Mater,* which, in the text attributed to Jacopone da Todi, still intoxicates us in music, from Palestrina to Pergolesi, Haydn to Rossini. *Eia mater, fons amoris.* I know nothing more sacred than that, and no love escapes it.

As for the feminine of man . . . a vast topic. I don't follow you when you write that monotheism closes access to the sacred, understood as a "transitional space" or "bisexuality." Without question, monotheism exhibits it much less than Hindu polytheism. Nevertheless, even Yahweh is said to have a "womb," and the Song of Songs describes the believer as the "beloved" of his God "husband." Moreover, the central place of Mary—not only as an acknowledgment of women but as an invitation given to man to identify in his faith with the Marian experience, since it is through and by it that Christ is human—is an open invitation to man's femininity. Christ himself, in his passion and the offering of his body, has often been interpreted, especially on the basis of the iconography that makes his flesh and the expression of his feelings excessively beautiful or ugly, as exhibiting man's bisexuality. As for the mystic, he completed the topos. You say you do not know of any Christian saint who identified with any feminine figure whatever. I don't know much about it, but I know at least one: Saint Bernard of Clairvaux (1091–1153). In his commentary on the Song of Songs, he insists at length on the ambiguity of the passage that describes the breasts of the beloved offering herself to the divine spouse, and does not hesitate to assert that the spouse himself possesses breasts: "Thy breasts shall be as clusters of the vine, and the smell of thy nose like apples." These are supposedly words addressed by the beloved to the husband . . . which suggests that the believer (if he is the beloved) and God (if he is the husband) would both be . . . equipped with breasts—hence maternal? As a result of which, God himself, the bishop, the priest, and Bernard in person would really and truly possess breasts! Which are nothing other—the analogical meaning requires it—than "patience" and "clemency." Oof! That was a close one. As for the painters, they don't make such a fuss about it: iconography abounds in representations of Bernard receiving the milk of the Virgin between his lips; others show that "milky way" emerging from his own breasts without mediation. Not surprising, all things considered, since that holy man, who was a crusader but also chronically ill, referred to his body, I told you already, as a cow—I come back to that to give you pleasure, you who adore the Indian sacred cows: "Our body finds itself situated between the spirit it must serve and the desires of the flesh or the power of shadows, which wage war against the soul, as a cow would be situated between the peasant and the thief." Breast body or cow body? For Saint Bernard, it amounts to the same thing.

I am not unaware that the same Bernard was criticized for having referred to women as "sacks of garbage"! No less! That does not surprise me coming from him, though his defenders claim that the image can be traced back to a medieval figure of rhetoric predating Bernard by a great deal, and that it was rather his brother André who designated their sister . . . Hombeline, that way—a dreadful socialite, she supposedly got the message and changed her life right then and there. . . . In any case, the body/sack-of-garbage is the male body as much as the female, before it becomes a glorious body through Christ . . . say the theologians. Duly noted . . .

All of which remains suspect, we agree on that. For myself, I take very seriously the allegations of Guizot and a few others who—speaking as anticlericals, that's understood, but all the same—remind us that the Church, not so long ago, maintained that women have no soul. In reality, that may be a misinterpretation on the part of Gregory of Tours who, in *Historia Francorum,* reports that, at the council of Mâcon, a "bishop claimed that woman could not be called 'man.' " Those who seek to exonerate the Church of all misogyny maintain that the poor bishop, quite simply, was not a very subtle Latinist and confused *homo* with *vir* and *femina* with *mulier*: he did not know, apparently, that Latin possesses a generic term, *homo,* to designate all human individuals, without distinction of sex. Let me enlighten you with an abridged version of that shady affair: even though she is *homo,* since she is not *vir, femina* has no soul. Which would mean that the soul is virile, whereas we know, thanks to Freud, Jung, and a few others, who came well after the council of Mâcon, I'll grant you that, that there are (at least) two souls, hence a psychic bisexuality. I will refrain from criticizing the council of Mâcon, and also Guizot, but we are well situated to observe that, whether or not woman is equipped with a soul, in the Church and elsewhere she is sacrément undervalued, despite the gentle efforts of Mary . . .

Nevertheless, the defenders of women in the Church remind us that, when God created men, he created male *and* female, and gave them the name "Adam" (Genesis 5:2). Others, on the contrary, are firmly rooted in their suspicions and learnedly cite the words of John 2:4: "Woman, what have I to do with thee?" And so on. The question is far from settled, that's the least one can say, since psychological daring (the daring needed to recognize the feminine of man, the masculine of woman, and other fine points of the maternal mystery) and institutional exclusions (to consolidate paternal power) join the fray. Christian women, though undervalued, are nevertheless protected, especially by marriage, until the latter becomes a new form of oppression in turn. Not to mention the fact that there is no obvious way to give a political (or religious) *equality* to the two sexes while preserving their psychological *differences* and the contribution these difference might make to the institution. Personally, I do not see what women could gain from being priests, from becoming like the priests, the faithful and acknowledged officiants of the cult of the father and the son. What interest do they have in that ratification by the males? Unless women want to introduce their strangeness, their irony, their latent atheism into that paternal cult? But then, why in the Church, what do they expect from the Church? That the Church allow itself to be transformed, invaded, reformed? Why should it? Shouldn't these anxious women instead found another sacred space, other spaces for questioning the sacred, who knows? Shouldn't they leave the Church, since it develops its own logic and would not know how to transform itself without destroying itself?

We will undoubtedly take up that institutional question another time, a question that, to tell the truth, does not interest me in the first instance. I must let you go now, since I still have to pack a suitcase for the hospital, and I am beginning to feel very tired. . . . It's not writing you that tires me, don't believe that. It's this feeling of powerless love that assails me when, with my son—even more than when it's just me—I am at the mercy of the medical system. And when I know that the more I love him the less I can do anything about it, and that the more powerless I am the more attached I am to him. I gave life, as they say. Or, more exactly, life passed through me, and I can't do anything about it, either in biology or physiology. Except to give of myself end-lessly, for the remainder of time and in the time remaining us, which is a great deal and, all things considered, keeps me going.

Julia

◆ ◆

Dakar
MARCH 12, 1997

Dear Julia,

WHAT AN ODD letter! Julia in archbishop's violet, with Vol-taire's irony lodged in her heart, in the face of an unprogressive ritual, Julia in a universe of men that recognizes her, without it being clear from what you say whether they are integrating her as a woman. . . . And, in conclusion, you call on me to unearth a religion just for you, capable of reconciling thought and the nothing?

It exists. I'm not sure you'll like it: it is Buddhism. Since, clearly, the "nothing" of your desires does not signify nothingness, the "noble truths" formulated by the Buddha correspond to your ideal. But you must let the first of them sink in: all is suffering. If you admit that, move to the second stage. The cause of all suffering is impermanence; nothing lasts. Directives: to avoid the suffering of impermanence, cast off the illusions of the self, move away from phenomena, situate your-self beyond time and duration, at the exact junction between thought and the nothing. Refute every position with a radical "neither-nor": neither joy nor suffering nor happiness nor unhappiness nor austerity nor debauchery nor this nor that. In doing so, discover the Middle Path. That is, place thought in a state of reserve.

An admirable approach, but perfectly atheistic, since God is not there. In his place appears the sum total of consciousnesses in the world, from which the equal dignity of every living thing proceeds. That is why Lévi-Strauss, invited by the National Assembly in 1977 to articulate a new formulation of human rights, sought inspiration from the three great, truly cosmological, philosophies, which are, in chronological order of their historical appearance: primitive thought, Buddhism, and Stoicism. Primitive thought is connected to the order of nature, which preserves animals and plants as the guarantors of material survival; because, in order to eat, one must hunt, but not too much. Stoicism is a cosmic philosophy defining a cyclical order in which the human subject has no power over anything but the-things-that-depend-on-him, his volitions and his desires. Obviously, primitive thought, Buddhism, and Stoicism are centered not on man but on the living thing.

Instead of championing the rights "of man," instead of restricting the universe to the rights of the human race alone (with the formidable ambiguity of the feminine hidden within the notion of "man"), these philosophies, Lévi-Strauss told the parliamentary committee, integrate the totality of living beings, of which man is a part, on equal terms. The new rights of man would thus require from man an absolute commitment to nonviolence toward the entire universe, beginning with respect for living species, plant, animal, AND human. In philosophical and legal terms, Lévi-Strauss's approach strives to reduce the perverse effects of the rights of the French Revolution and annihilates their reflex ethnocentrism.

There is nothing to be said about it, except that it won't work for you. As it happens, these three forms of thought, governed by the cosmic sacred, release the sorrows of individuals, and only individuals. The deliverance from suffering, the point of equilibrium of the boat in the middle of the river, the ingenious "neither-nor," have a price: indifference. In the true sense of the word, "in-difference" is not what people think: it consists of setting aside all differences—neither this nor that. These are philosophies that the West formulated differently. For example, Leibniz sought to diminish in-quietude, the opposite of quietude; but, at least, for him, the slight shuddering motion of inquietude at its best remained, a sharpened perception, a kind of vigilance toward the world.

The best of Buddhist indifference is expressed in the Buddha's smile. A wonder of bliss, of acquiescence, a splendor of vacuity, a luminous jewel . . . All right. I have often been to Bhutan, a Buddhist kingdom wedged between Nepal and Tibet, and to Sikkim, the old kingdom of the Tibetan religion that has become a state of India. The Buddhist temples there exude a peculiar joy, it's true. The idols smile, the simplicity is peaceful, and the parquets are gentle on bare feet. At the end of *Tristes Tropiques,* Lévi-Strauss hit just the right note for expressing the sensations the Westerner feels in a Buddhist temple. "The floor of thick bamboo, split and woven together, gleaming from the bare feet that had rubbed against it, was, under our steps, more supple than a carpet. That simple and spacious room, which looked like a hollowed-out rick, the courteousness of the two bonzes standing beside their straw mattresses set on bedsteads, the touching care that had been taken in collecting or fabricating the accessories of the cult, everything contributed to bringing me closer than I had ever been to the notion I had of a sanctuary." Yet he also noticed "the placid femininity, as if freed from the conflict between the sexes, suggested . . . by the bonzes of the temples, blending, because of their shaved heads, with the nuns, into a sort of third sex, half parasite, half prisoner."

After I had allowed myself to be won over by the tenderness of the place, I felt the same sickly sweet uneasiness. In that universe of gongs and handbells, an indefinable uncertainty hovers about. I understand that that uncertainty is the goal pursued. All the same, it left me perplexed. What was bothering me? Not the chants or the prayers. Was it the smile? No. It was olfactory. In temples in the Himalayas, the altar ornaments are sculpted out of butter. The predominant odor has the oily, nauseating subtlety of the still-undifferentiated primal maternal; there is something fetal in all that. And the monks and nuns cannot be distinguished from one another. That value of the bare skull is one of the mainsprings of Buddhism: indeed, if indifference is the goal to be achieved, the difference between man and woman is destined to be obliterated. The feminine disappears into uniformity; indifference is to be taken seriously, it gives rise to the undifferentiated. And, since nothing lasts, revolt is nipped in the bud.

I know I should not linger on personal sensations, and that Buddhist metaphysics is a grandiose construction, altruistic by virtue of detachment. That, in championing equality between living beings, original Buddhism, in its time, shattered the inequality of the caste system in Hinduism. That Buddhism wins hearts through serenity. And yet, in 1947, Lévi-Strauss was already stumbling over the "chilling alternative" of Buddhist morality: either confinement to a monastery or the practice of an egotistical virtue.

And yet, believe it or not, in a bizarre reverie on Buddhism, the "West," and Islam, the young ethnologist had previously indulged in a curious train of thought. The West, he wrote, because of its historical confrontation with an Islam that strictly separated the sexes, may have been able to "lend itself" to a slow osmosis with Buddhism. That may have further Christianized us, beyond Christianity itself. Then comes an extraordinary sentence: "It was then that the West lost its chance to remain a woman." What a fantasy! Not a word on Judaism, even though Lévi-Strauss's grandfather was the rabbi of Versailles, and the grandson owed his salvation during the war only to flight. . . . It is true that, in 1957, the year *Tristes Tropiques* was published, the hallowed term *Holocaust* did not yet exist; it took almost twenty years for the iceberg to reach the surface. And it was in 1947 that he visited the Buddhist temple of Chittagong. I understand how, in such a place, two years after the war had ended, a Jewish survivor could dream of the cessation of conflicts, even between the sexes. So, after the catastrophe, one can share the dream of that profound peace, which might be the "female" element in the world.

But is Buddhism the right way to "remain a woman"? That religion, which links thought and the nothing, veers toward the "neither-nor" of the sexes. Is that really your notion? That would surprise me. But I don't believe it's impossible that this "asexualization" attracts the Western believers who have converted to Buddhism. Finally rid of all that fuss about sex! Then you can really smile. One of my French friends, married to a Cambodian woman, told me in tears, regarding the twenty people in his wife's family who had died, that, with the Khmer Rouge, he came to understand the famous smile of Cambodia. That smile, he said, was indifferent. It was awful.

Why is indifference so constraining? Why restrict all heads, the same for men and women? And then, why interfere with the hair? There are so many examples. . . . The hair of virgins is sanctified, as is the Hindu baby's hair, which is thrown into the river in accordance with the rule; and that of Catholic nuns, who cut it off when they espouse God; sanctified, too, are the *nazirs* of God in Judaism—Samson and the Virgin Mary, who, conversely, must not cut off their hair for the duration of the oath. The single lock of the Brahman is also sanctified. It is as if that hair links heaven and earth. You keep your hair to sanctify it for God, or you shave it to get closer to Him. Either you weave the thread between us and heaven, or you pull it out and begin again from scratch. Monastic Buddhism chooses to begin again from scratch.

A sublime repression. What a quagmire! Forbidden embers; a prayer to extinguish desire. Buddhism, emerging from the depths of Hinduism, eradicates the latter's contradictions, its struggles, its blood-letting, its violent passions, the sperm spurting from its ascetics, and the feminine pleasure so celebrated in the sacred texts of India. You see, despite its infinite grandeur, Buddhism does not hold much charm for me. Let's just say you were struck by a sort of "reflex Buddhism," similar to the "reflex philosophy" of the scholars scoffed at by Louis Althusser. And let us go no farther. Because, in the end, you talk about the retreat of death into the "nothing," but then what? Give in to the asexual temptation, pass into pure abstraction?

After all, who knows? To be alone with one's thought, yes, really, who knows? I feel a twinge of hope. What if that were possible?

Perhaps that has never happened to me. I read here and there that women had no direct access to the symbolic, that they had difficulty with thought. Granted, but so what? I feel neither its poverty nor its pride nor its humility nor its disappointment. No hardship. My only criterion in the matter of thought is excitation. Nothing could be more opposed to the principles of Buddhism! It is bursts of enthusiasm within the mind, trains of thought so rapid that an ellipsis makes them jump the track, the electricity of a furtive current of pleasure and, to return to that, a short-circuit, which causes sparks. That is undoubtedly not the thought you are talking about, but that doesn't matter to me. I am a hedonist in the matter of thought. How can you understand that? I remember reading *Sémiotikè*, the dazzling book you published in the 1970s: hoodwinked, I told myself that you had a system of thought, a true one. That ate away at me for a long time. And then, with the help of analysis, it no longer had any effect on me. I am ready to confess my lack of a system of thought regarding the world. I believe that, on this point as well, I am truly an atheist.

I'm going to tell you what my own sacred is. The memory of the family lineage, "the head of my children" (on which one takes an oath), the alliances of love and friendship, respect for the dead, the Jewish lamp in front of the photograph of my mother during the year I have mourned her, the rites of ancestors. Am I a Confucian? No, I am truly Jewish. The rabbi who buried my mother last June told me that, for Jews, the only belief in an afterlife has to do with the survival of Israel from generation to generation: the afterlife is memory itself. That is my sacred; it is by definition faithful.

What is sacred in the English university ritual? Faithfulness to the rite. I agree with you, contemporary France has conscientiously destroyed its rites of passage. The result is edifying: no institution "takes." A rite is a sort of mayonnaise. It is not enough to mix the elements, you must get them to "set." A rite is an emulsion, and, to do it successfully, you have to know how to beat it. A little, not too much, especially not too long a time, a question of pace, duration, temperature. You learn on the job. If the rite is sacred in itself, that is because it refers back to that sort of memory. Proper to women? Of course not. But it is not difficult to understand why women can have more skill at it than men: in giving birth to living beings, they form a link between the generations.

Like the rite, the connections between generations are heading for the hills. The Roman rule of *pater incertus, mater certissima* required the acknowledgment of the father, which did not go without saying. That of the mother was taken for granted. Well, that's done for. That rule is giving way in the face of surrogate mothers on the one hand, genetic research on the other. It is possible not to have a mother, but, times being what they are, not having a father is becoming very difficult. What is that biological and social reshuffling? What does a child seek in his father's genetics? His chromosomal identity? What a mess. . . . So, filiation can be defined by blood, as during the times of Nazism and the Inquisition? Worse, because of artificial insemination, the order of generations has ended up in the gutter, grandmothers give birth at the same time as their granddaughters. And, since everyone senses the approach of a sacrilege, they seek to limit its effects. But, in fact, let us ask the question: In what way is it a sacrilege to reshuffle the generations?

After all, the great Greek infanticidal heroines savagely put an end to the generations. Medea cut the throats of her two sons, Agave the bacchante tore her son to pieces with her bare hands in her Dionysian delirium. I use them as examples because the danger, it seems to me, is on the same order as the current violations. Let us take the example of Agave. Queen mother and bacchante priestess of the God Dionysus, she antagonizes her son, King Pentheus, a good traditional Greek and very opposed to Eastern cults. The cult of Dionysus, imported from Asia Minor, is among them. Since Pentheus is a thoughtful sovereign, he prohibits it in his kingdom. But the offended god decides to take his revenge and, by ruse, leads the king to the heart of the nocturnal cult, as a way of showing him up close what it's all about. Intoxicated with rapture, his mother, Queen Agave, becomes delirious. Goaded by the god, she mistakes her son for a lion and attacks him. Death of Pentheus. Day begins to dawn. Finally, the queen sees what she is holding in her hands, her son's bloody head. In recovering the reason she had lost, Agave "rediscovers the purity of the heaven she has tainted."

Dionysus is a god who wears a robe, a god for women, in the first place; and then, he comes from the East, like the Hare Krishna of today. Mother against Son, East against West, delirium against reason, woman against man; in setting in motion the superhuman strength of the sacred delirium, the god transforms woman into a murderer, at night. Night against day. But there is something else, which I will call the "stranger." Queen Agave adopts a god who is not from her own land, and Medea, the other infanticide, kills her children in revolt, as a stranger abandoned by her husband, Jason. It is as a "barbarian" that Medea wreaks revenge on the children she gave her Greek husband. This mythical incident even appeals to the dangers imputed to the foreign woman, as attested to by the nature of the stranger Isolde, an Irish princess but also a witch who poisons her nephew Tristram, the Breton, with a love philter.

Oh, I see where you're headed. You were born a stranger! But these strangers come from beyond the sea. . . . Tristram brings Princess Isolde back in a boat, and it is in a boat, the one in quest of the Golden Fleece, that Jason kidnaps Princess Medea. In the times of myth and tragedy, the sea crossing is the risk of a journey from which one does not return. Medea's severed roots set her loose; in going off with Jason, she has burned her bridges—it's all over. And "id" returns. That infanticide, which she performs as a sacred sacrifice, is memory's frightening return to the native land. We experienced the diffuse reverberations of these memories of vengeance in the heyday of early feminism. We heard slogans about the return of witches, the moon, the tides, matriarchy, the primal. There was blood in the air and slaughter on the horizon. So, too, with the innovations in the systems of kinship.

So, who wrote, "The world belongs to women, that is, to death"? To life or to death? To both, General Sollers. To life to death. Understood: the one who gives life also gives death.

One question in conclusion. It concerns the Virgin Mary. I do not understand how she can make women hold their heads up within the heart of Catholicism. And, since you are so knowledgeable in Mariology, explain it to me. In return, I will tell you about the sacred dancing girls of India: they did not have the right to cut or wash their hair, they were prostitutes for the benefit of the gods; there are photographs of the last one of them, who died in the 1960s. Hair and prostitution, they introduce a curious difference into the sacred.

Catherine

My Dear Catherine,

PASSIONATE WOMAN THAT you are, you do not conceal your bad mood—your last letter, of March 12, which I received on the twentieth (our letters are crossing at the moment, no matter)—persuades me of that, if there were any need. The Virgin annoys you, thought as well, and the rituals of British academics no less. You prefer excitation and Buddhism. I suspected as much.

I won't fight for the English ceremonies. In that regard, and whatever my respect for the hospitality that the British cenacles offered Voltaire's works, I am inclined to share James Bond's sentiment. You know, when he returns safe and sound from his perilous adventures to the four corners of the world, his boss always offers him, as the ultimate reward, an invitation to dine at his club—one of the clubs whose male charm you assume captivated me, an absolute and incomparable ritual. Well, our agent 007 unfailingly responds that he is afraid he will have to refuse, since a personal obligation will detain him, that evening precisely, with a charming individual. . . . A ritual to top the first: James Bond is reason itself; I feel I am on his side, like every television viewer in the world.

First of all, let us not proclaim too quickly our sexual proficiency, in opposition to foolish "virginity"! The adjective *virgin* used to characterize Mary may be an error in translation: the Semitic term designating the social and legal status of an unmarried woman was replaced by the Greek term *parthenos,* which specifically designates a physiological and psychological condition. A discriminatory atrocity, an exclusion of women from sexuality, a punitive chastity? Of course, of course, we're against it, violently against that sort of chauvinistic manipulation, that goes without saying!

I like to imagine, however, that human beings were able to "think" . . . a beginning before the beginning. In their ramblings about "virginity," I choose to hear a protospace, a timelessness—wherever it was before the Word was. Before the Beginning: a non-imprint, a nonplace, beyond the grip of the original *techne,* of the primordial furrow? Rimbaud dreams of "that region from whence my sleep and my slightest motions come." When Meister Eckehart asks God to leave him "quit of God" (could I say "virgin of God"?), does he not envision as well that nonplace, that unthinkable outside? I like to imagine that the Virgin invites us not to cogitate on it but to dream it, to sing it, to paint it. A radical "transcendence" and, neverheless, one that gives itself, that becomes immanent to those who, like Rimbaud, consent to go that far: before time, before the subject, before the beginning. The fact that this nonplace before the beginning has been designated feminine or maternal is not likely to displease me, and it has led me to understand the "feminine" as something completely different from a symmetrical double of the masculine: did not Freud say, in one of those exorbitant intuitions, that the feminine is the more inaccessible for both sexes? More inaccessible because it is "before the beginning," and, in that sense, "virgin"? How many of us keep our ears open for that "virginity" in itself—for that unthinkable side of femininity?

Conversely, I am ready to fight for my Virgin. Yes, I say "my" Virgin, since to each her own, and I have somewhat the impression that mine is not in complete conformity with the canon of the Church. You'll grant me that I am not unaware of the traps that this sacré woman has set to snare our femininity for the last two thousand years: the body reduced to the ear and to tears; concealment of the sexuality I would not look at, under all the draping possible and imaginable by the best painters, and by the rest; sanctification of suffering and sorrow and, only afterward, the recognition of an incomparable power. Our queen of heaven may dominate the mystic depths, but she is rarely seen along the byways of power within the Church community . . . and so on. I am well situated to add that, in my tradition, that of Orthodox Christianity, the role of the Virgin as a power of intercession between the Son and the Father is extremely well developed. People have even gone so far as to suggest her immortality, since she is the only one in the gospel saga who does not die but is content to pass from life to death via the intermediary of the "Dormition"—you are familiar with the superb fourteenth-century icon of Theophanes the Greek, in the Tretyakov Gallery, as well as the well-known masterpieces of Andrey Rublyov. All that is possible, however, only at the cost of a "pilgrimage of the Mother of God amid the torments"—the title of an apocryphal text from the twelfth or thirteenth century, which recounts how Mary did not spare herself any torments suffered by the poor fishermen we all are—"the children of my son"—in the avowed goal of better pleading our cause before God, but, even more, of making herself the defender of the Son himself before the Father, whose pity seems very difficult to obtain. That Marian role is, of course, enviable, but it requires a boundless immersion in suffering; malicious people like you and me would say that Mary shows signs of an extraordinary predisposition to masochism.

Following close behind, modern thinkers such as Vladimir Solovyov and Sergey Bulgakov go so far as to introduce the cult of Sophia, divine wisdom, into Orthodox theology, with strong and often ambiguous feminine connotations. The experts observe, however, that that apparent promotion of the feminine under the aegis of the Virgin is, in the Eastern Church . . . cruelly lacking in women saints. With the exception of a few princesses and the very maternal Juliana of Lazarevskoy, my patron saint, women saints are rare in Orthodoxy. The Orthodox Marian cult has feminized the men, it may have virilized the women, but it does not seem to have contributed toward bringing recognition to the particular ways a woman feels and thinks. Be that as it may, and since a number of sublime constructions could be subjected to the same criticism, I continue to insist on the enormity of the enthronement of Mary in the Greco-Jewish synthesis of Christianity.

Mary's presence, very discreet in the Gospels, has continued to expand over the course of centuries, under pressure from popular paganism, which was eager to consolidate the role of a mother goddess within the prevailing monotheism. But also thanks to the painters—known to be sensitive to the maternal and the feminine, and who were dying to sublimate the so-called maternal. The theologians and philosophers themselves joined the fray, seeing Mary as a pretext for logical and dogmatic debates and refinements. Because the birth of Jesus was without sin, should not that of his mother, in a certain way, also be free from the same sin? Logical coherence requires it. Saint Bernard still bristled at celebrating the conception of Mary by Saint Anne and Saint Joachim, thus trying to check the assimilation of Mary to Christ. But Duns Scotus (1266–1308), a subtle logician, invented a *praeredemptio,* based on an argument of congruence: if Christ saves us through his redemption, the Virgin who bears him "must" be included in a backhand manner, beginning from her own conception, in what makes possible that redemption; in other words, she is the bearer of a "preredemption," . . . hence an "Immaculate Conception," which even goes so far as to remove original sin! You hadn't given it a thought, and you were wrong, since nothing is more coherent than Catholic dogma; and everyone knows that, without coherence, there is neither knowledge nor control over society. A word to the wise!

All the trickery to which the body of Mary was subjected, however, was very slow to take root as dogma, that is, as the law for believers. The proof: the dogma of the Immaculate Conception dates only from 1854, that of the Assumption of the Virgin . . . from 1950 (oh yes, that does not prevent Titian and many others from painting her in assumption, but all the same, that was not in the dogma: you were unaware of that, as was I!); I am also happy to inform you that Mary, who has worn the royal crown in paintings for centuries, and without batting an eye, was not proclaimed queen until 1954, by Pius XII, and that she has been the Mother of the Church only since 1964. A way of co-opting women by finding support in the image of the Virgin, the way the Church attempts to appeal to the Jews by canonizing a famous Jewish convert? In short, it entails recapturing or eliciting, within the official code, what has occurred or even taken root outside the official authorities, and which seems very useful in the eyes of those authorities. But then, why does the recognition of Mary seem so useful to them?

Far be it from me to reply in place of the authorities, except indirectly, that goes without saying. For example, it is often suggested that the success of feminism in Protestant countries can be attributed to, among other things, the greater initiative the Protestants grant to women in the ritual and social sphere. We may wonder, moreover, whether the militant and somewhat strained expansion of Anglo-Saxon feminism is not the result of a lack, within the Protestant religious edifice, where the maternal is concerned? The Catholics, in contrast, have elaborated that maternal aspect with all the ambiguity possible; we have not finished examining it, and it has made Catholicism difficult to analyze, as Lacan would say. Yet, clearly, the more difficult it is, the more agreeable it is to analyze, ad infinitum . . .

An odd little woman, that sublime Mary. The women and men who ask her to champion the secrets of female sexuality get nothing out of it and run the risk of going away disappointed. Like you. But then, what does she represent? In her beautiful book, Marina Warner quotes lines from Caelius Sedulius, who marvelously captures the uniqueness of that figure, who is really and truly steeped in mysteries: "She . . . has no peer / Not in the first woman nor in any others / who were to come, but alone of all her sex / she pleased God." A woman, Mary? Not so clear. Rather, "alone of all her sex." A clever construction, all things considered, which calms the social anxiety on the subject of birth, satisfies a male being anxious about femininity, and also satisfies a woman, no less anxious about femininity. In that way, a certain community can be established between the sexes, beyond their glaring incompatibility and their permanent war, and in spite of them. What if that were a version of the sacred, the version of the sacred that women bring to the fore: that is, the possibility of a life shared between the two sexes, just think of that! It is called the "rite of marriage," the family is considered sacred, and many take offense at such conformism. But, if we look closer, is it not sacrément difficult to join a man and a woman over time? With and beyond the conflict between rarely convergent, more or less incompatible, desires. Is it not increasingly rare, perhaps impossible?

Question: What, in the Marian alchemy, allows or at least facilitates "a certain agreement" between the sexes? Yes, let's not quibble, it's truly in Judaism and Christianity that the idea of the couple, of the emancipation of the person, and especially, of the woman, could develop, whatever the imperfections in relation to our modern requirements. It can be done better, no doubt, and that may be under way in a few protected circles that benefit from democracy, the economic independence of the two partners, the sexual freedom of the man and the woman, as well as respect for the other—who knows? We want to have it all and give up nothing, and some manage to do it perhaps, but, let's admit it, that remains a more or less frustrated desire. In the meantime, the Virgin holds no appeal except in Latin America or Africa.

I am writing you from the island of Ré, I can see the Ars steeple from my window, standing off in the distance, a pointed landmark, black and white, that cuts through the sky, the ideal place to discuss the subject. I therefore launch into a legal defense of Mary in three points, to move quickly.

Primo, from the Nativity to the Pietà, and including the Mater Dolorosa and the Regina Caeli, the Virgin is nothing like a lover: she is exclusively the devoted mother. The "good mother," as Melanie Klein would say, who gives herself body and soul to her son, to the extent that, without her, the dear son would have no body, since that god is a man, precisely, only by the grace of his journey through the body of Mary "full of grace." That grace is an extraordinary apologia for oblative motherhood, on the brink of primary narcissism: the origin of the love every human being needs to proceed. And the deficiency of same is the sinister source of all depression, if not psychosis. In short, Mary rehabilitates that primal bedrock of our identities, which modern analysts call "mother-baby coexcitation," and which Winnicott identifies with the serenity of "being"—in opposition to the drive-governed and phallic "doing," which develops later and is said to mark the phases in the evolution of the speaking subject.

In terms of "Being," I have always been surprised by the pages written by Heidegger, who, while visiting modern Greece, proves to be disappointed not to find the vestiges of Being inherent in ancient civilization but believes, all the same, that he has collected a few traces of them . . . in an Orthodox monastery. . . . Since I am somewhat acquainted with the popes, I have trouble reconciling them with the clearing of Heideggerian Being. Nevertheless, if the philosopher's impression could be justified, it would only be because of Mary. It is she, more strongly present in Orthodox Christianity than in the West, who imposes that serene tone, that *Stimmung* of Being, that "taste of brioche," as those who savor Russo-Byzantine sensuality say, preferring it to the Catholics and to Protestant austerity. Communion with the unnameable maternal bewitchment and the twilight of prelanguage are prolonged through Orthodox mystic exercises such as the "prayer of the heart" or "hesychasm"—a contemplation in prayer that makes it possible to achieve union with the deity once more, to transfigure man and nature. Mary, as "connection," "medium," "interval"—and not yet "other"—is the principal agent of that harmony between the inside and the outside, that restoration of narcissism. The desire to devour and murder remain, however, underlying every baby and every mother in their coexcitation, even if it is serene: you don't have to be a psychoanalyst to know that. But, via a strong cathexis of the breast—oh, the holy breast of the Virgin!—and the valorization of sorrow—oh, the sobbing of our Queen!—the aggressiveness inherent in that archaic link is obliterated, and we are saturated solely with the being of serenity. Which we miss so much, right?—an indelible fantasy!

In addition, that symbiosis of the son with the preoedipal—that is, not desirable but oblative—mother makes it possible to sublimate man's feminine traits. At one time, I took pleasure in demonstrating how a painter of madonnas, the magnificent Giovanni Bellini, put himself in the place of his mother (who, in fact, is absent from his biography: Dead? An unmarried mother? There's a mystery about that as well) to paint himself in Marian gentleness and melancholia. . . As for the daughter, whose case is not envisioned by the Christic family, by identifying with both elements of the duo (with the mother and with the son)—she finds the means to satisfy both her latent homosexuality ("I" am the suffering-and-male child of that mother who loves only me), and her need to be devoted to the other . . .

Secundo, around the child's archaic link to his mother, the entire continent, from the near side of language to its beyond, is set forth: the Christian Word, which metamorphoses the Greek Logos into the Christic and divine spoken word. Within the Word, two things will come about: on the one hand, part of the Son's trajectory toward his Father and, on the other, the rationality of Christianity, which will permit it to rediscover Aristotle and to clear its name through Descartes's cogito, before opening the way to modern philosophy. Well now, the Word, in fact, revolves around Mary. "The hole of the Virgin," says Sollers, by which he means—I'm simplifying, how can you help it?—that it is around an empty space left for Mary that the Trinity of the Father, the Son, and the Holy Ghost revolves. A hole, granted, I've made myself clear, but the artists have continually embroidered within and around it. Indeed, in that solemn adventure of the Word, Mary binds together *extralinguistic figures:* silence, music, painting. She elicits musical and pictorial representations, artists dedicate their experiments to her: the Virgin, at once the patron saint and the privileged object of art. It was in about the thirteenth century, with Saint Francis of Assisi (1182–1226), that the tendency to represent an earthbound Mary took hold: a human, very human Mary, and hence, a poor-modest-and-humble one: enough to encourage both humanist sensitivity and the glorious representation of the everyday, of nature—birds, animals, bodies of all sorts. This did not just involve giving the green light to the representation of cosmic destitution or female masochism. It was everyday lived experience, the natural life, that became the object of an uninhibited figuration of the Byzantine canon. Through the Counter-Reformation, the Jesuits, with Mary's help, would once more bring the ostentation of representation—Baroque this time—back to life: after Titian and Tintoretto came Bernini, Rubens, and Monteverdi.

Let's put it more baldly: the censorship of Mary's sexuality (here's a mama who has no desire, no eroticism outside her son) protects the artist from the anxiety proper to the Oedipal drama, and allows him to incorporate that denied jouissance by displacing it onto the deluge of forms that . . . he *himself* engenders. Forms that are at once an infra- and an ultralanguage, even when they take root in verbal art: is not literary "style" a vision, a melody, and also a silence infiltrated into everyday language? And the author is now the sole creator of these forms, at once subject and object. The consecration of Mary is the intrapsychic condition that favors the blossoming of Western art. Of course, in every civilization, aesthetic experiences unconsciously rest on the narcissistic connection and require the cult of the mother—and, at the same time, matricide—to modulate the signs of social exchange, which have become banal, into new, seductive, and regenerative signs. But, because that dependence has been made explicit, in a preconscious if not a conscious manner, the subject of Christianity has become freer within that archaic connection, more playful, more insolent. . . . In short, more artistic.

Tertio, Mary is in possession of a power, both recognized and denied, that holds up a reassuring mirror to women. As the Mother of God, the Virgin is more spoiled than her son, since she does not endure the calvary, passing rather through the intermediary of the very flattering Dormition and Assumption, before being enthroned as Queen of Heaven and of the Church. A superb canvas by Piero della Francesca depicts her as majestic, protecting under her skirts the kings and bishops who manage current affairs, whereas she is content to rule! What a fate! What an astute configuration, don't you think? On the one hand, she satisfies women's aspirations to power: I told you, she flatters our latent paranoia—every women who finds her reflection in the Virgin is implicitly destined for the same glory. . . . But, at the same time and on the other hand, she bridles them when she does not bully them: on your knees, ladies, you are only a place of transition, look after the children and the sick, no sex or politics, the ear and understanding are worth more than a sexed body, you can never be told often enough.

As of the thirteenth century, shored up by the implantation of ascetic Christianity, and especially, as of 1328, in the wake of Salic law, which prevented girls from inheriting and thus made the beloved very vulnerable, love for a woman became colored with every shade of impossibility. As a result, the Marian current prevailed over the courtly current. In the entourage of Blanche of Castile (d. 1252), the Virgin explicitly became the center of courtly love: the qualities of the desired woman were clustered around those of the holy mother. That made it possible to construct the ideal of the Christian woman, who makes every woman suffer and every man dream. For seven centuries, at least, a certain cohesion reigned within the couple: the war between the sexes could be forgotten, and cities, industries, and schools could be built . . .

Finally, even though it is possible, identification with Mary is far from encouraged: Mary, dear ladies, is unique. Does that mean that every woman is unique, that there is no point in comparing oneself to others, in seeking similarities and rivalries with others? It is a way, in any case, to plug up the aspiration for homosexual complicities, the secret societies among women, that the monastic life might have fostered but that Mary's uniqueness works to restrain, to eliminate.

I'll stop there: as you can see, the Virgin makes me verbose. The steeple of the Ars-en-Ré church, which is now cutting through the indigo night, illuminated by an internal reflection, incites me to continue, however. They're right to illuminate monuments. In this time of no values, monuments remain secure ones, to be displayed day and night, and preferably at night, urgently at night. . . . Relax, I'm tired and will spare you the possible consequences of my defense. As I told you on the phone, David's operation went well, despite the predictable postanesthetic difficulties, and we have come out to the island for Easter vacation. A moment ago, I received a call from Elisabeth, a woman I have known a little while: "Are you resting well?" she asked me. I was suddenly moved by that platitude: how long has it been since someone asked me that question . . . which I also never ask myself? There's no relation to the Virgin; it just seems obvious to me that, without work, there is nothing to be done—as an accursed writer says, and I am pleased to take that pleasure, which pushes us as far as we can go. Be that as it may, I very much want it to be Mary who makes me run like that, since she is, definitively, one emblem among others—but what a successful one!—of feminine endurance, of our ancestral courage that fuels the race after life and time.

Elisabeth's call moved me because of her caring and discreet proximity—I am not speaking of friendship, even less of love, that has nothing to do with it. Which leads me directly to what you say about your relation to Judaism: a sense of community, of the clan, of family. I cannot bear the eminent and Parisian vogue of those who, cram full of roots, social background, and complicities of all kinds, dream only of escaping from them to the solitude of the individual unburdened of all connections. You are well aware of those soldiers of freedom—I won't insist. In contrast, nomads like you and me share a different fate. As a result of our dislocated memories, we are left with the desire for discreet and reliable connections—like that telephone call: "Are you thinking about resting?" Minimal, familial perhaps, maternal if you like, essential. It is said there are no safe communities anymore (nation, religion, civilization) that are not in crisis. But that "networks" remain or are created. This friend's call is my own network in embryo: I want to domesticate it, cultivate it. A variant of that humble sacredness I told you about recently.

I've gone on about that minor event to tell you, above all, that I think I understand what you find in Judaism, an alliance of love and friendship. And yet, and yet, I do not agree with you when you identify the sacred with "the memory of the family lineage," "the head of my children," and so on. The biblical text, which serves as a reminder of erotic connections, connections of love and the conflict between men and women, in fact celebrates the reproduction of the living thing and the optimal conditions for its transmission from one generation to the next: genesis, numbers, and so on. But wasn't the stroke of genius precisely to have inscribed that genetic and familial—"maternal" if you like—connection within the loftiest symbolism? That which transcends the survival of Israel in a universal memory, an afterlife valid for all men? And does so, above all, through a certain positing of the feminine within Yahweh himself, within the people toward Yahweh, and even at the core of the robust fate of biblical women themselves! Now I want to give an apologia of the beloved in the Song of Songs, of Ruth and Sara, among others, but don't worry, that will be for the next letter. Assimilate the biblical message to genealogy alone? Certainly not. Others have done so, from within Judaism and from the quarters most fiercely opposed to it. As for you, you associate the imperative to ensure the survival of the generations with memory. On that, I follow you: it is at the *junction* of the genetic and of mind that Jewish election flourishes, and that, it seems to me, is another reason it is of such intense interest to women . . .

Just a word about Buddhism, to which you want to convert me, regarding indifference and the "nothing." In fact, the "nothing" I spoke of is part of the meaning of life—its appeasement and its limit, not its nullification. It has nothing to do with modern nihilism, the effacement of differences (especially sexual ones) and of acts of questioning (particularly revolt) that, in the West, is taken to be a "modern-style" Buddhism. The domestication of death, the acceptance of illness, in opposition to an ideology of health at all costs, the task of accepting euthanasia for the sick at the terminal phase—none of that prevents me from being a fervent proponent of life. A Judeo-Christian value, I have allowed myself to say. So what? I do not accept that modern Third World view of things, which takes the form of a battle against Judeo-Christianity by discrediting the desire for life and, on the pretext of disempowering the militant and commercial vitalism characteristic of technological society, in reality opens the way for a justification of death. For a culture of death, which is slyly insinuating itself at the end of this millennium, and whose victims, as if by chance, turn out to be the weakest, the most underprivileged: that can be seen in the ease with which we sacrifice the lives of Third World populations, but also in the poorer classes in the United States of America, and even sometimes here at home—on the pretext, for example, that the "gap" in Sécurité Sociale does not allow frequent enough screenings for one illness or another. . . . I think it is a shame that the pope is the only modern figure to defend the desire to live and the right to life. It is not because "eternal life" does not exist that life has no meaning. On the contrary, it is the experience of the "nothing" that gives the meaning of life, the fight for the most ordinary life, its sudden piquancy.

The north wind is picking up this evening, the water is beginning to hum in front of my veranda, and only the illuminated steeple stands fast across the way. Not me, it's time to go to bed, but you will hear from me soon.

Julia

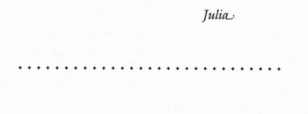

APRIL 22, 1997

Dear Julia,

DAVID'S OPERATION IS now behind you. I nearly wrote, "behind us," your last letter moved me so. It brought back memories. One day, the police found my son, on his way to school, writhing in pain on the sidewalk, in the middle of an appendicitis attack. . . . And the anxiety made my stomach churn in response. I don't know if that gut-wrenching feeling should be called "sacred," but it certainly crushes everything in its path. Omnipotence, you wrote me recently. And supernatural on top of it, that drive for the combination of feelings called "maternal love," which has such a powerful existence and such a weak name. Pardon me, but I am very angry about the misuse of the word *love*. In this precise case, I prefer the well-named *attachment*.

As it happens, at the moment David was going in for surgery, I was waiting for my daughter to give birth. I was surprised that I was more focused on her than on the child to be born—Is that normal, Doctor? Even so, the dear little boy made everyone wait for four days, during which time I found myself in a state of anxiety unlike any other. Thus, the maternal beast in me suffered quite a bit psychically, before the relief of the birth. Then I saw that child, "flesh of my flesh," an incomparable sensation. Incomparable, unlike any other, incommensurable, but for what? For the human race? He was two weeks old when I left again for Dakar, and the next time I see him he will have an eye color all his own. What if, fundamentally, the universality of the newborn were the midnight blue of the eyes at birth?

There is an omnipotence of maternal attachment, I grant you, but infanticide exists. It exists to such an extent that it is eagerly tracked in the news. An infanticide! The Villemin affair has shed light on that point for us; it's fairly recent. Someone had drowned a child bound hand and foot; and whom was everyone, including the judge, accusing with a single voice? The mother. Marguerite Duras conducted her personal investigation and, catching a whiff of Medea, wrote in *Libération,* regarding Christine Villemin: "Sublime, necessarily sublime." Terrific! Everyone applauded the artist. That written gesture, as grand as the classics. I know, art is not made out of the finer feelings, and so on. The frog Duras wanted to make herself as big as a sacrificial ox, and everything was for the best in the best of fantasized worlds.

No such luck, the mother was innocent. She lowers her tone, doesn't go on and on. The legal system, responsible for assessing "damages," calculates in francs the ravages of the social imaginary. Duras's notorious phrase ceases to circulate like the lyrics of a song. But, at the time, what psychic forces supported the shared desire for a son's murder by his mother? A perverse Oedipal stroke invented by Freud? No, thank you. Like love, Oedipus is undervalued. Well then, what?

Take the judgment of Solomon. As a result of family complications, two women claim to be the mother of the same child. The true mother must be identified. The king of Israel proposes to cut the child in two and divide him between the supposed mothers. A stroke of genius. The false mother agrees, but the true one begs: "Let him live!" She gives the child up to the other woman. . . . King Solomon is the greatest of the Judges. He knows how to identify a mother by the supernatural drive that inflames her in the face of danger. Because that drive is not miraculous, it appears "sacred" to me. To get it out of that nook, to make it shift over to the crime of infanticide, a very great envy is required. The jealousy that glorifies infanticide is a fierce one.

Indeed, to achieve fatherhood, fathers need a sacré salvage operation. There is no society that does not have formal occasions when
the child passes under paternal law. Rites of initiation of all kinds, cir-
cumcision, excision, seclusion in the forest, scarification. . . . In
India, the Brahmanic ceremony is called, with complete lucidity, the
"second birth": the first was natural, the second is religious. The
mother gives life but the father gives meaning. Elsewhere, he presides
over the marking of the body, and, if he does not wield the clippers,
he decides the moment when someone else cuts. The most beautiful
of the paternal rites, far removed from nicks in the flesh, is that of the
Romans: the mother puts the newborn on the ground, and, if the
man at whose feet the child is placed picks him up, he becomes the
father. There is still a little something of that in contemporary deliv-
eries, if the father agrees to be present, since then he will have the
child in his arms immediately. So it is that the father has the right to
give his acknowledgment, which, until the advent of genetics, was
not self-evident.

Positing is difficult. In its uncertainty (*pater incertus*), paternity requires unambiguous reassurance. How to avoid jealousy? The mother
is so certain. . . . That's understandable. Going from there to the desire
for the child's death at the hands of its mother is a leap that only
tragedy depicts. You have to believe that the desire for the tragic is just
as keen as ever! So, if we must find a mode of expression for the male's
motherhood envy, of which Duras—whose "Madame" and "Marguerite" I purposely omit—is a paradoxical example, I prefer the "nesting" ritual. Let men go to bed and mime childbirth, let them simulate
the mother's suffering and let people take care of them, that bothers me
less than these violent appropriations, these compensatory "second
births." For example, in terms of brutal appropriation, I think of the
way children are brought up in India. The child lives with his mother
until the age of seven, and then, yikes! He is handed over to the father,
the child is deprived of a mother. The result is disastrous: men are their
mothers' accomplices forever, petrified with anxiety before the figure
of the father. After you've lost the maternal intimacy of early childhood, how can you protect yourself from that strange man who makes
the law? That gives rise to the demand for the great goddesses I mentioned to you, these idols with a double maternal face, smiling and ter-
rifying. The sons, separated from their real mother, reinvent her by du-
plicating her. Near and far away. Tender and murderous, without tears.
Devotion guaranteed, fanaticism assured.

Here at home, paternal omnipotence belongs only to God. The fact that you were born in Bulgaria and I in France changes nothing: our Judeo-Christian heritage forces us to depict God as the Omnipotent Father. Omnipotence does not leave room for the absoluteness of maternal attachment. The latter exists, but does not prevail. The mother is honored, respected, but she has no say in the matter. The mother chosen by the Jews in exile is Rachel: Rachel, beloved of Jacob; Rachel, for whom he waited so long; Rachel, whom he won after marrying her sister—Leah, whom he did not love—under duress. Jacob and Rachel, or, deferred love. Jacob and Rachel, persecuted love. But Jacob and Rachel define two figures of God. After Jacob wrestles with the angel, he receives the sacred name of Israel; but, after the exile, Rachel receives the name "Shechinah," the shadow borne by God. When the people lament in the ghetto, then Rachel, veiled in black, appears. In misfortune, Israel needs Rachel's tears. More tears.

What then? The divine in power, the sacred in distress? The divine for the fathers, the sacred for the mothers? The divine for men, the sacred for women? The divine for phallocratism, the sacred for the oppressed? That would be so easy! But no. There's something not quite right here.

Let me get back to the ghetto. In this place of poverty where the dark veils of Shechinah could be glimpsed, the Hasidism of the "Just Men," the fanatical rabbis, originated in the eighteenth century. The rules that, even today, require that their wives shave off their hair and wear wigs also originated there. The wives do not sing or dance; only men have the right to do so. One need only read the legends of Hasidism to understand that the role of wives is confined to serving wine.

We know that the fathers of Hasidism had no taste for reading the Talmud, which is obligatory within the tradition, a tradition they shattered. The Hasidim preferred ecstatic dance and music to the Talmud. Like the Sufis of Islam, the Hasidim co-opted the feminine share of piety: in fact, in the Bible, it is Miriam, the sister of Moses, who is the first to dance with the Ark of the Covenant after crossing the Red Sea. The liberated Miriam dances, the liberated Moses does not dance. Conversely, the Hasid dances his freedom, his wife does not. Either she dances and he doesn't, or the rabbi dances but, consequently, not his wife. . . . In exile, the masculine appropriated liberation via the dance. Sharing it with women was out of the question.

Why so many separations? Why these missed encounters between the sacred and the divine? It seems altogether impossible that a man should dance *with* his wife in God's honor, as if the sacred constantly replicated the separation between maternity and paternity. What is there in the dance that makes it akin to divinity? Bisexuality, no doubt. In order not to confuse oneself with God, must one separate what God has joined together? Nothing can be ruled out. This phenomenon is not proper to Judaism. Sacred dances are done separately almost everywhere; the women dance, the men do not, or vice versa. The Koran radicalizes that separation of the sexes: when Adam and Eve are expelled from paradise, Adam ends up in India and Eve in Yemen. The Koranic separation is total—geographical, political, moral, and sexual. I admit that the Virgin Mary straightens things out somewhat.

But only somewhat. When does Mary step in? When she is fourteen, at the time of the Annunciation; then, during her pregnancy and Jesus' early childhood. When Jesus is twelve, Mary makes herself scarce. Once the presentation of Jesus at the temple is over, exit Mary, until the crucifixion. What an absence. What becomes of Mary for twenty-two years? It's a mystery. Her body has almost no story, or rather, it has only two: gestation without impregnation by the male and the final Dormition. I am undoubtedly too much of a pagan to accept a body that is incarnated but at the same time escapes sex and death.

On the question of "paganry," I promised I'd tell you about the sacred dancing girls in India. Today, the once sacred dancers live in the secular universe of an embryonic "show biz," with meager fees as compensation. But, until Indian independence in 1947, they danced in the temples in front of the statue of the god. Well and good. Who saw to their room and board? The Brahmans in the old days, and later, the rich merchants: in both cases, since they are of the higher castes, the Brahmans and merchants are "twice born." Hence the dancing girls served as sexual objects for the worthy paying members. We're closing in on the nature of "sacred prostitution": a tolerated brothel for high society. Nonetheless, there *is* something sacred in the matter: as it happens, a temple dancer did not have the right to wash her hair. Ever.

Have you seen that sort of hair? It is still very visible out on the roads in India. Those who have decided to leave the world never wash their hair. They are "renouncers." There is no longer anything human about their hair. It's like oakum. After a few years, that plant matter no longer has anything in common with the notion of hair. And that is precisely the goal of the maneuver: it entails connecting the renouncer to the "forest," the space of meditation, in contrast to the "village," the social space of the commonwealth. The renouncer's hair recovers the naturalness of the tree; it becomes vegetal and is not washed.

And yet there is nothing impure about these filthy bundles. According to tradition, the "twice-born" customers of the dancers are forbidden any impurity, and if you belong to the higher castes you don't fool around with bodily ablutions. The vegetal mass of unwashed hair is thus not for man's benefit, but for god and god alone. The model for this exists in Indian mythology: when the young girl named Parvati falls hard for the god Shiva, she engages in all sorts of mortifications of the flesh to seduce him. She perches on one leg, her hands joined, and remains that way for a thousand years. Liana envelops her, she becomes vegetal. Only then, when she is reduced to the state of the beautiful plant, does Shiva deign look upon her and marry her. By sleeping in the temple with the dancing girls with unwashed hair, the "twice born" man identifies with the god. And never mind the odor.

That vegetal question brings to mind Claude Lévi-Strauss's gripping analysis of the myth of Oedipus. After a meticulous and methodical comparison of the genealogies of the Oedipus line, Lévi-Strauss concludes that the myth of Oedipus is the expression of a hesitation between two hypotheses regarding the birth of the human race. Either man is born from the earth, according to the classical Greek conception—like a vegetable—or he is born of two parents, an enigmatic affair. Despite the obscurity of his birth, Oedipus is a man endowed with two parents. He even boasts adoptive parents, before discovering that he killed his father and married his mother. To be born of two parents comes at a high cost for the hero of the myth, as we know. But the fraud perpetrated on Oedipus begins with a mutilation.

From his birth, the child Oedipus has his feet pierced through with the rod by which his father suspends him, like an animal caught in a trap; let him starve to death, abandoned, this newborn who brings misfortune. Oedipus survives, but his name means "swollen foot." Like his father, Laius, whose name means "lame," "Swollen Foot" Oedipus is incapable of walking straight. It is this point Lévi-Strauss stresses. The myth of Oedipus, he tells us, corresponds to the moment when the Greeks changed their ideas about birth, moving from the plant world to procreation. The mental operation is so difficult that a myth is used to tell of it, and this is the story of Oedipus. If man wants to leave his vegetal status behind, then he walks crooked. The human plant born from the seed shoots up by itself, without designated parents, but, to accede to the knowledge of human procreation, the myth requires the full price: awkward gait, patricide, incest, monstrosity. It is, in fact, easier to assimilate the human plant to a liana touching God.

Many cosmologies make the story of men begin with a thread held between God and earth. A cord, a rainbow, a tree, leaves, or rope all equal hair. In that sense, the plaited locks the beloved gives the lover are sacred. Hair links them together. The things that happen with hair! Do you remember the violent scene between Mélisande and her jealous husband, Golaud? Maeterlinck's text in the libretto for *Pelléas et Mélisande* is incredible! Golaud drags Mélisande by her hair, shouting, "This long hair will finally serve some purpose!" Yet it has just served, spread out the length of the tower over the lover Pelléas at night. The jealous husband has understood the connection by means of hair. And when someone wants to humiliate a woman who is presumed guilty, he shears off her hair, as in 1945. Why?

The sacred has to do with odors, natural secretions, nail clippings, and, finally, with hair. In short, the sacred participates in all the materials that dear Lacan categorized under the generic name "object of desire," that is, the detail, the partial, the piece of body that is not the whole of the body, and even its waste. So, is waste part of the divine universe in the three forms of Western monotheism? For Judaism and Islam, the answer is no. Leviticus and the Koran absolutely exclude it. In the Gospels, the response is ambiguous, since Jesus heals impurities. He puts an end to the sick woman's vaginal bleeding, to pustules, to leprosy, to the decomposition of the body of Lazarus. Waste is there, obliterated by a miracle. Waste is to be avoided. One carefully purifies oneself of it. In following the texts of the *Corpus Christi,* based on the broadcasts of Gérard Mordillat and Jérôme Prieur, I was stunned to discover that the effects of crucifixion on its victims included, among other abominations, the physiological inability to control the discharge of urine and excrement. And, since the bodies of people being crucified were completely nude . . . Suddenly, I "saw" the real image of Jesus on the cross. All in all, no one talks about it.

It is more proper to have only the voice of God in one's ear. As a matter of fact, in the long list of material equivalents for the object of desire, there are nobles ones and there are ignoble ones. The voice, the tear, the breast, the milk, the breath, and the strand of hair are noble. The appropriate theology can be found for all these part-objects: the voice of the Eternal addressing his people, the "gift of tears" in the Orthodox religion—the exact count of tears in the writings of Ignatius of Loyola, which you presented in your last book—the breast of the Virgin Mary, the breathing technique in the exercises of the Orthodox Hesychast monks. In contrast, the objects of desire below the belt are ignoble: the sexual secretions, urine, and excrement. Nothing is said about them in the different forms of monotheism. To find theologies of the "ignoble," you must look elsewhere, in the tantric exercises of the left hand, of which I gave a long example in *Syncope*. Or you have to read Sade, who knows all about them.

Is the ignoble less sacred than the noble? That depends on the religion. That depends on the ennoblement of bodily waste or its symbolic fall. All forms of monotheism exclude the ignoble, but, in the religions of Africa, fingernail clippings occupy a privileged position. A sacred tree watches over the accumulated traces of animal blood, of milk; they are not cleaned up, they must ooze permanently. The sacred tree condenses the animal and the vegetal. Because of the absence of any cleanup, it is, rather, "of the left hand."

Yet nothing can prevent a woman from being confronted, within her body, with an acquaintance with the "ignoble": consider the vast number of ads for sanitary pads with a very blue liquid, to avoid the red of menstrual blood. Who's fooled by that? Not women; they are familiar with the "left hand." So it is, in fact, a trompe l'oeil effect for "the others," the men, who are treated like half-wits. They'll buy blue blood, is that it? . . . And nothing can prevent the birth of the child from occurring *inter faeces et urinas,* as Saint Augustine said; in his view, that's all it takes to impel you to seek salvation in the afterlife. And what to make of the ignoble face of the divine, my father? Purify thyself, my daughter, says Leviticus. Ritual baths exist everywhere in the world. Go off in your corner to bleed, and clean yourself up before you come back. What's that? You're bleeding in order to have children? We don't want to know about it! You can talk as long as you like, I'm not listening. All the same, it's because of the "ignoble" that the female body is directly linked to the sacred.

We need to examine that infamous "belt" that cuts the body in two, the noble above, the ignoble below. Such is precisely the emblem of separation between the upper and lower castes in India. In the Hindu cosmological system, the god Brahma partitions humanity by dividing his body into four sections: he creates the Brahmans with his breath, the warriors with his chest, the merchants with his thighs, and the servants with the rest, his feet, his bowels, his viscera. What about the sex organ? It is absent from the myth, don't you see. In uncertainty. There is a lack of certainty about the purity or impurity of the sex organ; better to have sexuality take the high road, the Brahman side, the breath of Brahma. That is what the ascetics do with gusto when they make the sperm "rise back up" to the brain via the spinal cord. Let us raise the ignoble up to the noble, that's safer. Let's get away from the lower regions, and let's catch our breath.

In Dumézil's footsteps, Georges Duby tracked down the system of Indo-European castes in medieval Europe and rediscovered it in the division among the three orders: the nobility, the clergy, and the "clerks," the latecomers. As for the servants, they did not belong. The servants are the "rest," the "remnants," of humanity. The aftereffects of caste divisions can be felt as late as 1789, in the Estates General. Hence, the three orders excluded the great mass of peasants from social representation: they were more or less "remnants" from below the belt, according to the Indo-European order. By that means, Duby takes off from medieval society and lands at the French Revolution, an aborted revolution in terms of the true liberation of the serfs.

The strange thing is his starting point, courtly love. In the twelfth century, European medieval society relied on the love of ladies to extend the life of its castes. Oh, what a fine invention was courtly love, explains the ironic Duby. A sanctification of love and a promotion of women? Come on! Read Duby. It's true that the suzerains recruited their clerks for a Platonic court of love for the lady, but only to keep the clerks at the castle. With their hearts committed, the clerks became better integrated at court, and it made little difference to the suzerain that it was a court of love. In plain language, this subtle connection to a sacred fire off in the distance was a mysticism designed for the clerks by their leaders. Then the image of the lady can coincide without damage to the image of absolute love. A charming game for the ladies, but a very exclusive one; outside the court of love, there are none of these niceties for the "remnants" of humanity. The peasants do not "love" in the noble sense.

Hence, perhaps, rebellion and its excesses. It is only one step from the frustration of love to the Reign of Terror, a step that the mother goddesses easily allow to be taken in India. What if one were to take the next step? What if "maternal love" were of the left hand, on the side of the ignoble, below the belt? I believe that is the lesson of King Solomon.

Catherine

Dear Catherine,

IT WASN'T POSSIBLE to send my letter of April 19 until a few days later, because of a broken printer. In the meantime, I received yours, dated April 22. Our correspondence is increasingly "crossed": perhaps we should switch to e-mail. Do you have an e-mail address?

Your concern about such ignoble things as pubic hair and other dirty hair does not really take me away from my intention to deliver a few reflections regarding Judaism, since filth and the sacred are adjacent to each other, you're quite right. Nevertheless, I will be less pagan than you and will play devil's advocate, since monotheism is now on the way to becoming the devil. It asserts that the sacred is, purely and simply, nothing other than . . . love. Is there an abyss between pubic hair and love? Or are there not similarities in the logic? Here's the little meditation I propose for you, and it comes at an opportune moment: today, May Day, is a sunny day in Paris, the silence of the closed streets and the fragrant lily of the valley touch my heart, David has gone away on a long weekend with a girlfriend, Philippe is meeting with journalists, and I have all the time in the world. I hope you do too.

I want to believe that the foul-smelling hairdos of your dancing girls are sacred, but what I'm sniffing out is that they are so by virtue of certain rules of separation or exclusion, which designate their place in an order. I already caught a nasty whiff of the more or less tolerable horrors and other abjections with which men have tried to purify themselves since the darkest times of humanity, while writing my book *Powers of Horror: An Essay on Abjection* in 1980. In reading Mary Douglas, Louis Dumont, and Paul Ricoeur, among others, not to mention *Totem and Taboo* by dear Freud (parenthetically, I was delighted to hear Alain Touraine, the other day, asserting that psychoanalysis has opened the way to sociology, and that, without Freud, anthropology and sociology would not exist: it's gaining ground, don't you see), I thought I understood that the sacred, which is always a purification, has a history. It can be traced on the basis of the specific characteristic of the filth that is gotten rid of.

To simplify, let us say that our ancestors began by ridding themselves of filthy substances: excrement and other waste products, but also blood, especially menstrual blood. You prefer hair, granted! One of your predecessors in our Western regions, the famous Socrates, was confronted with that business of foul pubic hair by Parmenides, in the dialogue of the same name; you remember, Parmenides asked him if it is possible to conceive of an Idea for "pubic hair, mud, filth, or any other of the most poorly regarded and foul things." That's where the entire problem lies: is that filth conceivable, is it nameable, and, if so, how can it be expressed? Well, in looking closely, researchers more patient and gifted than you and I have perceived that these substances (and I would like pubic hair to stand as the paradigm for them, a paradigm stemming from your own elaboration), are dirty or contagious or dangers "in themselves" only because they fall under the prohibition. In other words, humans are human because they speak—which means that, along with their speech, they constitute an order composed of exclusions and eliminations, in such a way that what is cut off and rejected from that order ceases to be "profane filth" and becomes "sacred filth," establishing, at the same time, that which is "proper" to a group. Or, in still other words, a *system of classification,* and not the substance itself, decides what is filthy or not. Hence, in India, with which you are very familiar, food is considered pollutive if its manufacture does not respect a strict separation but involves a mixture between two orders or two territories. For example, a food that has passed through fire is pollutive and must be surrounded by a set of taboos, as if fire, far from purifying—as our notions about hygiene assert—indicated a meddling of the familial and social hearth in the nature of things, as if it confused identities, favored their contagion, and, as a result, came to resemble . . . excremental objects of abjection, which, in another way, coincide with that same pollutive logic of the space between, by locating themselves between life and death, body and corpse.

Similarly, leftovers are dirty, according to Brahmanism, because they are a remainder of something or someone: they pollute because of their inadequacy—another figure for the breach in separation. In addition, the negative and borderline values of contaminating objects are reversible, and reverse themselves into omnipotent and positive values. For example, under certain conditions, the Brahman may eat leftovers, which, instead of polluting him, make him qualified to complete a journey, and even to perform his specific function, the sacerdotal act. Similarly, certain cosmogonies represent the remnant, after the flood, as a serpent who becomes Vishnu's helper, and thus guarantees the rebirth of the universe. Similarly, as well, even though the leftovers of a sacrifice are abject, the act of consuming them may cause a series of good rebirths and may even allow us to reach heaven. That is why the author of the Atharva-Veda (11.7) exalts the remnant (*ouchista*) as at once contaminating and regenerative: "On the remnant are founded the name and the form, on the remnant is founded the world. Being and nonbeing, both are in the remnant, death, vigor." The same is true for your hair.

I emphasize that boundary line that makes the dirty turn into the tainted, since it is then understandable how the ritualization of filth can be accompanied by a complete effacement of the dirty object itself, though it nevertheless underlies the rites. Definitively, the dirty object vanishes as such when it is transformed, within a particular logic, into "filth": it is no longer noticed, it no longer smells. That is what happens in the castes in India, where the ritualization of filth is extreme. Many travelers have noticed that Hindus defecate everywhere but that no one mentions their squatting silhouettes, either verbally or in books. That's normal, notes an anthropologist in conclusion: quite simply, the Hindus *do not see them*. It is not a matter of censorship due to a sense of decency. Rather, it is a foreclosure, a cleavage that seems to occur between, on the one hand, the territory of the body, where a sort of guiltless fusion with the mother and nature reigns, and, on the other, a completely different universe of social and symbolic allocations, where embarrassment, shame, guilt, and desire enter in.

That cleavage, which in other cultural worlds would produce psychosis, is perfectly socialized in India, perhaps because the institution of the rite of filth takes on the function of a link, a diagonal line: the two universes of *dirtiness* and of *prohibition* lightly touch each other, or ignore each other, but do not reject each other as an *object* and a *law* do. Hence the human being who inhabits that universe, where the sacred is filth, moves back and forth in a state of flexibility—or hallucination?—between the unnameable (what lies beyond the limit: dirtiness) and the absolute (the implacable coherence of the prohibition, of which no one is unaware, no more in India than elsewhere, and which generates meaning: exclusions, impossibilities, various and varied norms, and so on).

That regulation of the opposition between pure and impure via the intermediary of filth determines a social and symbolic order that is not binary in any way, but intensely hierarchical: a stratification of differences between social groups in behavior, in verbal and artistic codes, and so on. I don't need to tell *you* that endogamy, precisely, is part of that order: I leave aside the question of whether endogamy produces the order or whether it is its consequence. I simply observe that, in endogamy, the individual is prohibited from marrying outside his group. In the Indian castes, there is, in addition, a specific filiation: the transmission of the status of member of the group by both parents at once. A balance, both symbolic and real, is achieved in the role of the two sexes within the social and religious unit constituted by a caste. A caste can be defined as a hierarchical mechanism that, apart from professional specializations, assures an equal share to the mother and the father in the transmission of one's status as a member of that group.

You will notice that the Hindu system differs in an essential way from "our" exogamic systems, founded on a strict separation between those who belong "properly" and those who are "strangers," between same and different, man and woman. It would seem that, when one avoids the binarism of the exogamic system at the level of the institution of marriage—that is, the estrangement between father and mother, man and woman—the differentiations—the abjections—at the level of ritual multiply: hierarchies between the sexes, between subjects, objects, castes, foods, and every sort of "hair" under the sun. That proliferation of rules and their hierarchical arrangement set in place a logic of "nonviolence," in opposition to a logic of "cutting" proper to monotheism, the sharp edges and passions of which we know only too well. Yet the nonviolence of that polytheistic and hierarchical pantheon, so close to the sacred/filth, is, in fact, far from absolute: outbreaks of every order and recent acts of carnage have marked India's past and present.

You seem to think that this variant of the sacred is the "true" sacred and that all the rest is "religion." And you imply that women, because of their familiarity with the body, would be inclined toward that particular sacred. I disagree, and not only for the pleasure of enlivening our correspondence.

Even though the sacred is constituted through a logical system of exclusions and does not dwell in the natural substance themselves, I maintain, contrary to Mary Douglas and certain anthropologists not associated with psychoanalysis, that these substances are in no way a matter of indifference. Filth, which is always related to the orifices or boundaries of the body, as so many landmarks constituting the corporeal territory, is, schematically, of two types: excremental and menstrual. Tears and sperm, for example, though related to the edges of the body, do not have the value of pollution and/or filth. Excrement (and its equivalents: rot, infection, illness, cadaver, hair, and so on) represents the danger stemming from what is external to the "proper" or to the "(logical) order"; conversely, menstrual blood threatens the relation between the two sexes and represents the danger stemming from within sexual and social identity. (The rotten hair of your dancing girls stands as an opaque conjunction between bodily waste and maternal power.)

Now I can set forth my idea: through these two prototypes of filth (excrement and menses), what is fundamentally warded off is maternal power. Why? Just think of the maternal authority that oversees the training of the sphincters, through archaic frustrations and prohibitions, and forms a first cartography of identity out of our autoerotic baby bodies, well before our identity cards, a cartography composed of zones, orifices, points, and lines, between "proper" and "improper," to be precise, possible and impossible. A primal cartography of the body I call "semiotic," which is the precondition for language even though it depends on language, and which suffers and takes pleasure in an other logic, complementary to the logic of linguistic signs imposed and consolidated by paternal laws. The sacred rites founded on filth unquestionably celebrate our difficult—impossible—separation from that authority, the mother. Is it the only form of the sacred that is in complicity with women? Surely not. Does it vanish under the other variations of the sacred? No to that too.

I am not the kind who attempts to constitute, in the direct line of Hegelian logic, an evolutionary history of increasingly perfect religions, up to the last, which would be the universal religion. Let us confine ourselves to speaking of "types." Next to *filth,* there is an *evil.* It is always what departs from the "logical order" but takes the form of a *transgression of every prohibition*—and not only that of an exclusion of excrement or blood. That evil may be the *collective fault* or *sin*, an age-old debt that avenges the iniquity of the fathers by visiting the punishment on the children. It is also *individual guilt,* which pulverizes the collective sin and internalizes the realism of the sin as an individual responsibility. Such is the trajectory of the Bible—from the Levitical abominations that exclude certain substances, to the conflicts in which the descendants of Abraham are engaged, and to which they are handed over, to the superb and intimist movement of the guilty consciousness, known as the "suffering just man," the "suffering servant," Job, whose sorrow is absurd and scandalous, defying judgment in the strict sense. Guilt now changes horizon and deserves mercy. Finally, a third type of sacred links guilt to remission. The Christian faith does not say: "I believe in sin," but "I believe in the remission of sins"—*Kippur. Forgiveness.* A "sacred" that suspends judgment and time: it wagers on a fresh start.

The Jewish Bible completes that extraordinary trajectory, which is not unacquainted with filth or collective sin, nor with individual guilt or forgiveness. The Bible is obsessed with filth, but metamorphoses it into election, that is, into the rite of love.

Take the Levitical abominations. First, taboos have the advantage of saving you the trouble of a sacrifice. "Thou shalt not kill" implies "Thou shalt not eat": an apparently illogical list of dirty foods follows. What relation is there between food and the prohibition on killing? It's quite simple: the first separation between man and God is alimentary—thou shalt not eat of the "tree of life," says Yahweh, but Eve does not want to hear it, any more than does Adam. It takes a cataclysm, the flood, to prompt the authorization to eat "every moving thing that liveth" (Genesis 9:3), and, in fact, it is not a reward but an accusation: "For the imagination of man's heart is evil" (Genesis 8:21). After the flood, the biblical concern with separation takes new forms: on the one hand, bloodless flesh (destined for man), on the other, blood (destined for God). Blood connotes the penchant for murder, which is precisely the major prohibition. But blood is also the vital element, an allusion to women, to fertility, to the promise of fecundity. Blood then becomes a lexical crossroads, an auspicious place for fascination and abjection, where death and femininity, murder and procreation, the end of life and vitality repel each other and join together. "But flesh with the life thereof, which is the blood thereof, shall ye not eat" (Genesis 9:4). "I am the Lord your God, which have separated you from other people. Ye shall therefore put difference between clean beasts and unclean" (Leviticus 20:24–25). . . . The list of sometimes specious prohibitions contained in Leviticus—alimentary prohibitions after the burnt offering Moses and Aaron make to Yahweh, and after that which Noah makes to Elohim—becomes clearer once we understand that what is at issue is to keep man from eating carnivores. For that, there is a single criterion: eat herbivores that chew their cud. Certain herbivores depart from the general rule of ruminants with hoofs: theirs are cloven. They will therefore be excluded. The result, already perceived in other religions in pursuit of filth, is that the "pure" will be what is in conformity with a logical order or taxonomy, and the "impure," what disrupts, what favors intermixing and disorder.

What about woman in that taxonomy? Leviticus adds, to the food considered impure because it does not conform to the taxonomies, the body of the menstruating woman and of the woman in childbirth. The mother goddess, a fertilizable or fertile body, a pagan power that poses the danger of threatening the logical order, haunts the imaginary of a people at war against polytheism, which is always operative. The various chapters of Leviticus list varied abominations: illnesses, sexual and moral deviations—we are moving farther and farther from the substance of blood/mother and murder, we are becoming integrated into "abstract" moral laws. Nevertheless, a recurrent precept holds our attention, since it associates the alimentary prohibition with fusional maternity: "Thou shalt not seethe a kid in his mother's milk" (Exodus 23:19, Deuteronomy 14:21). It is not milk as maternal food that is being called into question, but milk used in accordance with a culinary whim, hence a cultural fantasy, establishing a mixture (an incestuous connection? a narcissistic connection?) between the mother and her child. That new alimentary prohibition is to be understood as a prohibition of incest, in the same capacity as the prohibitions that prevent one from taking the mother from the nest with the young or an egg (Deuteronomy 22:6–7) or from making a burnt offering of the cow or the sheep with its young (Leviticus 22:28).

The biblical text, concerned with that prohibition of incest, seems very harsh toward women. And, starting from there, no one misses the chance to take aim at its misogyny. That violence, justified by the history and context of paganism, should not lead us to forget that, through it, in spite of it, and thanks to it, we witness a process of "subjectification" of the feminine substance, a true alchemy of that substance ("blood" or "milk"), which is transformed into an autonomous, vigorous, responsible, loving subjectivity. For me, *the sacred resides in that transition, in that passage,* and not in its edges, lower (filth: pubic hair) or upper (the strict prohibition that veils or cuts off heads: the horror of monotheistic fundamentalism). I do not know Hebrew, I read the Bible as a layperson and without proficiency or real assiduity. But literary texts send me back to it endlessly, as well as a number of dreams, and certain moments in my analysis of patients—unbearable or magnificent. . . . I detect in it a destiny specific to the feminine to which I cling, in that a transition occurs that turns that "maternal" element—which paganism sanctifies and polytheism cleaves and disseminates—into a highly sophisticated moral edifice.

Let us begin, as is only right, with Yahweh. Jewish mysticism, well known now thanks to the works of Gershom Scholem, mentions a fe-male deity whom some call "the Hebrew goddess." In the beginning, it is demonstrated, Yahweh is represented with a female partner. Later, when it is prohibited to represent God, the woman will be reduced to the position of guardian, represented by two female cherubim. After the destruction of the first temple, the idea takes root that God alone pos-sesses the two aspects, male and female, and, as a result, the cherubim no longer signify anything but divine attributes. For the Talmud, the male cherub represents God, and the female, the people of Israel. The Kabala, finally, develops the mystical theory of the *sefirot*, and considers the king and the Maronite two divine entities. American feminist stud-ies have recently established a filiation between Hinduism—and the place it grants to the mother—and the couple in the Song of Songs, proposing a "depaternalizing" interpretation of Judaism.

We all know—but do we know it really? Who still reads these texts, apart from believers?—the very famous four "mothers of Genesis" and their supernatural power: beautiful, rebellious warriors, they were as sterile as they were gifted with longevity—as if to ward off the natural pagan fertility through a completely different destiny, stemming from the Other, but to which they did not adhere any less, body and soul. Hence Sarai, whom Abraham passes off as his sister, becomes Sarah when Yahweh promises her a son, Isaac . . . at the age of ninety-two. After that utter and complete adherence to the word of God, Sarah can live to the age of one hundred and twenty-seven. Could that be a vari-ant of incest, from which one must separate oneself through laughter, given that "Isaac" means "he who laughs"? Rebekah is beautiful and virginal when she is sought out to marry Isaac. Rachel, a shepherdess and daughter of Laban, is loved by Jacob because she is "beautiful and well favoured," but she is also sterile and jealous of Leah, the other wife, who will give Jacob six sons. QED: procreation is indispensable and heartily recommended, but that is not the only thing for a woman, and even the best of them can be deprived of it—especially the best of them. All the same, it is not a matter of punishing them, each will have her child, but only near the end of the story: ultimate reward, or un-likely? Oof! Yahweh "remembered Rachel, and God hearkened to her, and opened her womb. And she conceived and bare a son . . . Joseph."

As far as women warriors go, I prefer Judith—probably because of Artemisia Gentileschi, who left behind her immortal *Judith and Holofernes*: the cruel decapitation of Nebuchadnezzar's general, which she (Judith or Artemisia?) carries out in cold blood, by the greatest female painter of all time (Artemisia), to save her people and confound the Assyrians (Judith). She lives no fewer than 105 years and remains faithful to a single man, her husband, Manassi: once a general has been decapitated, there's no reason to complicate matters or split hairs, even less to leave them dirty, since that erotic frenzy is truly only a miserable attempt to remedy castration, as everyone knows. Esther, the wife of Ahasuerus, and Deborah, who impels the men to vanquish Sisera, as well as Jael, Susanna, and a few others are no less heroic or less historical. No relation to any archaic substance or disorderly mystery whatever—they chop, they lead, they smash the heads of the enemy, or they choose to die. In short, they accelerate history rather than abandoning themselves to nature. I very much like Deborah the priestess, that "bee" who "arose a mother in Israel" to whom "the children of Israel came up . . . for judgment." Although more discreet, she does not cede in the slightest to the male word of the other prophets, and her song, which celebrates the victory of Israel over a Canaanite king, one of the oldest texts in the Bible, begins by celebrating . . . yes, hair! Not jammed-down hair, but the liberated hair of the soldiers of Yahweh: "Praise ye the Lord for the avenging of Israel, when the people willingly offered themselves."[6]

There are also the queens. Esther, a sublime beauty whom Ahasuerus married, saved the Jewish people from the first "pogrom," the massacre ordered by her husband, the Persian king. Racine loved her in turn, as demonstrated in his famous lines, which rival the Hebrew psalms in grandeur, modesty, and pathos. Jezebel, the mother of Athaliah, was, in contrast, violently pagan and idolatrous, to the point of erecting a temple to Baal: the soldiers of Jehu killed her ruthlessly, her body was thrown to the dogs, and only "the skull, and the feet, and the palms of her hands" remained. You know the engraving by Gustave Doré commemorating that sacrifice, which does not bother with the hair but by rights disperses even the slightest remnants of that dirty woman, as abjection requires. Athaliah, also passionately recalled by Racine, exterminates everyone to keep herself on the throne, but can do nothing in the face of Joash's innocence—nothing, above all, before the Law supported by God. There was Bathsheba, the seductive wife of one of David's officers, whom the king married even while killing

---

6. In French: "when in Israel, hair floated free"—Trans.

her husband, despite the reproaches of the prophet Nathan, and who became the mother of Solomon, and, subsequently, has continued to seduce us from her bath in the paintings of Raphael, Cranach, and Rembrandt. These queens are not always sympathetic, I grant you that, but all are subversive, nonconformist. . . . Strangeness, or, let us say, the female power, insinuates itself into the social order, threatens it, is sometimes integrated into it, even while remaining rebellious, desirable, never passive or docile.

The monotheistic battle against "dirty hair" takes very strict institutional forms: not only must there be no priestesses, but the presence of women at readings in the synagogue is optional on the Shabbat. When women do go, they are relegated to the back or to a platform: let them remain in their place! An Israeli architect cousin of mine recently wanted to set up the balcony for these brave women to make it more comfortable, bring it closer to the rabbi, and allow them, almost, to participate in the prayers. He had cause to regret it! Out of the question! He had to demolish his balcony! Of course, little girls do not attend the yeshivas, nor do women teach in the yeshivas.[7] On that score, malicious people do not miss the chance to cite a few extremists, who were not lacking in the past and persevere in the present: Rabbi Meir in the second century C.E. ("Praise be to God, who did not make me a boor, who did not make me a woman, because woman is not obliged to observe the commandments") or Rabbi Eleazar in the first century C.E. ("To teach the Torah to my daughter is to teach her obscenities"). Within my own family line, I have the advantage of a maternal grandmother who called herself Jacob; legend has it that her community was among the followers of Shabbetai Tzevi, a mystic who proclaimed himself Messiah in the Balkans. . . . In that region, at times the melting pot for the three forms of monotheism, these ancestors went over to the side of Christianity, and, as for my father, he did everything he could to reinforce that latter tendency, but without neglecting to have me learn French from the Dominican women, to better assimilate a culture of doubt and reason, he said, thinking of the Enlightenment. The height of confusion or of lucidity, tell me that! In short, you won't be surprised if I tell you that my favorites among these biblical matrons are the lovers of borderlines: Ruth the Moabite, naturally, and, of course, the beloved of the Song of Songs.

---

7. This is, in fact, no longer true in Israel or New York: there are now women's yeshivas. —Trans.

Ah, Ruth the Moabite, a stranger and nevertheless the ancestor of Jewish sovereignty, since she is the ancestor of David! The story dates back to the year 2792 (968 B.C.E.), it seems. A time of ordeals, a chaotic moment in Jewish history, the Law was in a state of deterioration, forgotten. A venerable man, you remember, by the name of Elimelech, leaves his country, Judea—instead of helping it in that time of depression—and dares settle in Moab. A foreign kingdom, and banned from the alliance for an additional reason: its inhabitants had not welcomed the Jews fleeing Egypt. The exile of Elimelech is thus a grave sin and must be duly punished: he dies, in fact, like his two sons, who leave no heir. The mother, Noami, remains, and her two daughters-in-law, Orpah and . . . Ruth. The punishment, if it is a punishment, is not so severe, since Ruth is saved from disaster and even becomes the matriarch of Jewish royalty. Did she convert? Nothing is clear on that matter, but the text explains that Orpah returned to her homeland, while Ruth stubbornly accompanied her mother-in-law to Bethlehem. Her words attest to a beautiful fidelity to Yahweh, but especially to an intense connection between the two women: "Entreat me not to leave thee, or to return from following after thee: for whither thou goest, I will go; and where thou lodgest, I will lodge: thy people shall be my people, and thy God my God. Where thou diest, will I die, and there will I be buried: the Lord do so to me, and more also, if ought but death part thee and me" (Ruth 1:16–17). As a result, Naomi's duty will be to find Ruth a "redeemer," who, according to the rules of the levirate, can only be the closest relative of the deceased husband, whose place he takes when the widow is childless. Of the possible redeemers, the second in line is Boaz, cousin of Elimelech, her deceased husband.

A beautiful story of a gleaner in a wheat field follows, a combination of innocence and ruse, until the so-called gleaner overlooks the young reapers, and, in the end, attracts the proud Boaz, aged eighty, who knows very well that this beauty is a Moabite. Ruth, hardworking but also richly perfumed, duly instructed by Naomi but full of her own charms, appears to the patriarch to be worthy of a "full" reward: "The Lord recompense thy work, and a full reward be given thee of the Lord God of Israel, under whose wings thou art come to trust" (Ruth 2:12). "And now, my daughter, fear not: I will do to thee all that thou requirest: for all the city of my people doth know that thou art a virtuous woman." (Ruth 3:10–11). "So Boaz took Ruth, and she was his wife: and when he went in unto her, the Lord gave her conception, and she bare a son" (Ruth 4:13). Tradition has it that Boaz died the very night the marriage was consummated, whereas Ruth conceived a child and took her place in Jewish history. Her name is never again mentioned, however: as you wrote in a recent letter, only the family line counts, and here, it is saved by the birth of an heir, hence exit the woman—exit the foreign "bearing mother."

Things are less simple, however. Like the other "great women" of the Bible, Ruth enjoys an extraordinary longevity, since she sees her descendant Solomon take the throne. It is Naomi, the grandmother, who is recognized as the mother—"symbolic," let us say—of Ruth's newborn: "And the women her neighbors gave it a name, saying, There is a son born to Naomi; and they called his name Obed" (Ruth 4:17). (*Obed*, or, he who "serves" God.) The child of Ruth the stranger serves, in fact, as an intermediary between two peoples, between two mothers, and is inserted into the line of Boaz and Naomi. The race of kings is his descendance: "He is the father of Jesse, the father of David" (Ruth 4:17). As for the descendant of Orpah, the sister of Ruth, who did not choose Naomi-Yahweh, he is none other than Goliath, who will be beaten by David.

You are wrong, dear Catherine, to rebel against "baptisms" and other rites for accepting children into the father's symbolic line. Not only is Ruth wiser than you, but her role as intermediary, it seems to me, goes beyond the service rendered by a stranger to the Jewish community, since it reveals the profound meaning of the sacred function, the function of intermediary, of a mother: biology plus meaning, childbirth plus symbolic choice. The story of Ruth still needs to be reflected upon, to revalorize the maternal vocation of today, in the twenty-first century. It is truly a vocation, in fact, when we have the technological freedom to dispose of our bodies within an eroticism liberated from the "threat" of procreation, and when we can make it a "free choice." It is a vocation as well since we will reach the point—we are already reaching the point—of reproducing the species artificially, more or less well. That is why, if present-day and future Ruths are not vigilant, if they do not experience that fierce adherence to wheat and blood on the one hand, to the transcendence of a moral contract on the other, our species is destined to be manipulated or to become extinct.

Ruth was praised, I praised her in *Strangers to Ourselves,* for opening the sovereignty of David to an ineffaceable strangeness: it is she, in fact, who opens royal security to a permanent inquietude and spurs the dynamic of its drive for perfection. "How long will they speak to me in anger, saying: is he not of an unworthy line? Is he not the descen-

dant of Ruth the Moabite?" implores David, speaking to God. The letter *dalet,* which means "poor," occurs twice in David's name, because he
integrates the poverty, the fall, the filth of the dirty stranger—without
whom there is no sovereignty. If David is also Ruth, if the sovereign is
also the Moabite, then that means his royal destiny will never be quietude, but a permanent quest for the acceptance and the transcendence
of the other in oneself. I know this interpretation of Judaism is not
everyone's, but it is mine, and I know others share it; that's already
something. . . .

This role of intermediary, for which I have such a fondness, the role
of the one who opens the way from the "lowly" (the stranger, the substance, the body) to the "beyond" (Yahweh, the line of the fathers, the
transmission of the Law), I also find, in a different way, in the beloved
of the Song of Songs. The Sulamite is, in fact, the one who speaks the
words of love, though their author, it is said, is King Solomon. It is
truly *she* who speaks, it is *she* we hear, it is *she* who *loves*—whereas *he*
flees: "The song of songs, which is Solomon's. Let him kiss me with
the kisses of his mouth: for thy love is better than wine. Because of the
savour of thy good ointments thy name is as ointment poured forth,
therefore do the virgins love thee" (Song of Solomon 1:1–3). This *Shir
Ha-Shirim* is a superlative, which, from the outset, sets the loving in-
cantation apart from other speeches, songs, or forms of the sacred. It
is said to have been composed by Solomon himself, the son of David,
and its earliest date is set around 915–913 B.C.E.; others maintain that
it may date from the third century B.C.E. Recently, the Solomonic origin of the text has been under reconsideration, and its date pushed
back to the second millennium B.C.E. The Indian influence—this will
please you!—supposedly manifests itself in the fact that it is a woman
speaking, that the rebirth of nature is often evoked, and that the dominant note of the feeling of love is the languor of the beloved—beyond
a certain aggressiveness of the male. A cross between Solomon and
Tamil poetry? A parallel between the Song of Songs and the Gita
Govinda? A similarity between Krishna, a sensual and mystical deity,
and the Sulamite?

The novelty of the biblical text appears indisputable to me: the
woman who speaks in the Song of Songs is an independent and free *individual,* a sovereign person, and not a cosmic diffusion, be it fascinat-
ing or abject. This is the first time that, in the love literature of the
world, an *autonomous* subject appears who can name her desires—their
strengths, their goals, their obstacles—and this subject is a woman in

love. The Song of Songs is allegorical, understood as a song of the chosen people (of the beloved) addressed to its God, of course, and the
Christians did not miss the chance to see it as the church's aspiration
toward God, or even a presentiment of the love of the Virgin. Whatever the symbol might be, it is a woman who is the source and center
of the invocation. Dramaturgy and the Greek lyric, as well as the
Mesopotamian cults of fertility, no doubt irrigate that song with its
often pagan accent, which nevertheless occupies a natural place in the
Bible. The rabbis understood this in about 100 C.E., when they finally
accepted, not without reservations, a lover's dialogue at the very heart
of the sacred Scriptures. Might the woman, the individual in love, be
the premodern variant of the sacred? Your addition on courtly love at
the end of your last letter, in the form of a correction on the proofs,
leaves me unsatisfied; yes, you'll have to endure (in our book) my long
development on the metamorphosis of filthy body hair into a woman
in love.

As the crossroads of bodily passion and idealization, of sex and
god, the love of the Sulamite is that privileged experience handed over
to us, we who read it thousands of years after its composition, like the
sacred par excellence. It is said that there is no Jewish "faith," no
"credo," but—what then? A *love*? In the sense of the Song of Songs?
"By night on my bed, I sought him whom my soul loveth: I sought
him, but I found him not" "I sought him, but I could not find him"
(Song of Solomon 3:1, 5:6). The heartbreak, the thrill, the outburst of
love: between presence and absence, visible and invisible, physicality
and transcendence. Sensual and deferred love, body and power, passion and ideal: all the tension of Judaism resides in that experience of
love, of which both man and woman are capable—and perhaps woman
a bit more than man.

So I say nothing about the snares of that ideal, of that Great Other,
of that superegoistic tension? Snares for man, further snares for
woman? You know I am not unaware of them. I was listening to a patient who, evoking the agony of her anorexia, said she has the impression that she submits to it out of "duty." Naturally, I'll tell you her
story, inevitable when you're circling around the sacré "sacred." But
that will be for the next time. Today, let me stay with that search for
love, "sought but not found." With that thrill of the lovesick but in no
sense startled body, neither tragic nor pathetic: limpid, intense, divided, quick, upright, suffering, hopeful. The sacred body of a woman, sacred because at the crossroads of love. I assure you, the sacred is not

pubic hair! Don't believe that! Let's be more ambitious, the sacred is love. The black dirtiness is passed through, the anorexia set aside—the Sulamite eats and drinks greedily because she maintains the connection beyond separation: she loves. "I am black, but comely, O ye daughters of Jerusalem, as the tents of Kedar, as the curtains of Solomon. . . . He brought me to the banqueting house, and his banner over me was love. Stay me with flagons, comfort me with apples: for I am sick of love. His left hand is under my head, and his right hand doth embrace me" (Song of Solomon 1:5, 2:4–6).

Julia

◆ ◆

MAY 1997

Dear Julia,

YOU ARE A Christian atheist and I a Jewish atheist; we are both "bound" by our history. Obviously, getting away from it is out of the question. Well, then. Let's remain within it.

Here is why I cannot always abide "your" virgin.[8] *Encadrer* is a trivial word. Yet I like it very much. One cannot "abide" someone when one comes across something in that person that is somehow unsettling. Who is that person? Bad for me, that's clear. . . . In the same way, one does not succeed in "framing" [*cadrer*] a painting when it is overburdened by too much gold, too much black, too much steel. I often remove the frames from paintings; I prefer them naked. Hence I cannot "frame" or "abide" the Virgin you show me. Let's say I would like her better naked.

No doubt the benefits of "your" Virgin have played their role in the history of women, but even so . . . Remember the way her Son roughly pushes her aside. "How is it that ye sought me?" Woman, what do

---

8. *Encadrer* means "to abide" but also "to frame"—Trans.

you want? Me? Just a little tenderness. But Jesus explains that He has come to divide families, not to unite them. Leave your earthly cares behind, abandon your family in the name of love, follow me. As we know, separating the follower from his family circle is the fundamental gesture of every sect at its birth. Granted, it is shocking to rediscover that sectarian mechanism in the birth of Christianity. But the fact that Christianity became a universal religion does not change a thing in that historical truth: every future religion begins as a reformist sect, Christianity like the others. If not, how is change possible? How can the old be forced to give way to the new? The revolt against the old order requires a fidelity in the face of every ordeal, hence the sect: this was true of Buddhism's revolt against Brahmanism, of Protestantism's revolt against Catholicism, and it is also true of early Christianity, which originated within the rigid context of an old Judaism already being gnawed away by numerous sects. The sect becomes a religion by virtue of its endurance, the number of faithful, its capacity to organize, and the charisma of the man who founds it. I say the "man," since I have yet to find even one female founder of a religion.

Female founders of sects can be found by the dozen. But of religions? Not one. From this perspective, the theologians' discovery of the Virgin certainly guaranteed the splendor of Christian churches. I agree. But, like Freud, I will tell you that the more the repressed surfaces, the better religion is tolerated. That deserves a little explanation, I believe. Let me warn you that, in the matter of theology, I am intentionally heretical.

In *Moses and Monotheism,* Freud sees Christianity as a successful attempt to lift the repression of a human sacrifice, the murder of Moses by the Jews on the border of the Promised Land, for example. As often with Freud, the hypothesis is fragile, but the demonstration is not lacking in audacity. The crucifixion of Jesus would thus be a return to human sacrifice, which a father applies to his son. But father and son are God, *bound* by a common breath, the Holy Spirit. God is in three persons: must they resort to the Trinity to carry out the sacrifice of a son of God? No doubt. If I listen to Freud's demons, I conclude that, with the Trinity, the repressed content of a religious system, to which Judaism put an end by appearing in the world, is lifted. That repressed content is familiar to us: it is polytheism. I thereby conclude that, the more polytheism returns, the more the repressed surfaces. The path is open. And Christianity will add one more to the three persons of the deity: the Virgin.

I cite as proof how simply the Hindus, past masters in the art of religious appropriation, assimilated Christianity when they converted: in their eyes, the three persons could only be their trio of gods, Brahma the Creator, Vishnu the Orderer, and Shiva, Master of Life and Death. By way of Sanskrit, that trio bears the name *Trimurti:* it's from the same root as Trinity, everything is fine. And the Virgin? Well, for them, there can be no god without a goddess. Only one for those three? That's been known to happen in the Hindu pantheon. I know of superb portraits of the Virgin Mary with four or six arms, with her halo and her blue mantle. In India, the essential thing in the conversion to Christianity does not bear on trinitary theology, but, much more important, on the equality contained within that religion with a universal vocation.

To convert to Christianity is to rise up from being an untouchable or a member of the lower castes, period. You have to realize that, to reach that objective, every method is valid, especially new gods in a country that is not stingy about the number of deities. It was the same in India for all the other egalitarian monotheistic religions: in chronological order, Buddhism, Jainism, Islam, Sikhism. And the distribution is significant: 120 million Muslims, 16 million Sikhs, 16 million Christians, 10 million Jains, and a few hundred thousand Buddhists. Hence, in the monotheistic register, Islam is essentially in the majority, because, on the question of equality among men, the Koran makes no concessions. The fact that women's status in the Koran makes them creatures both equal and secondary has in no way dissuaded masses of untouchables from converting to Islam. Social status, given priority over all the rest, has prevailed.

There is no option but to observe that the only religion in India where women achieve theological freedom is Sikhism, which makes equality between the sexes an unassailable point of dogma. The result is clear: Sikh women do not wear the veil or a red dot on the forehead; they have a proud bearing and are the heads of businesses. Their hair is loose, braided, or cut short: unlike their men, they are not constrained as to clothing or hair. They are freer than their Hindu sisters. Why? Undoubtedly because the status of sacred warrior, that is, of the Sikh man, always ready to defend his persecuted religion, leaves them a margin for maneuvering to which the Sikhs are, in fact, vitally attached. The men may well wear fierce costumes, exhibit a hirsutism they are forbidden to touch with scissors, wear "battle shorts" night and day (an object that the libertine young Indian women of the capital collect); it is no use, they need independent women. It's as if they needed the "irony of the community" to mock their large sabers and daggers. And it's true that the women are cheerful, mocking, very free in their tone, like peasant women of the lower castes. It is high time our— French—ethnologists notice that irony in the obscene songs the women shout out at the men in the fields they cultivate together.

Now, let's not leave India and let's return to the hair of my dancing girls. That consecrated hair is not "rotten": on the contrary, it is perfectly dry. There is nothing wet about it: I compared it to oakum, hemp residue ready to catch fire. That hair falls on the side of fire. It is forbidden to put water on it, something that deserves attention. Indeed, whereas ablution purifies the body, only fire puts an end to filth. Water is for prayer, but fire, that's something else.

For example, Hindu asceticism is "fiery" because it consumes the flesh and its desires. Before becoming the Buddha, the prince/re-nouncer became an accomplished Hindu ascetic, and certain statues of Gautama in an ascetic state show him without flesh—just skin and bone. He "burned" everything in him. He departed from the natural raw state by being spiritually cooked. Let me reiterate the alimentary laws of the human race, as explained by Lévi-Strauss in *Mythologiques:* to become a man means to eat cooked food. The raw is natural, the cooked is cultural, and the first gesture proper to the human race is that of lighting a fire. But "to cook" is to wait. To respect the time of cooking, muzzle impatience, know how to defer. The same is true for marriage, which, unlike rape, requires waiting, for trade, which is not pillaging, and for war, which is not murder. Yet asceticism in India takes an entire lifetime. A long wait, explicitly defined as a cooking of the flesh: the mind commands the body, which is gradually stripped of flesh.

These are not metaphors. The first sign of the progression toward ecstasy is traditionally visual: the skin on the chest of the novice in asceticism starts to glow. It is red, probably because of the irritating effects of the breathing exercises. It is said that the novice's skin is "golden," like good bread. The future Buddha is such a perfect ascetic that he is "cooked." Then—and this was the turning point on the path of the future Buddha—that interminable drying-up process appeared sterile to the prince. Breaking his fast, he excitedly ate the rice that a woman held out to him. He stopped being a Hindu. And, renouncing the mind's cooking of the body, he began meditation, where neither body nor mind exists.

tion, the large train station in Bombay, stacked every morning on enormous luggage racks that move up and down the platforms. These carefully numbered tins are carried by the workers to their workplace, since they are thus assured that *their* meal, prepared by *their* wife, will certainly be that of *their* religion, *their* rank, *their* caste.

A strange paradox! "Woman" is impure because she secretes "raw" blood, and yet it is she who assures the transition from raw to cooked. One thing is certain: only a mother offers the child the first food of its life, mother's milk, a mysterious substance that is neither "cooked" nor altogether "raw." Added to that gesture we have in common with the animals are those that distinguish us from them, the cooking of the first mush, the first purees: and they're off.

As for the women in myths who refuse to do the cooking, their goose is cooked. They are punished, as Lévi-Strauss demonstrates in one of the most beautiful passages of *Mythologiques*. The event takes place among the Indians of Brazil, who are fond of honey. A very high-calorie food for undernourished peoples, the honey collected is so strong that it cannot be consumed without first being diluted. It is collected and water is added to it; otherwise, those who eat it become dangerously intoxicated. Above all, the precious calories are shared with the community. Once there was a naughty girl who was so crazy about honey that, in defiance of the rules in force, she went into the forest to gorge herself on it in a hollow tree trunk. Sacrilege!

She had not respected the table manners, she had demonstrated her retarded development, she had not waited for the honey to be diluted, and, above all, she had consumed the precious liquid herself. . . . The punishment must fit the crime: she is cut up in pieces, cooked, and eaten. The story of "Girl-Crazy-About-Honey" illustrates very well the importance of the sacred act of sharing, which requires a wait. Here is a girl who is not married, who wants to escape the law, who does not want to share, who refuses to cook, who consumes an invaluable product in secret, especially one as sacred as honey, an element not found in nature, and which is . . . neither raw nor cooked. Honey, raw because it stems from nature, but "cooked" by the alchemy of the bees, escapes the culture/nature dichotomy. The punishment of Girl-Crazy-About-Honey demonstrates the price of rejecting the order of the commonwealth: neither being unmarried nor being a solitary bulimic is allowed. How well we understand her, however, that beautiful child! Today, we are girls crazy about every sort of honey. Gluttonous, in a hurry? No doubt. We have to be.

Men who cook have an intentionally alchemical vocabulary: creation, research, science, art, quest for the substance never yet experienced by the taste buds. . . . Well, the vulgate of the chefs of "haute cuisine"—as one says "haute couture"—is well known: to cook is to create. You can make masterpieces. Every day? That's questionable. I never miss an issue of the cooking magazines, and I have observed that they too get bored with concocting combinations to entertain the servant women stuck in their daily routine. An exciting body of literature, where metaphors are played out on the table, where, to give servants the nerve, the authors enjoin them to place cress on the strawberry tart and jam on the salmon. A little imagination, what the hell! So they advise. But combinations follow certain laws, and these laws eventually give out. I dare a servant-wife to serve her family meals like that every day. . . . The family chorus: hamburgers, noodles, french fries! Innovation gives rise to resistance. The mom who is a heretic in the matter of cookery has discontented children. The sacred requires repetition.

In fact, in your repertoires of the Virgin Mary, can you find me one who cooks for the Holy Family? What does the Holy Virgin cook? The divinity of her son, her own sorrow, or bread? She offers the breast, that is not very difficult—although . . . But the rest? You tell me she is not a woman, and you are right. Crazy about honey, the Virgin was almost certainly not. The feeling of intoxication she is known to have had at the time of the Annunciation is her only breathing space, but that sublime exaltation came from a divine order.

I prefer the exaltation of the bacchantes, authorized, by a god clad in a tunic, to share the wine, the men's drink. Granted, the god is quite a rat. He can require a mother in ecstasy to tear off the head of her son while mistaking him for a lion. Woman's excess can be seen in her very real potential for violence, that's true. But the same drive animates Girl-Crazy-About-Honey and the bacchantes: to escape the order. You see, I am cautious. I do not say "the order of men." No, I speak of the order in itself, and that's not the same thing. From that perspective, the theological disorder occasioned by the Virgin Mary is quite beautiful.

Is it possible to conceive of a form of the sacred without disorder? Yes and no. The sacred shatters the order and introduces a new one. The sacred is "of another order," as we have seen among your mystics and my healers, in "my" trances and "your" ecstasies. For men, this other time establishes a transcendent relationship with the deity. As for women, they undoubtedly rediscover the "rawness" of their intimate self, as the inner labyrinths of the mystics prove. It is neither the same relation to the order of the world nor the same relation to the well-named "supernatural." The male officiants are there to dodge it in favor of the transcendent, the female ones, well, I'm not sure about them. It's a long way from transcendence to the supernatural . . .

As the word indicates, transcendence extends beyond oppositions. Now, in the construction of the word *supernatural,* there are still remnants of opposition, nature on the one side, supernatural on the other. The supernatural is intertwined with sensation; it is physical. It seems to me that transcendence is not situated within the register of the raw. In a sense, it is "cooked." I imagine a secret division between masculine transcendence and the feminine supernatural. One is within the order, and the other within the counterorder. That will not surprise you: like Girl-Crazy-About-Honey, I am mad about honey consumed at the wrong time.

Catherine

✦ ✦

Paris
JULY 4, 1997

Dear Catherine,

YOUR SUMMATIONS, WHICH are not lacking in brutality, fill me with joy! For example, when—after my letter on the women in the Bible—you see me as a Christian atheist and, on the trail, you unearth "the sign of the sect" in Christianity, while inviting me to "get fed up with Mary"! Come on, come on! I'm sure you'll compose that differently should our publication plans take shape. If atheism did exist—which is not certain—it would belong to no religion, but rather to the depletion of all religions, in full knowledge of the facts, as old Hegel wanted it, without forgetting the Universal, the Christian. Yet the tendency to forget Christianity, which sometimes puts on the airs of a liberating blasphemy, characterizes a number of modern "atheists." A forgetting, a denial, which, naturally, makes them squirm a little. Could you be one of them?

"My" Virgin, as you say, and who grieves you deeply, is certainly not a model for women at this end of the millennium. If I thought so, even a little bit, we would not have undertaken this correspondence. It is nevertheless true that cornering her for her lack of experience with babysitting, baby mush, and other cooked meals for adults or little children is, of course, very funny, but avoids the difficulty of the cunning and, I maintain, splendid construction of the Virgin-Mother-of-God. Which has the merit of raising, in its way—far from definitive, and for good reason—a question that has remained painfully unresolved: how to combine uterine cookery with the fire of the word; how to unite the logic of passion with the order (as you say) of the ideal, of the prohibition, of the law. The order of the superego, explains dear Sigmund.

The bosom of the Virgin—I refer to both her belly and her breasts—is offered precisely to bring about that transition: it has produced magnificent paintings. The Renaissance rehabilitation of the erotic female body would have been impossible without that glorification of the virginal body—pace the purists and the puritans, be they Christians . . . or atheists. Even though a follower of Mary (which I am not, your keen-edged fugue may have "framed" her, to borrow your expression) can have breast cancer—just like a Jew or a Parsi—you ought to recognize that no one has really succeeded in hiding that breast, which I could not fail to see, in spite of the drapery of Mary's blue robe, or thanks to it. . . . If there is still female guilt—to give to eat or to allow oneself to be eaten, in pleasure or in pain—well, with Mary, that guilt has some chance of not escaping people's gaze. . . . That of painters, perverse fetishists, granted; but, after all, that of women as well . . .

A sacré history, then, that conjunction between the appetite (which the woman experiences, provokes, or maintains) and duty. If you will allow me, I'll tell you about my analysands.

I just left Agnes, as I shall call the anorectic patient I mentioned in my last letter. A tall thin girl, translucent, taut as a piece of wire and crumbly as dry clay, I always wonder whether she is about to fall to dust or, on the contrary, sharpen like a blade. She eats nothing for weeks on end, then suddenly stuffs herself with chocolates and other sweets, before making herself vomit until she's dying from dizzy spells and pain, and then the cycle begins again. Of course I am touched by her, a bit too much, no doubt; don't tell my psychoanalytic colleagues, who would naturally find that I am not properly controlling the counter-transference, and who would not be altogether wrong. Nevertheless, I was never an anorectic. Not really. But I know I was weaned very early, Mama had a breast infection, and, as I child, I had little tolerance for milk—sheep's milk, cow's milk, goat's milk, concentrated, skim, whole, nothing did the trick. The slightest dash of cream made me vomit. Necessarily, because I had been taken off my mother's milk very early, too early, said my mother. I tell myself that rather simplistic but no less painful story to be done with sick breasts, to analyze my countertransference with Agnes, to hear her and only her—and not my own little dramas about cream, which have to do only with my mother and me.

In short, there is nothing like an anorectic to give you that impression of an impoverished religion, perhaps because it reveals a poverty in religion. When I say "impoverished religion," I do not seek to denigrate religion, on the contrary: it is because it domesticates poverty that religion gives life and, perhaps, cannot be transcended. And the more impoverished it is, the more it affects living flesh. Nevertheless, religion, in the proximity of distress, stands side by side with the symptom. Agnes is not a believer, she comes to complain about her symptoms. To swallow and digest her mother, whom she adores and loathes: an impossible task, but what passion! The scenario is replayed, naturally, with her friends and superiors in the hierarchy, and day by day with what she has at hand, that is, with the man in her life. Agnes's partner, as you will have guessed, is a very feminine, very maternal man, not really effeminate, but a true "breast." Take a new lover. That occurred to her: a real man, the kind they don't make anymore, and who imposes his virility by hurting—in the literal and figural sense—his female partners. She had to go dig up one of those. I'll give you a sense of the subtleties of the labyrinth we are passing through, she and I, during the sessions, between her desire to be the young page who would satisfy a frustrated mother and the desire to run off with the father, who is loved as well, and who abandoned the family home to the greater despair of mother and daughter. Agnes the woman and Agnes the man, Agnes playing out in her mouth, in her stomach, in her anus—through voracity, vomiting, constipation, and diarrhea—the desired and impossible coitus of the two parents, since she is both and neither at the same time. . . . "It's funny, so to speak," she whispered before leaving me just now, "but, in that fall, I have the impression I am performing a duty."

Duty! That is truly the issue. Agnes's separation from her mother was apparently both too abrupt (a brother was born when she was still under a year old) and never completed. Maternal depression, violence and absence of the father, early comprehension of the little girl, who became the "big girl" at the age of one: and that is why your daughter is not "mute" but . . . violently superegoistic. The technical terminology of psychoanalysis has the advantage of calling a spade a spade—which is lacking in subtlety, of course, but makes it possible to move quickly, an appreciable advantage, especially in a correspondence between accomplices such as ourselves. That necessary separation, which allows us to separate ourselves from the maternal bosom—oh, very little, little by little, never enough!—to take off, one day or another—that separation, I say, became frozen for Agnes into the most rigid of prohibitions: thou shalt not eat of that mother!

First and foremost, that rigidity protects her: Agnes eats words, books, becomes an excellent student, a brilliant intellectual. A sacré daughter of the father, if you see what I mean. But the taut piece of wire in that leap toward the place beyond, in that passion for the symbolic, in that straining in the direction of the Other who never stops running—as is only right and proper when one is truly Other—stands side by side with unfulfilled fusion and burning desire. Duty cuts off but does not appease the pleasures of the senses. Agnes abandons herself to them only to better reject them: sadomasochistic drama on the surface of the body—in the lips, the teeth, the tongue, the throat, and even deep in the belly. And, since duty protects the mother—"Thou shalt not eat of that mother"—the drama is played out between self and self. "I swallow you / I spit you out. I love you/ I kill you" becomes: "I swallow myself / I spit myself out. I love myself / I kill myself." Freud wrote that women did not have the capacity for a superego. I am well aware that he was thinking of his Vienna and his protected middle-class women, but that doesn't ring true for everyone, far from it. The anorectic is welded to her superego: hypermoral, hyperscrupulous, hyperdevoted to the Law, to God, to the One—call them what you like. It is because of that rigidity, which both sustains and destroys her, that she has come to me, to ask that I get rid of it. Does that mean I must deprive her of her duty, of her obligation to be All, male and female both?

Certainly, Agnes is going to lose—is already in the process of losing—her tyrannical religion, but not her sense of duty or her morality. Neither the superego nor repression disappears in analysis—at most they become more flexible. And tyrannical religion is replaced by what? By tenderness, which is nothing other than the possibility of telling oneself the story of duty, and which is called the imaginary. Let me tell you why, for me, the sacred is also the imaginary, and perhaps only that. But first, I want to recall another anorectic, Catherine Benincasa, known as Catherine of Siena (1347–1380). I return to Christianity, you see, but to lead you back to what you do not acknowledge, its revelation of the violence of the Word. I say violence, the other face of love, which, for its part, benefited from all that publicity . . .

This remarkable woman, who preached the passionate love of God, a fervent Dominican and patron saint of Italy along with Saint Francis of Assisi, was a doctor of the church in the same capacity as Saint Thomas Aquinas. She miraculously healed people stricken with the plague and wrote down her raptures in *Dialogue of Divine Providence* — one of the first masterpieces of Italian literature. At the same time, she was a kind of anorectic. In addition to her own writings, the biography written by her confessor, Raymond of Capua, has bequeathed a true legend to us, in which anorexia explains nothing but crystallizes, nevertheless, that extreme sense of love and duty without which Catherine would not have been Catherine of Siena.

Your namesake was a twin and, as often happens, the two baby girls were very fragile. At their birth, their mother, Lapa Piacenti, was about forty and was already the mother of twenty-two children, only half of whom had survived. She had to separate herself from one of the twins, Giovanna, who was put out to nurse and soon died. As for Catherine, she latched onto the maternal breast and recovered her strength. Satiated, filled: she was the chosen—enough to confirm the analytical hypothesis that beings who are orally satisfied are capable of hope and . . . of faith. Another Giovanna was born two years after the twins, and Catherine became attached to that second sister, double of the "first double"; but the second Giovanna died as well . . . in 1363—the very year Catherine converted to a radical saintliness. You begin to sense that the thorny path to duty is strewn with corpses, female corpses— doubles and beloveds. When her sister Bonaventura, whom she also admired, died in childbirth, Catherine felt responsible, accused herself of that death: like the death of Giovanna? Of the two Giovannas? As the highest duty, Lapa, the mother, demanded that Catherine marry . . . the dead sister's husband. You see the psychodrama. Question: how could our future saint get herself out of that maternal and sisterly embrace— loving, of course, but lethal, an inextricable double bind?

It was fairly simple, but it had to be done: Catherine cut and sliced on her own, she decided that she herself was the law. She prohibited herself the lethal delights of incest and promiscuity, but by taking that fierce law upon herself: it is not you who oblige me, *your prohibition* is only *my duty*. I am even going to intensify it, make it more powerful than you could ever imagine. For I alone am the one who gives orders: in a private dialogue with what you are not, with the Other, with God.

That game was set in place fairly early: Catherine had her first vision at age six or seven, when she was visiting, in the company of her brother Stefano, her already married sister Bonaventura: Jesus, dressed in white, smiled at her. For years, Catherine did not say anything about that vision to anyone, but she tended its compensatory and comforting images in her solitude, thus relishing her personal and indissoluble connection to a sacred ideal, the divine spouse granted to her alone. At age ten, when her mother scolded her for coming home late in the evening ("Cursed be the gossipmongers who say you will not come home!"), Catherine replied, "My mother, if I do not do what you ask of me, I beg you, beat me as much as you like, so that I may be more attentive the next time: that is your right and your duty. But I beg you not to let your tongue curse other people, good or bad, for my own misdeeds, for that does not befit your age and will give me great pain."

Do you hear that power? Catherine does not reject the punishment her mother is preparing to inflict on her: she appropriates it and transcends it. It is not the mother who punishes, but the daughter who corrects the mother and punishes herself. The daughter takes the upper hand, she makes it her duty to transform the mother's displeasure and their separation into a personal moral triumph. She undoubtedly draws great satisfaction from that mind game, by mortifying herself. But the same game builds up her moral being . . . and her capacity to overcome every privation, every ordeal, beginning with disgust—the oral ordeal. Catherine refuses to get married, devotes herself to Jesus, and stops eating. The fast begins at age sixteen—she allows herself only bread, raw vegetables, and water. After her father's death, she gives up bread. By about the age of twenty-five, she is eating "nothing." Shrewd souls and gossipmongers say that, in secret, she rewards herself with a few treats . . . but that is commonplace. What is less so is that, in tending to a woman's cancerous breast (the breast again!), she recoils in disgust at the putrid odor; but, resolved to suppress any reaction by her body, she collects the pus and drinks it. In the night, Jesus appears to her, and asks her to drink the blood of his wounds, and Catherine receives that invitation as a consolation for her stomach, which now "no longer wants food and can no longer digest."

The biographers have not missed the chance to dissect the father of that woman of duty, as you may suspect: Giacomo Benincasa, a dyer, not always prosperous, but a man of good sense, in possession of a few belongings in these times of plague. Yet Catherine's strength is obviously bound up in the mother's milk—Lapa naturally weaned her children fairly early, since she was pregnant almost continually, and Catherine was the only one to be fully cradled in that milky way for an extended period. The moral of the story is that one can escape an overly satisfied mouth only through an extremely demanding faith. But not everyone who wishes to be a saint can become one, and even Catherine, with her eccentricities, provoked the distrust of the Church, which had to call a special committee to examine her case before sanctifying her all the same, to be done with it, won over by so much uprightness. Such an extraordinary effort to master oneself, to suppress the passion that connects you to your mama and sisters—not only through hunger but also through flagellation and absolute silence, all the while perfectly alert—cannot help but elicit admiration. With that, Catherine is so persuaded of her mystic union with God—Jesus and Mary appear to her and slip the wedding ring onto her finger—that, when Lapa falls ill, she orders (rather than asks) Jesus to assume his part of their supernatural contract by restoring her mother's health—and by inflicting illness on her in her mother's place.

Her influence increases with the popes of Avignon, whom she convinces to return to Italy, but she does not succeed in preventing the Great Schism. Nevertheless, her self-mastery is increasingly perfect: the little girl becomes the mama of the company of disciples that surrounds her. The cycle of anorexia and vomiting continues, however, until she decides to die . . . refusing to drink even water for an entire month. Three months of death throes: unspeakable suffering and brief flashes of lucidity punctuate her end. And this last sentence, spoken on the brink of death, the most sublime of all, reveals that Catherine is even succeeding at challenging the "vainglorious" control she had constructed for herself with God's help: "Vainglory, no, but true glory to praise God, yes." Could she have been trying to suggest that true saintliness is not magisterial self-mortification? That her masochistic triumph was in vain? That it is only vainglory to be Saint Catherine of Siena? That something else . . . was needed? But what? To return to "the plainest poverty," that of Meister Eckehart's "unborn" (*ungeboren*), "that which has nothing": not even a name, not even a force of duty— with and in hunger, with and in disgust?

What am I getting at? Quite simply at the snares of the sacred, in other words, of the sacrifice: to succumb to duty, to immolate oneself for a tyrannical ideal, with all the jouissances that mortification procures, but all the uneasiness as well, even unto death. The lethal sacred drives the machine of spiritual improvement, and, quite simply, the social machine. Granted. Catherine's works, her influence on the papacy, do not allow us to forget the psychic suffering she endured, the disavowal of life.

So I'm defending different values? Those of another time? Of modern times? We embrace these values, and happily so, as well as a new idea of happiness that might seem bland when compared to Catherine's, and even Agnes's, passions. Such a benevolent, reasonable notion of happiness! So, abolish that draconian ideal? Certainly not. Ease it. No doubt. But how? Does a nonsacrificial sacred exist?

I'll stop here. My cell phone is ringing. It's Ghislaine, who pushed me into the recent electoral campaign and wants me to continue. And, even though I hardly feel I'm of the political fiber, what can I say, it's my way of performing a duty. . . . At least, I listen to it and engage in dialogue.

Julia

✦ ✦

Dakar
JULY 7, 1997

Dear Julia,

HOW MANY MORE letters will there be on the subject of the Virgin, Julia? I understood the lesson: without her, Eros would not have had right of citizenship in the Christian world, or women either. That said, when I wrote, "I cannot *abide* her," it goes farther than the Virgin; I prefer profane paintings to sacred ones. The feeling I get in front of a sacred Western work is bizarre. I experience the sensation that someone wants to impose a vision on me; that I do not have the choice. I no longer have anything but an antagonistic perception. It seems to me that this muffled hostility is similar to Freud's in front of Michelangelo's statue of Moses; I am afraid I'll bow down before the forbidden representation. In short, I feel vaguely guilty. And, like Freud, a little too Jewish.

And yet, since I do not have the slightest hesitation before depictions of non-Western deities, I have to admit this feeling is defensive, even hateful. I am ashamed of it. To discover in oneself the most secret roots of fundamentalism, when one has tried by every means to battle it out in the open—how humiliating! In short, I would probably have never opened that door if you had not chased me down with the Virgin Mary. I will no longer prefer profane works to sacred. At any rate, I'll try. I would still prefer to open the file of the sacred on a global scale rather than confine it to the West. In its present form, as "globalization" with the mug of an economic goddess, I dislike it intensely. If the sacred signifies the displacement of a limit, perhaps, as you say, we shall manage to remove that silver cope. Not without risk, however.

Indeed, the sacred is a no-man's-land that both of us are entering equipped with a weak light. It must be said that there are snipers in any no-man's-land, and that is frightening. No-man's-land, the place where snipers have their fun. In reality, it is a territory of many lost souls, men and women. In Africa, the new nomads of globalization are called "the cleared-out." They are expelled during civil wars or coups d'état; they are evicted from their slums, or hunger drives them out of their villages. They clear out and go elsewhere to set up a provisional household. So, in the spiritual territory of the sacred, what I call "the lost" are those who do not stay in place within the boundaries of religion. Those who go elsewhere, chased out, pushed toward an emotional nomadism that will never end. These are the "cleared-out" of religion. These two gifted women you let me discover are cleared out of their religions.

One attaches herself to Mama's vomit, the other fashions her unsatisfied hunger into saintliness. Astonishing, that power of the sacred, which transforms mud into gold and pus into nectar, don't you think? That reminds me of a short text by Lacan, *Kant with Sade*: Lacan based that incongruous comparison on the publication date of Sade's *Philosophy in the Boudoir,* namely, eight years after Kant's *Critique of Practical Reason*.

In Kant's book, Reason grounds the sovereign good; in Sade's, it founds sovereign evil, a reflection of a "being-supreme-in-its-wickedness." And Lacan insists on Sade's attack on decency, a term rarely used by psychoanalysts. Decency, "amboceptive of the conjunctions of Being," he writes. (Sometimes, all the same, he uses such words!) From the etymology of the term *amboceptive,* I believe it means that, between ambivalence and perception, at the boundary lines of being, the terms of an opposition vacillate, but not with reference to each other. And, in this precise case, the indecency of the sadist attacks the decency of the other. It seems to me that I find the same indecency in your outlaw "cleared-outs," who attack the decency of Being. Your saints and my priestesses abolish decency in the face of God; now we have returned to square one of the sublime according to Immanuel Kant.

Again! Yes. Because, like the sacred, the sublime according to Kant is the result of a short-circuit. For principles of morality, life in common, and the relation to the other, we have our reason, which errs when it wants to know, since that is not its job. The function of that reason is to prescribe formulas of moral law, of the sovereign good, and, hence, of God as principle of the ideal commonwealth. Fine. But, when objectless contemplation spurs a feeling of being invaded by an incomprehensible grandeur, then decency in the face of the real disappears. Hence the effusiveness that characterizes the sublime. People have even been known to cry over it. And, in this brief instant of "amboception," nothing keeps them from sublimating vomit, spittle, and even excrement.

The same short-circuit occurs in Freud's vocabulary, which makes the sublime an act, the act of sublimation. To sublimate is to move from sexuality to the ideal by short-circuiting neurosis. Of course, this entails the repression proper to artistic creation, since no one escapes repression in the strict sense. But, whereas nonsublimated repression produces only unhealthy disturbances, sublimation produces art. Unlike neurotic disturbances, which make life untenable, the artistic disturbances produced by sublimation socialize the artist: the short-circuit of the sublime thus involves insertion into society. In a sense, Kant says nothing else when he bases the sublime on Reason, since the latter is moral in function.

We are making our way through that wasteland of the sacred, where the aim of the abject is the ideal and where it achieves it. Your Agnes is in psychoanalysis only because her "impoverished religion" is not socially recognized as saintliness in our world. And today, like Madeleine, the delirious mystic whom the psychiatrist Pierre Janet treated for twenty-two years early in the twentieth century, Catherine of Siena would probably be in treatment at a psychiatric hospital. Nothing is more revealing than Janet's hesitations in *De l'angoisse à l'extase* [From anxiety to ecstasy]: Is Madeleine delirious, or is she a mystic? In the end, Janet settles the matter. Yes, he has a true mystic before him, one who, in other ages, would have become a saint. Yes, if she had not lived in the twentieth century, she would not have had dealings with the police or with medics. In other ages, instead of reporting her for wandering the streets at night, passersby would have venerated a woman who bore stigmata in her side and on her feet, who set out on a pilgrimage on tiptoe, who gave her belongings to the poor, who relived the delivery of the Christ child. . . . She would have been successful with that mystical repertoire up to the nineteenth century. Madeleine was living at the wrong time, Janet concludes. The signs of the sacred have not changed in Christianity, but the territory has been reduced. Madeleine goes astray because of an excess of memory.

As for Sade, the logic of sovereign evil impels him to wish that his mortal flesh not become the object of any tomb, so that the particles of his body will not become a pretext for any memory, to be precise. Oaks and acorns will have the task of annihilating what will have been, for a short time, the support of the subject named Sade. It is planned, organic disappearance with, Lacan suggests, the hope that these particles will never again reassemble. That desire for obliteration has no equivalent, apart from Sade's renown. It's a game where, if you lose, you win, which the mystics of the world play through the denial of the body.

But, notes Lacan, Sade took little risk in reality. In the contemporary world, the new sects play for keeps, with the rejection of medicine, the acceptance of death, in short, with an effective and dangerous denial of the body. This is a recurrent phenomenon. The Cathari, for example, who despised the flesh, practiced sacred debauchery to better degrade the body, and the "strongest" among them underwent the supreme ordeal, the *endura,* that is, fasting to death. To force the body to let itself die, what a request! Freud—and hence Lacan—repeats that "true love" ends in hatred. And, in that reversal of love, the same ambivalence is at stake as that which operates in the sacred: noble/ignoble, purity/impurity, eternity/time, decency/indecency, even including sacrifice. To leave everything, even one's body. To let go of everything.

This love is fiercely attached to an object of desire with a human face. Sometimes, it is called "mad love" [*amour fou*] and quite rightly, since the sanctification of love leads lovers to their deaths. Let's quickly pull out our Tristram-and-Isoldes and, outside the West, let us not forget the lethal couple formed by their Arabic equivalent, Mejnûn and Laylà. Even Mejnûn's birth name is unknown; he is the madman, period. He is mad only from love, but absolute love is madness, that is what "people" say. Mejnûn dies in the desert while exulting Laylà, whom he did not have the right to marry, and she dies as a result. In the Arab countries, the mad love of Mejnûn and Laylà is still celebrated, a love nothing could eradicate from their hearts. The Koran may have regulated polygamy, divorce, and the whole lot; it is no use, it could do nothing against the madness of love, which a good Muslim ought to reserve for God. So there!

"So there!" because there's a certain childishness on display. I leave everything behind, I am no longer anything but love. Whether it is for a man, a woman, a master, a god, or for God, absolute love is sacred, not divine. Narcissistic, bulimic, exhibitionist, mortal. Indecent and conspicuous. As lethal as the love of mothers who force-feed their babies, thus condemning them to anorexia. I love—the Other no longer exists. Isolde is no longer Isolde, she is Me. And I, I am no longer anything but love. I am everything: neither God nor Master. I love myself in a state of love. So there! And that childish protest, an onomatopoeia in French (*Na!*), is that of followers who go off to obliterate themselves in sects. "They don't want me to go. So I'm going."

In India, until the legal ban on the practice in 1988, there was a peculiar conjugal situation where the protest "So there!" took a curious turn. Here is the story that, for many long centuries, sent the bodies of widows to the flames. There is still a great deal of indignation about the "obligation" Hindu widows had to set themselves on fire on their husbands' pyres; the custom often went awry, that couldn't be more true. But the nature of the rite has been forgotten. Was the death of the widow on the pyre obligatory? No. It is the widow who must decide to be burned alive in order to become a suttee, that is, a goddess. A tribunal of Brahmans authenticates her wish. In appearance, there is no greater sacrifice of love. But that's not at all the case, it's just the opposite.

When he was alive, the husband was the wife's god, according to the ritual formula of marriage. Her duty was not to love, but to worship the husband chosen by her parents. The wife had the right to love him if that suited her pleasure, but it was not her duty. When he is dead, the husband is neither divine nor the object of worship. In return, or in revenge, the wife can choose to accede to divinity. And it is a mistake to think of this as an act of love. The question lies somewhere else altogether: in the woman's revenge against the family order.

She has only to make up her mind. In *Ashes of Immortality,* a wonderful book on that voluntary sacrifice, the ethnologist Catherine Weinberger-Thomas proves, via numerous examples, that the notorious suttees, the widows burned alive, sometimes had trouble convincing their close relations of their determination to die. Sometimes, they roasted an arm without flinching, as a way of proving their words. There is no doubt that widows were often burned of their own free will. Why? By way of proof. Proof of their asceticism, of their virility. "I can do it too." Once the decision is made, the future suttee is venerated as the equal of an ascetic, since she will accomplish in a minute the equivalent of a whole life of asceticism. A minute: the time to give a sign to a brother to thrust the torch into the straw, the time for the flames to attack her, the final suffocation. Getting off the pyre at the last moment is out of the question; she would be banished from the village in shame. Not only would she endure the unhappy fate of Hindu widows, but she would be dishonored. Between downfall and heroism, the choice is understandable. Better a destiny as a goddess worshiped till the end of the world. A beautiful suicide.

Where is the sacred? In the brief instant of the signal the wife must give of her own free will. Alone in the midst of the community that already worships her, and omnipotent. The author of *Ashes of Immortality* observes that, in the hours preceding the ceremony, the future immolated woman had the right to dictate as she wished the fate of her family: she could then express revenge against the stepsister, the stepmother, and so on. I am a goddess; I order. I can do it too. "Death be damned," as the back bumpers of trucks on African roads say.

It is the misdeeds of asceticism that Prince Gautama abandoned. Except for the fact that, in India, these sad heroines roasted "for real," I see very little difference between the decision of a suttee and that of the legendary Valkyrie, Brünnehilde, who leaps onto the pyre of her dead husband, Siegfried. In Wagner's work, that leap into the flames concludes the opera known as *Twilight of the Gods*. That mortal twilight, succeeded by a new world, is a perfect definition of mad love. Whether it is Sufi or romantic, the essence of mad love is protest, the "So there!" It must be acknowledged: mad love makes it possible to reject in bulk the rules of the commonwealth. Till death? Slow down, please. Not so fast.

The modern Western norm wants love to play the madman for a reasonable period of time, in the manner of an initiation rite. As in an initiatory seclusion, the smitten couple cut themselves off from the world; work, time, and hunger fade away. The lovers are emaciated and beautiful. Money no longer counts; it's money to burn. And then, time passes. Things take a turn for the worse. You have to walk away from rebellion one day and make a peace compromise with the social. You have to come back, mutilated but alive, from the "So there!" Yes, but the whole issue is to emerge from it before going to your death. In general, you succeed, but not always; sometimes you still lose your hide. Notice that you could hardly have an initiation without any danger. And it's true I often tell myself: "Woe to those who have never known it!" Yes, the same is true for mad love as for all sacred experiences: they are not democratic, and some people go their whole lives without experiencing them even once.

We stand at the crossroads of the rite of passage, which always socializes moments of advancement in life. Once the ordeal is completed, one can go on living. That's exactly what you propose when you want to "ease" the draconian ideal of Catherine of Siena. Go on, try! It's not easy. If the sacred walks along the borderline between the social and madness, what can you do? If one of its functions is to cross over, how can you stop it? I imagine you want to hold onto the ideal and discard the draconian. And yet. Might you have in mind some little notion of joyfully accepted constraint? What do you do with the "draconian"? Knowing you, I'm not at all sure you get rid of it entirely. Because you emphasize that Catherine of Siena exerted an influence on the papacy. Is that the price to be paid? Influence for influence, let me pull out two of another nature for you, women who profited enormously from the sacred. When I tell you their names, you'll see I do not locate myself within the religious: Eva Peron, Indira Gandhi, or, how to transform oneself into a consecrated object.

Eva Duarte was a bastard and lived an impoverished childhood. Indira Gandhi, the daughter of Jawaharlal Nehru, was a little girl left to her own devices, whose absent father was sometimes a prisoner, sometimes a militant, and whose tubercular mother was cast aside because, as a Hindu woman from a high caste and a member of the illustrious tribe of the Nehrus, she did not speak . . . English. Two humiliated children. The embalmed dead body of Eva Peron was stolen on several occasions, physically profaned by soldiers who hid it in outlandish places; then it was housed for a time in Spain, before coming back to its own country. Indira's dead body was burned within the prescribed time: twenty-four hours maximum. But, contrary to the Hindu rite, her ashes were not just cast onto the river. They were also scattered from an airplane by her son Rajiv, over the Himalayas. Two corpses, dispersed against all the rules.

Nevertheless, Eva and Indira marked their people as few leaders have. During their lifetimes, they transformed their images into a sacred icon. Hence the oddities of their posthumous fates, since sacrilege befits a goddess. What did they do to reach that point? Eva Duarte went through a phase of semiprostitution before meeting Peron. There was no passion between them, but an agreement regarding their conquests; for Peron, the Grail of power; for her, the Grail of the people. Once she married, Eva Duarte de Peron become la Señora, the Lady. Not the First Lady, no, the Lady; there was no "second." Her stroke of genius lay in a simple demonstration: Peron is the savior of the people because he saved the poor girl and married her. Hence Evita was the people. Jewels, furs, clothes, nothing was missing to signify the salvation of the People-Evita by the Savior Peron. The case of Eva Peron goes much further than a mere metaphor of social ascension. As the lady of the Argentine people, she invented courtly love at the popular level. As long as ecstasy lasts, the suzerain crushes democracy.

Soon, in her own lifetime, she is Saint Evita. She does nothing for the people, except to bring them images in the place of social transformations. And, when she dies, millions of Argentines parade in front of her coffin in the union hall. I was a kid, I remember crying in front of photographs of the people's tears. I lived the same scene in miniature when formal vigil was kept over the body of Elsa Triolet by Communist Party militants in the *L'Humanité* building. People paraded in front of the remains of the Beloved of the Poet. I wanted to see. So, that consecration of a mad love, as false as it was popular, fulfilled its function fairly well in the French manner: a little short-lived cult, a stay-at-home version of Evita.

It was harder for Indira. She had to fight, she did so with such passion that she was the only Indian prime minister to slip into despotism, by decreeing a state of emergency on the grounds that her election had just been invalidated: a police regime, abolition of freedom of the press, campaigns of forced sterilization of the peasants. She lost power. She was believed to be done for, and that is when the stroke of the sacred intervened. She begins another electoral campaign "at the grassroots level," a superb and very Indian expression, brings help to villagers during a storm on the back of an elephant. There she is, perched on the animal, letting the villagers call her by a new name: Durga, the goddess who, perched on a lion, crushes the demon of Evil. Indira is depicted as Durga on posters. And, as in the case of Evita, it works. . . . She is reelected and believes she is strong enough to lay siege to the Golden Temple of the Sikhs, which has been invaded by the proindependence forces of Punjab. People think they know what happened next. They think she was assassinated by two of her Sikh guards. But pay attention.

If you look closely at her schedule in her final days, what do you see? Indira learns that the plane tree that has served as the family's protector has withered, and she takes a helicopter to verify it on-site in Kashmir, the birthplace of the Nehrus. The tree is dead. The next day, she summons back two Sikh guards, who have just spent six months at home, in proindependence territory. The next day, in a meeting at the other end of India, she pronounces these astounding words: "When my blood has been spilled over India, it will fertilize her." Two days later, she is assassinated. During the night, her son Rajiv is elected prime minister. The game is won; Durga kills, but she is a mother. I believe that, in weaving politics, the nation, myth, and motherhood around her, Indira, up to her death, fancied herself as sacred.

Eva was neither tall nor strong; as for Indira, she came up to my chin, and I am not tall. Their voices were not powerful, their faces were not perfect. Indira had a sweet, high-pitched little voice, the look of a sparrow. They had no inclination for sex—they are not known to have had any affairs once they acquired power. But they conquered the sacred of the political field: the love of the people in its madness, its absurdity, in the danger it poses for freedom. Their two images, worshiped and hated, haunt the national conscience of their countries. And they violated freedoms. The sacred, my dear friend. I told you it was risky.

Take a good look at the heroines to whom absolute political power falls: the symbolism in play around the image of their bodies goes far beyond that of the three-piece suit or the general's uniform. Evita's elaborate chignon, her feathers and evening gowns, her ascetic thinness; Indira's well-kept saris, the white lock flashing through her black hair, the eyelid of her right eye permanently fluttering after a stone was thrown at her during a political meeting. . . . Those women are too unique to have heirs. The men would like to reissue the miracle: Peron tried with a second wife, Isabella, but in vain. The Indian Congress pressed Sonia Gandhi, Indira's daughter-in-law, to please replay the role; she agreed to conduct the electoral campaign but refused the post of prime minister in advance. She knew. The true sacred in politics understands the death sacrifice to which Eva and Indira had the right.

Where is God in their stories? Nowhere. They did not need him, since they had become goddesses without the support of a clergy. I will not say, "all alone," since, without the people, they did not exist. Eva and Indira were no more alone than the suttee on her pyre. They found their ecstasy in the meeting where they raised their voices. Have you ever stood at the rostrum in a political meeting? I imagine so. When it happened to me at the Mutualité, which is not a very large room, I was sweating with anxiety in front of the dark swell. But I had the real sense that, if I sublimated just a bit, it would not take a great deal to make the vocal cords vibrate, and to slip into danger. It was an exhilarating, frightening palpitation. I hated it.

Apparently, that jouissance of the collective body is the political personalities' object of desire. It is their sacred. But they need the stomach to digest the breathing of so many, the voice from everywhere and nowhere, the indistinct presence, the mass being, and above all, to confront the brutal effacement of identity, on the people's part and on the leader's. A borderline is crossed, that of the identity of the proper name: the leader's name, shouted, chanted, or hissed, is no longer truly his own. Nobody belongs to himself any longer, not them or him or her, if it's a woman. The sacred thing about that operation is that the private sphere no longer exists. As in rites.

It is clear I am beginning to mark my distance from the sacred. You don't need very much of it, otherwise, it'll make you crazy. So, what easing can you offer, my divine one?

Catherine

+ +

Dakar
JULY 8, 1997

Dear Julia,

I'M PICKING UP on my letter of yesterday, which felt unfinished to me, since I'm afraid I'm not done with Eva and Indira. I did not say enough about the hatred they were able to inspire. If Evita's embalmed body underwent that kind of treatment for so long, and if, even today, Rajiv Gandhi's widow and their two children are under police protection, then my harpies, because they stirred up the hatred of the subsequent generations, must be the object of posthumous curses equal to the blessings they received during their lives! After living the lives of saints, now they are awarded the immortality of witches.

I understood the greatness of witches from Michelet's romantic book, *The Witch*. In it, the author tells of the life of a poor peasant woman who calls on goblins to help her calm her baby's cries. Where does the peasant acquire the forest goblins? In a long-standing inheritance transmitted from mother to daughter. It's a pagan secret, that of the lares, which all Romans honored under their own roofs. And yet, beginning with a certain decree from Emperor Theodosius, "paganism" was banned throughout the territory of the Christian Empire, including Gaul. In the Middle Ages, the prohibition was already age-old, but the legends survived. The goblins clandestinely replaced the gods. The baby of the peasant woman cries unremittingly, and the obliging goblin flies in. The baby calms down.

Then one thing leads to another, and the goblin tantalizes the peasant woman, brings her balms with a sap and plant base, teaches her to use them. She becomes a healer, an abortionist when necessary, in short, she helps women like herself bear the harsh misfortunes of existence, when the priest offers only threats and prayers. Could hell be worse? The witch says no. The cruelty of the times requires makeshift solutions, tinkering, and the women tinker with what they have at hand, without suspicion. What a magnificent idea it was to invent the benevolent character of the witch therapist, to describe the indomitable tenacity of "paganism" under the mantle of Christianity! The more time I spend with healers on every continent, the more I verify Michelet's intuition. Magic uses the implements of a now-proscribed past, and it is always women who hold its secrets.

Michelet decides that the witch will be arrested when she has finally become beautiful—in insolently good health, too comfortable in her own body, not sickly enough. She wears a green dress, the color of the devil and of Islam, and walks straight ahead, in a rush. Have her burned at the stake! Yes, braving unhappiness without the Church's help is not allowed. That poor woman is too beautiful, too brave; it's not normal. For explanations of that anomaly, bring in the inquisitors, equipped with the *Malleus Maleficarum*, the instruction manual for apprentice inquisitors, written by Heinrich Institoris and Jakob Sprenger.

Examples: Woman is more vulnerable to the devil than man, because she is carnal; because, coming from Adam's rib, she is "twisted" (I quote). Also, the etymology of the word *femina* comes from *fe* plus *minus,* which obviously means that woman has less faith than man. The voices of women "empty the purse" (a direct quotation), take away one's strength, and force one to lose God. Woman is insatiable. Her boundless desire means that man "binds his soul" to woman. And finally, the high point: "A woman who thinks by herself thinks of evil" (*sic!*)

In the first edition (Strasbourg, 1486), the "Apologia" begins with a sentence that needs to be savored: "In the midst of the calamities of a century that is falling away, the old East, which, having fallen under the irremediable sentence of its ruin, from the beginning has not ceased to infect with various heresies the church that the new East, the Man Christ Jesus, fertilized with the dew of his blood, nevertheless is especially about its work today, when, with the world at eventide descending toward its decline, and with the malice of men growing, it knows in its rage, as John bears witness in Revelation, that it has but little time left." Reread it slowly. By definition, the East is ruined, old, heretical; but its rage is still infecting the "new East," that is, the West. As for the infection targeted by our inquisitors, it is called Heresy of the Witches. So Michelet got it right: the infection comes from an old fallen empire.

More important, the Dominicans, quoting Saint Augustine, enumerate the means to attract the demon. They are: "stones, herbs, woods, animals, songs, musical instruments," later subsumed under the generic name "herbs and music," *melio ancor.* Half-nature, half-music, such is witchcraft. In reality, the one in charge is not the devil but Orpheus! But the inquisitors don't know it. They linger over the danger of music, like any self-respecting fundamentalist. It's just crazy how much these two streetwise characters anticipate the Talibans of Afghanistan; in Kabul, women no longer have the right to keep caged birds, on the grounds that they sing. In 1980, as women were being forced to wear the chador over their mouths—can you imagine?—classical Iranian music, one of the greatest in the world, was banned in the Islamic republic; Khatami, the president of the republic elected in 1997, managed to have the ban lifted. Music and women, as we know, are always the first to be targeted. And it is not just recently that music has become bewitching: the Protestants also banned it, and, in *The Republic,* Plato proscribed certain musical modes as being too emotive for his liking.

Maria Callas—"the Voice"—of popular origin like Evita, underwent that transformation of the poor woman dressed up in chic clothes, the object of a persecutory adoration. Hence her tomb was profaned. Callas was a diva; everyone knows that. But only the specialists use the word *divo,* in the masculine, for a singer. "Diva" equals divine, nothing could be more pagan. It must be said that opera seems purposely designed to escape the maneuvers of the Inquisition: with setting, illusion, machinery, pagantry, music, and voice, everything is set in place to cast a spell over the soul, in defiance of the Church's rules. The *Malleus Maleficarum* dates from the fifteenth century; in the sixteenth, the card was played. In the courts of Italy, opera was born, relief for the powerful. . . . In the countryside, witches were still hunted down; two million of them would be burned at the stake in Europe.

Our two Dominicans examine the air transportation of witches, since all the witches talked about it. According to historians, it is nearly certain that witches coated their bodies with ointment before "taking flight" for their infamous Sabbath. But let's be a bit more technical. In India, the exercise called "leaving the body" is learned methodically. How does one leave one's body? Generally, through a prolonged suspension of breathing; it is then that the spirit journeys. But it is believed there were also ointments, revulsive hallucinogens. Even so, the lovely illusion of "leaving the body" is as old as the world. It can be found in Plato at the end of *The Republic,* in India at every crossroads; you run into it in animist Africa and in its voodoo versions in South America; it can be recognized in the well-known drug techniques of Castaneda, or in extreme sports. It is the "trip." The most recent version of leaving the body coincides with the experience of being brought back to life: people who have been resuscitated often report a euphoric moment of leaving the body at the time of their short-lived deaths, followed by an extreme repulsion when the doctors force them back into their sack of skin. These are the near-death experiences, theories of which are raging in the United States of America, that great country of witch-hunts, as we know.

In all polytheistic regions, the act of leaving the body belongs to both sexes. But, in fifteenth-century Europe, only women take flight at night. To leave one's skin, what freedom! But, say the inquisitors, those women must really be doing something with it! And the inquisitors reply in their place: at night, witches do everything backward: kiss the ass of the diabolical Great Goat, force the Host into its anus, sacrifice a living child, run through the repertoire of medieval anti-Semitism.

For the little offense of flying above the rooftops, merely throwing caution to the winds, they are condemned. That minor transgression was not very much, however. . . . To leave one's body, whatever one makes of the journey, is simply to leave behind the rhythm of collective life, to stay awake instead of sleeping, go out when everything is closed. But it is also to pass into the sacred, and the inquisitors did not want any of that.

In fact, the time and space of the rite contradict the time and space of civil society. You don't get to a site of worship any which way. A threshold has to be crossed according to precise rules, by covering or uncovering the head, for example. Then the space and time of the commonwealth vanish: in the journey of Parsifal, Wagner did a fine job of setting that phenomenon to music. The forest becomes sacred, animals friendly, and the borders of the real disappear, with the help of drugs. Everything is done to break the tough husk of the temporal routine; the sacred appears only at that price. The initiates of forested Africa remain in convents for a long time: it used to be for several years, it is three months in Casamance in 1997.

If the universe of men is forward, the sacred is always backward. Not "normal." For a non-Christian, it is not normal to go to a place where an officiant holds up a flat white disk, saying, "This is my body." It is not normal to speak from the balcony of the Casa Rosada to assert that you are the people saved by Peron. It is not normal to swallow the spittle of the sick, to refuse to wash your hair, to use excrement as a plaything. It is not normal to regress. Regression, as Lacan explains very well, is not the effective return of childish gibberish and gestures, but the return of signifiers for which there is a prescription. We've got it now. To take flight is child's play. But when you become an adult, you don't play anymore. You no longer have the right. Come on, don't be a child!

Yes, I will too, the cut of the sacred is needed. That lack is felt to be desperately lacking. Within the order and the discipline, Leviticus fixes it for one day a week, empties that day of its occupations, destines it for thoughts of God, and calls it the Sabbath, a word later recycled by the inquisitors. And to think that they transformed the repose of Being into madness! There is no better way to say that women in flight rested from the day that was so cruel to endure. And, as it happens, at nearly the same time, the Jews in exile changed their ideas about the Sabbath. The repose of Being turned feminine, became "Princess Sabbath," who was crowned during festival time. This was a time when magic permeated the Jewish communities. In Palestine in about 1540, the few rabbis who had come back to the region began to speak the language of insects; in the place of the Sheol, the pit into which man falls at his death, reincarnation returned in force. The old Orient, a little farther to the east, reappeared with the Diaspora. Of course, when life is too hard and you no longer have a temple, when you don't know the date of the return to Jerusalem, which is put off to an eternal "next year," then you leave your body, like every other place. That is what Rabbi Luria in Safed did in the sixteenth century, and what the Hasidic rabbis in Poland did in the eighteenth.

Does that mean there is no sacred in "forward" life? I think so. One must truly "go into reverse" to accede to the sacred. "Id" occurs in the blink of an eye, it exists "in the house of being," as Heidegger would say, a man who knew a great deal about the question. As the flip side of life, the sacred lies down with death. Now we need to tie in death, timelessness, and women, by harnessing them together with an approximation.

Catherine

♦ ♦

Ars-en-Ré
JULY 15, 1997

Dear Catherine,

THE LONGER THIS correspondence goes on, the more convinced I am that an infinite distance separates us. What do we agree on, other than the urgency of examining the feminine way of approaching that obscure territory called sacred: not "religion," not "sacrifice," not even "value," but, certainly, and through all that, a borderline; or, better, an "economy" that gives meaning to the human adventure? We don't agree? Another reason to make these disagreements visible, without confrontation. A long time ago, I made the choice, in all my activities, not to get into arguments, and even less to impart lessons: especially to you, since you have an answer for everything! I loathe fits of anger, invective, sarcasm. I prefer to move on and pursue my argument. How many letters on the Virgin? Ad infinitum, if necessary, to undo that knot that is taken for a hole. Besides, you do the same thing, in your own way, with your "So there!"

Nevertheless, there would be a great deal to say, about that poor West, for example, on which you heap every evil, including that of ignoring the existence of the sacred among the Indians of Brazil, and even among the Greeks! Are you serious? Ethnocentrism, granted, but why forget the efforts to transcend it? Efforts that other civilizations have not yet undertaken! Moreover, the anorectic analysand and Saint Catherine, whom I supposedly "served up" to you, are not composed solely of "brutality," as you write; but you'll undoubtedly smooth out the rough spots. . . . They manage, within monstrous suffering, to negotiate the violence of the prohibitions imposed on them, and which they impose upon themselves—without prohibitions, always more or less violent, there would be no social tie. What the history of religions demonstrates is that the sacrifice represents and appeases that violence because it builds a logic around the rite. And psychoanalysis teaches us that, without that violence-sacrifice-castration-lack-etc., there is neither language nor subject. Beginning from that point, the panoply of failures and successes of the so-called negotiation are set in place. Love is one of them, and I tried to unpack the multiple figures of it in my *Tales of Love,* which is already ten years old: Eros, Agape, sadism, masochism, homo-, hetero-, Don Juanism, melancholia, and all the rest. . . . As for Agnes, she does not suffer just because psychiatry has now replaced religion, which would have sanctified her. Oh no! One cannot sanctify all anorectics, and Catherine of Siena does not belong to the realm of psychiatry. A real effort must be made to accompany their symptoms with a certain use of language. A language that, precisely, can ease the morbid fixation of the symptom, the short-circuit of "body" and "soul" (we'll put them in quotations marks, if you like, to show we are not the dupes of binary Occidentalism). A language that, without necessarily suppressing the symptom—though that can happen—translates it and exhausts it in connections with others. What language? It is not enough to place bits of religions side by side to dream of a globalization of the psyche. Every particular memory appeals to a singular discourse. And that singularity, Duns Scotus's "haecceity," is truly a sacré acquisition of monotheism. Not of other religions. I am aggravating my case, I'm insisting on our Western merits, I will not give in to the lure of your Third World views. Not immediately. Agnes suffers because she has not found the *rhetoric* or, let us say, the *economy* (in the Byzantine sense of a "crossing," a "dialectic," a "ruse") of her experience: because she has not found the language of the senses.

No, politics is not the rhetoric or language of the senses, as you seem to believe. Political meetings sometimes give me a thrill, it is true, but one that is not exempt from something religious: paranoid or fusional or osmotic. Not in any way the peculiar lucidity that the word *sacred* conveys for me, at the intersection of the same and the other, nature and culture, drive and language, at the origins of the human . . .

Of all the arts, music is no doubt the closest to that elevation without words, before words, beyond words, the passion made voice, sound, rhythm, melody, and silence that the sacred communicates. From Kathleen Ferrier to Billie Holiday, the vibrating bodies of the great women singers incarnate absolute perfection and mystery. And music, all music: Monteverdi, Mozart, Bach, Armstrong, whomever you like. Human, transhuman precision, you can't go beyond that, it is the beyond, it is sacred.

I follow you when you recognize the "sacred" in Maria Callas, but surely not when you impute it to Evita: why not Madonna while you're at it, she who named her daughter "Lourdes"? You can't escape the Virgin, but that one doesn't belong to me.

To return to politics, there is an exception all the same: the celebration of July 14. Just yesterday, in front of the TV, I was overwhelmed by *La Marseillaise* on the Champs-Elysées, I got up out of my chair, a lump in my throat. A republican religion? Of course. But I maintain that it has better succeeded where others fail: in preserving both the community and the individual, the practical and concrete improvement of the human condition. Not enough, never enough, with many mistakes, but who can top it?

I know there are plenty of people who recognize the sacred even in Hitler, especially in Hitler, who has appeared on TV recently. Well, I'm not one of them. For me, that fascination with the feeble body (Hitler's), or with that of a woman one would not expect on the political platform, but who is all the more exciting for that, and who manages to get a hard-on to ensure the power and cohesion of the group, stems from a secular religion. It is all the more dangerous in that it entails neither hell nor moral code. It seems to me that that political religion is the most pernicious culmination of Religion in the most illusionist sense of the term, and it has nothing to do with the sacred.

What else? You claim that only female bodies took flight in the West in the fifteenth century. What about Giotto? What about Dante?

Men exist as well, let's not be "homophobic." I won't go over regression with you again, which is supposedly a "prescription of the signifier"—there would be a great deal to say about the overflow of the drives without any "signifier" whatever! What if the drive were the devil of your divine "signifier"?

No, I don't want to argue. A saying of Goethe's comes to mind: "What is the sacred?" he asks in a distich. "What unites souls," he replies. The sacred is what, beginning from the experience of the incompatible, makes a connection. Between souls, if you like. I almost want to get back on my hobbyhorse concerning the sacredness of maternal love, but I'm afraid I'll be brushed off. I owe you a confession, however: I truly believe in it, and that sacred seems to me both essential to women and very threatened in a world that knows how to do everything except "unite souls." I have sometimes thought I have gotten to the bottom of its alchemy: a violent push, biological perhaps, surely narcissistic, propels us toward our children, it sweeps away everything in its path, yes, I say everything, and can abolish the other as well as ourselves, make us mad, possessed; but, curiously, the connection prevails, an appeasement comes along to defer the violence, Eros and Thanatos are transformed into tenderness. Here we are at the source of words, where love becomes a so-called mother tongue. I imagine Goethe embraced that love in his vision of the "sacred" that "unites": he wrote, for example, that a hero is a man very beloved of his mother. Let's move on . . .

Let me pick up the thread of my last letter: supposing that a nonsacrificial sacred exists, might not the *imaginary* be one of its possible variants? The imaginary as eternal return, which opens the mind and body to an inquietude without end, and makes it possible to stand straight and lithe in the world?

The other day, an American friend of mine who gives English lessons to David, but also to your humble correspondent, since I really need to improve in the use of that idiom, had me read an article in the *New Yorker*. The author was making fun of books on "health sex," which are flooding the American market. Generally produced by women, these books give a thousand and one recipes for the clothing, behavior, and gestures to achieve a terrific orgasm, capable of ensuring well-being and success, both conjugal and professional. The author of the article takes great joy in mocking, and rightly so, these priestesses of sexual technique: don't they go so far as to propose their merchandise as a progressive battle against American religiosity, without realizing that they are championing nothing less than a religion of sex—perfectly symmetrical to the religion of Providence? And our instructor concluded: "American culture is a culture of Providence—divine or sexual, you can't get around it, we require salvation. You French are different: your culture is a culture of the Word, and everything always ends with distance, if not laughter or atheism." That makes sense, what do you think?

America is in quest of Providence through its technical perform-ances of "health sex," through extraterrestrial potentiality, and through other cults aspiring to Nirvana via suicide: that seems staggeringly ob-vious. I am also convinced that French culture, which has bound pleasure to the word, cannot, ought not to, succumb to that religiosi-ty. Those who said with Rabelais that "to give the word is an act of love," or, with La Bruyère, that conversation is a military art ("There are more risks than elsewhere, but fortune is swifter there"), or who, with Bossuet, have defied death by transforming it into rhetoric ("I enter life with the law to leave it, I come to fashion my character, I come to show myself like the others; afterward, I must disappear"), they are not ready to bind themselves to the Providence of sex or other health techniques. It is in France that psychoanalysis was understood less as a technique for healing than as a speaking of the truth. But, apart from the couch, can the word still be an art of living, a military art, a welcoming of death? Can it assume duties and connections, make fun of them, bring them to life?

I like to think that, if Catherine of Siena had not allowed herself to die of thirst, she would have sought to tone down her self-control— the "duty" of my analysand Agnes—by writing down that tension that led her to dominate her mother and speak to Jesus as to a close friend. Agnes writes poems and, increasingly during our analysis, tells stories: a way of undoing her knots of anxiety, debt, and guilt. The narrative, the novel, are simple forms, less demanding than poetry, commonplace even. They know how to conquer ordinary existence and never give up the task of giving it meaning: a sort of "duty," but worn down, neither absolute nor fierce, simply livable.

Catherine's confessor, who successfully defended her against her in-quisitors, and who persuaded the superior of the Dominicans, as well as the pope, that the thoughts and conduct of that sister were in con-formity with Catholic doctrine, apparently allowed himself to be sub-jugated by the young woman. He certainly accompanied her; he helped her to bear and sharpen her superhuman endurance to the ex-treme; he did not appease her. Because time has gone by and some of us have become more humane than those mysterious beings in the fourteenth century, allow me for a moment to take the place of that venerable Raymond of Capua. I would have proposed to Catherine—oh no, not an analysis, let's not kid around about that!—but that she go meditate among the builders of cathedrals who were her contemporaries, and reflect on their tools. Because of her tension, her propensity to take upon herself, to harden herself to, the most demanding ordeals (hunger, pus, death), I would have proposed that she choose a tool as humble as it is straightforward. For example, a mason's perpendicular: that she meditate on it, that she measure her gravity and aspirations by it, that she come tell me the most important things about it.

The overpowering superego of my anorectic analysands, and of a few others, often makes me think of that instrument: how can I direct them to keep what they need from their superego to make it a plumb line? No more, but no less either. Without lethal control. Just the tension necessary to stand up. Would they be capable of standing up?

That meditation exercise would be a sort of writing workshop, or a narrative account of oneself based on a symbolic support. It appeals to me by virtue of the humble dignity of the perpendicular—a sober uprightness, not overpowering in any way, simply indispensable. But, even more, by the fact that it is possible to talk about it, weave the associations that this taut line might unwind (for Catherine, for Agnes, for others). The imaginary apprenticeship relieves tension, does not make it disappear, but plays on it. It awakens curiosity, feeds the hunger for meaning and significance, but without satisfying it or frustrating it; it avoids both the absolute and the void, indefinitely.

So let us imagine. Let us imagine the plumb line. Women who are annihilated by a duty, more or less conscious, will at first have trouble perceiving the interest of that commonplace instrument, which builders, ancient and not so ancient, have used: a central symbol, it escapes attention, as obvious things often do; its elegant modesty keeps people from being curious about it.

To begin with, the perpendicular/father (oof!) is in league with duty. I like its function, which is to even out the stones of a structure: to get them in line, avoid deviations. Nevertheless, I believe I got through communism and achieved freedom as a woman, an intellectual, and a writer by wagering on the "exceptional," when not on the "strange." I have an infinite appreciation for the biblical and Christian idea that it is only from a "poorly squared stone," a "stumbling block" that the Light of Yahweh shines forth, and from which Christ and his Church arise. I acquired the certainty, however, that that libertarian gap is possible if, and only if, a perpendicular exists, and if I incorporate the sense of *alignment* into myself. In addition, like you, I know that the modern world easily plays to the gap, but doesn't care to know what rectitude is made of. Since we have not undertaken this correspondence to seek the emotional excitation or the childish naïveté or the absolute grace of a religion, but, perhaps, after all, the possibility and meanings of a *rectitude that makes a connection,* I propose that, as an image of the sacred, you contemplate that taut line as an invitation to that alignment.

I have read inspired and scholarly research that designates the perpendicular as the symbol of a deep-rooted knowledge, concerned with digging "lower and lower" and farther into the "center"; it has been compared to the trajectory of Dante, who, guided by Virgil, is not afraid to descend to the last circles of hell before coming back up to paradise. The downward-pointing tip of that modest metal, the lead plumb bob, is a good indication of what is at stake, and I have the feeling that the descent to the "low," or to the "center," might be associated with my practice as an analyst, concerned with the most commonplace aspects of memory and the body.

But, of all the other possible connotations, I would like to privilege three meanings of the plumb line, which seem unavoidable to me in this digression, after the impasses of the duty of my modest Agnes and the magnificent Catherine of Siena: rectitude, secrecy, and depression.

Everyone is familiar with that line: it becomes taut because it is pulled down by the attraction of the earth, manifested by the lead bob, but also because it is suspended from the ceiling. Uprightness is a tension between a point of attachment and a weight: uprightness is a maintained contradiction, it requires an up and a down, a roof and a weight. That taut line unfailingly calls to mind the erect posture—the verticality of the spinal column; and, metaphorically, in the figural sense, the perpendicular evokes soundness and justice. It seems to me that the erect posture is too easily considered natural to the human being. No, it is a constantly threatened achievement, which we must readjust—to which we must stretch—endlessly. "Stand up straight!" my father used to say. My father, the foremost being of uprightness—of an exceptional uprightness—that I ever had occasion to meet. People cannot imagine how unnatural it is to stand up straight, how difficult it is to stand up straight. Especially if one is a woman, with a husband, child(ren), lover(s), male and female friends, work and home, the list is infinite. People cannot imagine how difficult it is to stand up straight when one is a woman with a husband unlike the others, a child unlike the others, a profession unlike the others—and when these various points of attachment are as much elevations as handicaps (it being understood that each of us is "unlike the others" and that she has her own plumb lines "unlike the others"). They can't imagine!

Myself, Agnes, Catherine, and the others—we can try to imagine and realize that. I might manage to maintain the rectitude of my body (of my spinal column, which I have so much trouble not curving) and the rectitude of my mind if I fashioned myself in the image of the plumb line: never forget the plumb bob of my handicaps, never unhook myself from the ceiling. Yes, it is only in that way—pulled between its dangling weight and its fixed point—that my tension is not necessarily a tightrope that runs the risk of breaking. On the contrary, it can have the precise suppleness of a perpendicular. In sum, I get my rectitude from my weight, I would not be so upright if I did not have all these weights. But, even so, I must be properly hooked up above.

With Agnes and Catherine, I look at that plumb line a second time. Nondescript metal, gray-black, a long way from the nobility of gold or silver, a tip like an arrow pointing toward the ground. Yet we know that, above the point of suspension, the rooftop rises and the light of day unfurls. I see in that solidarity between surface and depth, light and shadows, the image of *secrecy*. It is well known that the sacred and secrecy have journeyed side by side throughout history. But the Greeks defined truth as an unveiling, and the Catholic Church made the mystery universal, available to all. Far be it from me to argue the present-day scientific and democratic benefits of that procession of "phenomena," "insights," and "openings." Let me say, nevertheless and simply, that it entails the risk of the spectacular and of the artificial. And I maintain that the rehabilitation of secrecy can be a salutary counterpoint to such tendencies, to such dangers. Not a secrecy that would revel in itself, that would be content with itself, or that would degenerate into corruption, which, in that case, would be as harmful, if not more so, than a complacency with appearance or display. But a secrecy that, like the plumb line, can be measured in the dignity of its focus, which, like the plumb line, does not forget that it functions so that rectitude shall become visible—that is, so that it shall appear in everyone's sight in the visibility of the building, which remains the sole proof of the utility of the secret plumb bob. To respect Agnes's secret, Catherine's secret, my own—a trauma? an untranscendable desire?—and to give expression to, allow to be expressed, make readable and visible what Catherine, Agnes, and I are capable of formulating here and now, at our own pace: such is the meaning of secrecy in psychoanalysis. And undoubtedly that of the best secret societies: that of friends, accomplices, philanthropic organizations.

Let us look a third time at that plumb line. There is something desolate in the modesty of that metal, a nostalgia for light and depth in the tension of that line. Late symbols, as we know, have a nostalgia for earlier religions, of which they collect only eclectic fragments. Nostalgia is the sister of melancholy, it stands side by side with the depression of individuals and the loss of meaning. At this point, I would like to make myself the advocate of that nostalgia and that depression. I say they are indispensable. I say that it is only in mourning the old seductions and beliefs of our ancestors, in exhausting their artificial spark in the accounting of a sober meditation, that we can move in the direction of new truths. No, the symbolism of everyday things is not sadly nostalgic. It benefits from that fertile moment of depression, when I assume the loss of the old and undertake a rebirth. But I stand between the two. That moment between the two, that stage of transition, that space of suspension—which the plumb line makes present in its gossamer sobriety—makes me think that the narrative that gives meaning to our daily objects is the very site on which nostalgia turns itself inside out into "something to come." How so? We do not know, we will never know perhaps. What if the truth were only that? Not "a meaning" but a "tension toward." Let us confine ourselves to remaining upright and sound. Let us work toward meaning, but let us leave it . . . indefinite, always "to come." In the face of religions and ideologies, I would say that our attention to the sacred is "transitory" (rather than "nostalgic") and that, paradoxically, that transitory quality is its strength. A nondescript but true strength. Like the strength of the mason in the past, equipped with his plumb line, still far from complete, always too far from the finish, but which draws its rectitude and soundness from that nostalgia for the infinite.

It is something of all that that I am trying to introduce into my brief interpretations and comments during the sessions with Agnes. As for Catherine of Siena, was she not thinking of that when she mentioned a "true glory" in opposition to "vainglory"? Who knows? She hangs over us with her superhuman experience, we who were born after humanism but have, nonetheless, not forgotten the sacred.

Julia

Dear Julia,

WAS I RIGHT to pull your leg? Looking at your last letter, I'm beginning to doubt it. I therefore assert: 1) that the Virgin is not "yours," but a liberating theological invention that excites you for that reason alone; 2) that the "So there!" in my last epistle was not mine, but a "So there!" of the lethal bolt of love at first sight; and 3) that if I rave against the sacred, it is because, in moving like a she-cat around the tom, I get an inkling of all the places it has been.

Let's dig in. First misunderstanding: the "So there!" of love. Love, as negotiation with the prohibitions, is indispensable, I grant you that. But the myth of love in the West is, I believe, just the opposite. The prohibitions are transgressed with extreme violence, with a mortal effect of overabundance, which is extraordinarily moving, extremely beautiful, especially at the opera. As you may remember, I attempted to show, in one of my books, that the sublime operas of the nineteenth century were also machines for savoring, with tears in the eyes, the death agony of the victims of that myth of love, women especially. At the time, I focused on the women. I was partly wrong. It's true that men often die beautiful, agonizing deaths in operas. But, in the nineteenth century, whether they were men or women, the ones sacrificed were always sopranos and tenors, the tessituras of youth and innocence. Of vulnerability and childishness, if you like. Let us call it the regressive imaginary of love, still fairly powerful today. Yes, it is a "high-risk" stereotype. In any case, it played enough nasty tricks on me that I have not forgotten it; yet, even so, I managed to escape with my life.

On politics, we have no disagreement. You offer me sacred-love-for-the-fatherland on a platter, something that seems political to me, in the original sense of the word, since the "fatherland" concerns the community in which we have chosen to live, or to remain. And when you attribute a charge of osmotic "fusion" to a political meeting, that's the right word. I agree fully about the republican sacred. As for republican religion, that's another matter, about which I am less sure.

Second misunderstanding: Eva Peron. The political aspect of that bizarre self-made creature disappeared the day she became sacred. Up until the time that Colonel Peron took power, you are right. She stirred up the masses enough to get Peron out of prison, she was his main political asset. But as soon as she became the wife of the president, she was not the "First Lady," she became the Madonna, and that was such a different thing that Peron was no longer able to get rid of her. For a time, she plugged up the holes of poverty with her evening gowns. But then, she got in his way. What didn't he do to shatter his wife's myth! Impossible, because of the sacred. Politically, he did not exist without her, but her own concern was a dual saintliness: that of the people and that of the Argentina she claimed to incarnate.

Cunning, scheming, yes, until the moment when she was physically swallowed up by popular devotion. She died just in time: she was about to be named vice president. It's attested that Peron was greatly relieved by her death (wrongly so—he lost her power). As for Madonna, you think you're joking, but, in terms of a caricature of the sacred, you're telling the truth. The enormous cross on her punk chest in her early films, the role of Evita, which she forced on the public, not without difficulty, the daughter baptized "Lourdes," her repentance for her youthful blasphemy, and finally, her stage name: an excellent business to be in, since there is great demand for that supply. Indira was able to identify herself with the goddess Durga, Evita was able to become the madonna of the *descamisados,* and Madonna was able to mimic the sacred. But I have not forgotten the tyrannical drift of my political actresses. As for Hitler, however intolerable the question, I don't see how to avoid it. In politics, Hitler experimented with almost everything relating to the sacred: from the amplification of the voice with microphones to the naming of the scapegoat, from fires blazing in the night to clandestine murders, from the mad love of one people, the German, to the secret plan for the Final Solution, which would have annihilated the other people, the Jewish, from terrorism to suicide, accompanied by the music of *Twilight of the Gods* . . . I don't see how he can be exempted. Hence my worries about the excesses of the sacred. To remain within the private sphere is an imperious necessity. If not, there's danger.

Third misunderstanding: witches. I am not unaware of either Dante or the paintings of Giotto, or, in the *azulejos* of baroque churches in Brazil, of the crucified saints in rapture, equipped with giant wings and in flight. As far as I know, male saints were not burned at the stake. . . . In contrast, the Dominican inquisitors sought out a means to identify the accursed women. And the sole demonstration of their major work is that only women are witches, because they fly. Who is forgetting Giotto? Or rather, who is ignoring him? The authors of that manual of the Inquisition.

Fourth misunderstanding, but in this case, you've gone too far. Did I brush you off concerning maternal love? I applauded! But since you're angry, I'll go on. Yes, maternal love is on the order of the sacred. Does appeasement necessarily follow violence? Well, not always. The mothers of anorectics and Jewish mamas (I am one, I know) don't succeed at it. In fact, you describe in admirable passages the hard work required to tame the maternal sacred in oneself. Really a tough job!

All things considered, our only disagreement has to do with the risk factors of the sacred. But first, let me emphasize this, I call "religion" any organization of the sacred that relies on a clergy, rites, constraints, and sanctions. That is why republican "religion" does not suit me entirely: I see too many constraints in the word *religion*. Look at the United States. The curious thing about that nation is the dramatic tension between a democracy that functions and the referent "Providence": the president's oath on the Bible, religious paraphernalia. A matter of connecting pleasure and language, you say; I believe you've got it right. A technology of images, hard-core sex, gore, extraterrestrials, violence, and puritanism, that's their witch's brew. The true freedom of pleasure is banned. I've wondered for a long time about the perverse effects of the First Amendment of the U.S. Constitution, which considers freedom of opinion indefeasible. A sacred value of the United States of America, to be sure. But sects thrive on that soil, and one of the most recent to be recognized by U.S. law was purely and simply . . . satanic. You can laugh about it. You can also remember the satanic ritual crimes in California.

In any case, I am delighted by the idea that occurred to you, that you were dearly sorry you couldn't "analyze" Catherine of Siena on your couch. . . . Oh yes, the "impoverished religion" of your Agnes is loosening its stranglehold. Of course, because you are there! You do the work together. You inform me that Catherine of Siena did not go her way by herself. All right, but her confessor, Raymond of Capua, did not know how to unfasten the yoke of rigor, in spite of all his efforts. Fortunately! Imagine if he had succeeded. No more saints, and no more commentaries by Julia Kristeva.

I marvel at your metaphor of the plumb line. And I'll take you back to India, at least if you're not tired of it. It is so unnatural to stand up straight that it took yoga centuries to analyze that difficulty proper to the human race, which has a back that becomes stooped with age. Not the yogis' back, to be precise. To understand the straight back of the yogis in India, I took some thousand or so lessons. And, since it is possible to explain to the master that you're not interested in mysticism, I benefited from a course of study based on physiology. From that materialist angle, the yoga lesson is of great simplicity. First, you practice breathing from the stomach, which expands the rib cage, and thus lifts the shoulders. Try it, you'll see. When you breathe deeply with the stomach, that pulls apart the clavicles, mechanically. Try it with the lungs, without the belly: it's the ribs that stretch out. Obviously, yoga breathing includes other, more complex exercises, but none exists without that basic correction of the back.

The main posture consists of holding the feet in the air for ten minutes maximum, with the back vertical, pressing on the back of the neck, supported by the arms on either side; or—but this posture is not recommended for women—directly on the head, without the support of the neck. Head down, feet up, that's "standing up" backward, straight as a plumb line; let's call it equilibrium. It is no longer a case of descending toward "the low" but of raising it. And the work is being done by the abdominals—the belly—and by the neck, on which the equilibrium rests, and which is not allowed to be rigid. From what my yoga master told me, that pressure on the neck massages the thyroid gland, which, as you know, regulates mood. Isn't that what you're looking for with the plumb line?

Finally, the position that we call "relaxation" has been called, for two thousand years, the "corpse pose." Back flat, head, hips, and body touching the ground; only the hollow space between the neck and the back is an exception. It's the full horizontal. And, if you slip into the mystical theory of yoga, which is not at all my cup of tea, it's the moment of meditation on the indifference to death, the detachment of self: the yoga equivalent of Bossuet's words. In that posture, since I am suspicious of mysticism and not gifted for meditation, I relax without worrying about what comes to mind. Free association, in short. Once the phase of internal unblocking is over, similar to the beginning of so many analytical treatments, thought calms down, and then it's productive. As for emptying the mind, frankly, no thank you. . . . All the same, I'm well aware of the posture I'm in at that moment. It's called the "corpse pose." You live vertical and die horizontal. Might thought occur between the two postures, the mind alive and the body simulating death? It cannot be ruled out.

In the twentieth century, the "yogini," the women who practice yoga, are very visible. And, in the same realm of ideas, female dervishes are increasingly numerous in the Sufi branch. Same exercise in the

"Sama" of the dervishes: it's the back that allows you to spin. The sharing of an apprenticeship in the "straight back" is thus in progress; that is to say, once again, that it is not self-evident. Not symbolically either. Indeed, if it is hard to learn to hold the spinal column straight, it is no easier to learn to hold straight the column of the person, in the sense of the moral person, the civil person, the identity. The Latin word *persona* means "stage character." Bossuet again.

At this point, I'll introduce depression, since, when a person is depressed, the "stage character" has collapsed. The wires are limp. The body is no longer straight, but beaten down. Identity wavers, morality no longer holds sway, the heart is empty, suffering is infinite. On that point, you and I are perfectly agreed. In the only one of my books where, I believe, I approached philosophy (*Syncope: The Philosophy of Rapture*), I wrote that depression was the only rite of initiation remaining for industrialized countries. Yes, depression is really and truly indispensable. Yes, it is a useful retreat. Yes, the posture of prostration is a withdrawal that does not do any harm: head down, eyes invisible to the other, body curled up. Yes, depression makes it possible to stand back up. Yes, it precedes a rebirth, and that is why I compare it to an initiation. The "work of mourning" is one of its versions, and it belongs to life, not just to death. If the depression lasts too long, in fact, it turns into melancholia; the void of the sacred becomes lost in a chasm, and rebirth does not come about. Now I'm back in the danger zones. But can the danger be avoided? There is real danger only in excess, said the Greeks. That is the very definition of the tragic.

On that score, there is still a difference between us that is not on the order of disagreement. You say "cathedral" and I reply "yoga." Undoubtedly, with our hobbyhorses, one Christian, the other "Indian," we aggravate each other like two goats on a bridge. That is because our biographies are noticeably different. Before choosing to become French, you were a foreigner—alas for us, too often you still feel treated like an alien in my country. I was born French of Russian grandparents on one side, Bretons on the other; the alien in me is more distant. You were communist in your youth, and I in adulthood. You were in Bulgaria and I in France. Your parents experienced Communist oppression, my Russian grandparents were gassed by the Nazis at Auschwitz. You are not divorced, I am. You have only one son, I, a boy and a girl. Finally, you are a psychoanalyst and I was simply in analysis. In short, my life is more ordinary than yours, easier to live, in a sense. I know that. I do not draw any consequence from it, except that it seems to me that I find a tension between us there, in the musical sense of the term: soprano on one side, mezzo on the other. One rises to the high notes, the other descends to the bass. The soprano is heavenly, the mezzo hellish. Since, in opera, the mezzo is often assigned the roles of witches and other nasty characters, I take on that symbolic tessitura and I assign the soprano, albeit a bit victimizing, to you.

But neither of the two voices can sing without a straight back, it's a matter of breathing. In singing, as in yoga, you learn to hold, to retain your breath. In singing, it's quite necessary; the melodic phrase demands the note be held. In yoga, suspending your breathing for a long time makes it possible, by cutting off the air, to achieve ecstasy. When you lack air, you get dizzy, your head becomes fuzzy—that's easy to understand. There's no point in telling you that, in translating the lessons of yoga in this way, I am committing a great sacrilege against the doctrine of the yogi. But, since I am a materialist, that's my grasp of things. Is it so different from singing? My friend Ruggero Raimondi says no. The objective is not the same, but the effect produced surely is. And what interests me in these techniques is the idea of suspension, which, as you say, is connected to your plumb line. "Holding" or "retaining" is not bad either, but "retain" comes from "retention," which indicates a diversion from the path. The retention of sperm in coitus to the point of rapture, and, hence, the refusal to procreate, the retention of the breath to the point of death. Maria Malibran almost died of it. Excess.

To suspend, then, moderately. The back straight, but not rigid. Rigidity is paralysis. Light rather than dazzlement. Brightness rather than the paradisiacal illumination of the immediate afterdeath experience of those who are brought back to life. Finally, let's talk a little bit about secrecy. Granted, it is necessary in the same way as depression. But, at the risk of angering Sollers, who makes it his moral rule, I am not crazy about absolute secrecy. Secrecy may be a moment of gestation, granted. It may be the plumb line of the psychoanalytic cure, yes. But I am not happy with the idea that it might be the golden rule that will never be lifted. Look at Freemasonry. The reasons of circumstance that historically made it a society of secrecy are understandable; there was danger. Secrecy about membership, a common phenomenon in the birth of religions, seems prudent to me. And it seems altogether normal that there are, in Masonry, other reasons for secrecy, associated with a system of initiation by degrees, without which the initiation, which works on surprise, would no longer have any meaning. But that secrecy about membership has endured for several centuries! That verges on a travesty, or sometimes even on farce. The secret brotherhoods were able to do damage–remember lodge P2 in Italy!—and, when you use the word *accomplice,* which seems innocent to you, it also expresses guilty deviations within the idea of secrecy. Decidedly, Freemasonry ought to be reformed: the plumb line is sacred there, the ideal admirable, but, even in Masonry for women, secrecy has turned financially complicitous many times. . . . Do you see how suspicious I am?

Now, as for negotiation: psychoanalysis is an apprenticeship in it. Away from the couch, true mediators are rare: a few true diplomats can be found sometimes, two or three journalists with enough gray hair to exercise authority, a few individuals whose biographies have provided the ordeals needed to learn the art of negotiation. In the past, trade unionists knew that art. Today, I find that the only voice for true negotiation is a woman, Nicole Notat (while rereading, a few months later, what I wrote, I observe that filthy words are spewing from the mouth of Marc-Blondel-who-is-not-"queer" in reference to that woman; so much the better! He's discharging himself, he's a sewer, he doesn't know how to hold back).[9] And, to negotiate, one must weigh one's words, assess the moment, the tone. One must stop and begin again, suspend in order to advance. A question of breathing.

The time for secrecy in negotiation seems to me the proper example of equilibrium. As in analysis, the time of negotiation is clandestine and limited; as in analysis, the practice relies on language; as in analysis, negotiation requires compromise, that disparaged word. Let me describe the processes of negotiation I was able to see operating at close range in twelve years in the diplomatic life. Nothing exists but the word. It begins with the secret, which the negotiator and his partners share, knowing that, one day, it will have to be revealed: there, in the future of the public announcement, the plumb line of the matter can be found. The essence of the secret in negotiation consists of its being revealed at the right moment; thought is riveted to the future.

The beginning of a negotiation takes place in a sort of anxiety that verges on the sacred. Everything has been prepared in secret; the ad-

---

versaries prepare to meet each other. They appear in person, catch sight of each other, exchange glances. "We'll talk." Already, they've moved from "they" to "we." Time flies. Depending on the case, it is imperative to keep the secret or to reveal it partially: if freeing hostages is at stake, total secrecy. If there's a question of a peace compromise, partial secrecy, even false secrecy, a diversionary maneuver. Example: the Israel-Palestine conference officially opened in Madrid, but the real negotiation unfolded in Stockholm. When the negotiation is public, it doesn't work, and is thus often accompanied by a work of displacement. The official work is open, but the latent work is dealt with in secrecy.

Whether it has to do with freeing hostages or reaching a peace compromise, the negotiation has no meaning except with the end of secrecy. A peace treaty follows; in transcribing the secret in writing, it reveals it. Whether the peace is observed in actuality or not essentially depends on the proper use of the symbolic in the language of negotiation. Even today, in many places on the planet, gods, rituals, the consultation of diviners and other astrologers must be accepted as part of the process. . . . In that, I see no contradiction with the political, or even economic, aspects of the negotiation: indeed, the spiritual aspects are part of the negotiation apparatus. All that language work begins with a sacred moment, experiences the same ups and downs as analysis, and ends in the same way. That short-lived phase is key: a brief instant, and sometimes parodic in the case of misfires (I'm thinking of the countless African peace treaties that were broken as soon as they were concluded).

That is what you express so aptly as the "transitory quality" of the sacred. As long as it is provisional, the sacred is indispensable. If it "holds" too long, pathologies get mixed in with it, the unsteady structure reconstitutes itself with even more assaults than before, nothing new comes of it, and the conflicts increase. The "blow"—the salutary shock—of the sacred is a miss. The sacred is thus productive only in the transitory. This time, we are truly in agreement. In point of fact, transitory or transitional?

But why are you cryptic about regression as the return of prescribed signifiers? Why do you invoke the name of the Lord, and without a capital letter? What does that "good god" mean when you write it in reference to the excesses of the drives?

Catherine

Dear Catherine,

YOUR LAST LETTER gave me a good laugh. Me, a soprano? If I could sing, I'd be an alto instead, but I don't know how, and you run no risk of hearing me, therefore the question does not arise. In addition, and since you were using it as a metaphor for the tone of my letters, I do not believe I am hitting such high notes. But, after all, to each her own ear.

My PowerBook is transparent today; I can't see it. I see only the geranium on the low wall in front of me, bathing its red clusters of petals in the blue of the Fier River, the pyramidal salt crystals lined up in the marshes, the landmark of the steeple in the distance, and an oyster light, the dazzle of midday blurring into mist. It is the auspicious hour for waves, fine sand, the language of skin, and the silence of eyes. No "signifier," "prescribed" or not. There are states of regression—and of progression—where the signifier no longer exists, a rhythm has taken its place, the beat of a sensation, like the rustle of this sea before me, a breath that makes a mark but is the bearer of no meaning. You see, I am not in a mood to "respond," unless, precisely, this is the ideal moment for a subject like our own. As for "secrecy," we run across secrets, deep or open ones, throughout our correspondence, and "excesses" of every sort even more so. No question of clearing everything up, am I right? Or of saying everything—a word to the wise. And just because the secret has been "capitalized on" does not mean it is not the most favorable site in the search for personal truths, and also for collective ones. Otherwise, how do you proceed without *sharing* your sacré secret? Then, so that everything does not deteriorate into a sect, there's only one solution: let's continue the battle, that is, the permanent questioning of everything, of oneself, and of secrecy itself.

If you find me cryptic about regression, it is because I observe in myself and in my patients bodily states that make meanings and all possible and imaginable signifiers implode. After Freud and with Lacan, we return again to Freud, but this time with biology, to perceive that there are strategies of *sense* without *signification,* "memories," if you like, but far below language and the signifier. When "id" submerges you, "id" produces a psychosis—or rapture. Depending on the era, on chance, and on the few possibilities humans have at their disposal to

create. Precisely, you'll tell me, as soon as you say "create," you introduce the "signifier"! Not only it, don't be too hasty. Creation comes
out of a cut, the gap that opens within the signifier, and there is no
Word there. Not yet. I would go so far as to remind you, since you are
such an expert, and your Théo is the proof, that it is even from that
separation that the Bible proceeds: in the beginning, God *separates*—
my emphasis.

No, I don't put any trust at all in the sacred, or any devotion: relax.
Parenthetically, let me also point out another disagreement between
us: I find nothing sacred in Hitler, he fiddles with the sacred and ex-
ploits it in religion, from the outset he pushes himself forward as the
founder of a movement, as the maker of myths. If I accord any interest to the sacred, through and beyond the religious, it is because we
have an interest in not forgetting it. It stems precisely from the cut,
bereshit, that opens representation without becoming confused with it:
heaven and earth, man and woman, and other divisions as well, each
on its own side. Humans have difficulty sorting it all out; yet, as soon
as they exist as beings of meaning, it is the cut that preoccupies them.
They begin with the act: rites of decapitation (I'm working on a report
right now on the catalog of my exhibition at the Louvre), the skull, castration, ritual murders, and so on. But no, the God of the Bible tells
them, what makes you evolve into human beings is not the act of
killing so that you can imagine yourselves stronger than death, it is not
even the sacrifice. You can "sacrifice," quite simply and logically, by
confining yourselves to observing the *prohibition*. In the beginning was
not the sacrifice, in the beginning was the prohibition. Know that, it
will allow you to vie with one another in verbalization, morally speaking. You will continue to transgress that prohibition or that morality,
that's life. But, if you forget them, they will catch up with you from
within—you'll be slashed from the inside, you will bleed, you'll be ill;
or from the outside—you'll lose your place and your composure, you'll
be attacked, possessed, dispossessed, paranoid, mad.

So, some people are fed up: they want to be done with the cut, the
prohibition, the sacred, and their sadomasochistic retinue. No more
sacred, they pay off the account, long live reason, everything will be
"managed" quite properly! A little diplomacy (as you say), a little computer, a little central bank. . . . But then, one fine day, our management
diplomats find there's another attack in the heart of downtown. Or, in
the end, they notice that their wives are suffering from vapors, which
neurochemistry cannot cure. And that democracies are swarming with

mystics, founders of sects who want them recognized as religions by the courts. What relation is there between a terrorist act, a psychosomatic illness, and a sect? I ask you: that's a question for a TV quiz show, it can bring in a lot of money, billions in tax relief, combined with a little test of republican secularism. Why that commotion? Purely and simply because, on the other side of the prohibition, the abyss remains. It does not allow itself to be mopped up by the administration of signification and signifiers. It waits, or, rather, does not wait for its due.

Others, like me (and you, despite our discordant voices), think we have only one way remaining to stay alive, which is to think: yes, I say "think" and not "calculate." To visit, the best we can, that cut, that prohibition, that reversal of meaning, where meaning is born on the edge of the geranium or of the water of the Fier, on the edge of nothingness. To go along on both sides, from nothingness to being and back. I call atheism the meaning of that labor of meaning, its delivery into the world, its long life. The depletion of transcendence in transcendence itself. "A cruel and long-term enterprise," wrote Sartre. Today, in front of these seagulls that cry for joy as they come to drink near my old stone wall, I do not find it so cruel, that long-term enterprise. I am left with only the certainty of solitude and the desire to share it. Which means, after all, that we are not so alone as all that . . .

Julia

◆ ◆

Le Thoureil
AUGUST 20, 1997

Dear Julia,

YOUR LOVELY SUNNY epistle comes close to the theory of life. Splendid! Clearing things up is out of the question, you say: nevertheless, on those states you describe as "id," you express yourself with the only means possible, poetry; geranium, seagull, oyster. And, already, in reducing your words to flower, bird, and mollusk, I elaborate, I distort. I obliterate the transitory quality.

In the meantime, I have moved from Dakar to the Loire, the regressive site of my childhood, as well-stocked with seagulls as your island by the sea. In addition, there's the passing moment of unsettled strangeness that accompanies the return to the capital of one's own country. To see Paris once more at dawn—the plane landed around five o'clock in the morning—is to discover its façades restored by virtue of absence, a window with medieval panes one has never seen before, a caryatid, a curious-looking roof. The Place de la Concorde, entirely empty, recaptures a revolutionary look, in spite of the fountains. It doesn't last, but an empty city is nice. What relation does it have to the sacred? For me, the return, strangeness, the void, and early morning.

We agree on the most feminine of the "fundamentals" of the sacred: the atheism of the labor of meaning. But let me give it a somewhat different name: the "atheistic mysticism of meaning." Let's not leave the word *mysticism* to the fringe elements of religions, and let's use the connotations that word has in its very etymology: mystery and initiation. In the beginning, the Greek *myste* simply meant "initiate." As Georges Bataille has demonstrated, there is nothing incompatible between that atheistic mysticism and the exercise of reason. Provided, however, that one takes a proper survey of it, does the owner's tour with posts and measuring tape. I will not try to "clear things up," since you don't want to. But I would like to draw my bow and clear a few shots, as a way of not losing the space between atheism and mysticism.

Each in her own way, you and I have both explored the apparent "returns to" in the forms the sacred takes. Return to childhood, to dirt, to the anal stage in initiation rituals; the return to the body, both pure and impure, internal and external, in the precise lyricism of the mystics. The "return" to motherhood, which you are right to say is the source of the sacred. But it's a long way from the "about-turn" you express so well to the dangerous illusions of "return" denounced by Lacan, which I mentioned previously. So then, what is that danger?

The very term *regression* implies a return to a bygone past. Real or imaginary? That is one of the pivotal points of Freudian thought. During a discovery phase, Freud groped around before settling the matter: no, there is no original primal scene, duly established by the facts. There is no real return to the past in the psychoanalytic cure. The traumatizing "origin" is only a reconstruction, a fantasy made of bits and pieces "arranged" by the unconscious, in the way a saxophonist "arranges" a musical theme. In the place of a primal fallacious truth from which all the repetitions of an individual's life would originate, Freud posits the "screen memory." This much is clear: there is a screen, which it is point-less to knock against.

That is why regression is not a return to the past, but a return of the past in adult life, in forms contrary to the codes of behavior. You know it better than I—the unconscious is not polite at all. It is barbaric, poorly behaved, foul, like Poenia, the poor hungry girl Aristophanes dreamed up as the mother of Love in Plato's *Symposium*. But just be-cause a human being bleats for love doesn't mean he becomes a real sheep. Freud's lesson is also that the past remains in disguise. For ex-ample, under the fallacious appearance of a geranium sky and an oys-ter-colored gull in flight.

Now, the mythology of origins uses and abuses the sacred, making it the foundation of countless, not to say all, religions. The repeated celebration of a sacred event necessarily borrows the notion of mystery from the idea of origin, indefinitely repeated in the rite. The Christian Mass repeats the Last Supper of Christ, the rigorous pilgrimage to Mecca that of the last pilgrimage of Muhammad, and the dual African burial repeats the journey of the familial ancestor from life to death, and then from death to life. The establishment of the rules of repetition becomes a code—which Freud would call obsessional—and the sacred is framed by the schedule of the rite, which begins, unfolds, and ends according to an immutable rule. "Introibo ad altare Dei": I shall rise to the altar of God, and the rest follows.

But the starting point of the sacred is as buried as the elements of the screen memory. Hence, there is not a great deal known about the exact process of revelation. We do know, more or less, what landscapes predispose one to revelation—high mountains, steep cliffs, vast snowy expanses, deserts, dark caves. That does not tell us anything about the state of revelation. The philosophers have trouble with these bound-aries. Apart from Kant's reflections on the sublime, I am thinking of a few emotional outbursts of Nietzsche in Sils Maria; I remember Pas-cal's words when he was in a state of rapture—"Joy, tears of joy"—and certain passages by Kierkegaard on the "internal leap" into the state of anxiety, but I do not know much more about it. During his period of revelations, Muhammad suffered violent headaches: what state was he in exactly? What about Jesus in the desert? The question does not arise. Then, every religion plasters imagery onto the strange psychic trans-formations of those who experience the state of revelation. The Prophet received the inspiration of the "Angel Gabriel"; Jesus in the desert was tempted by Satan. As for the content of the process, it has disappeared from the scene. The Romans, without knowing as much as we do on the neurological plane, were intuitive enough to attribute sacred power to their epileptics. At least epilepsy's short-circuit of consciousness has the merit of being complete; inspiration is found in the set of phenomena known as the "aura," before the seizure. Blue lights, shaking, hallucinations, bizarre odors. . . . With the convulsions, everything disappears into darkness.

Don't put words into my mouth. . . . Epilepsy is a special case that does not explain everything about the content proper of the sacred. Of course, we have learned more about it since the mystics, women or men, took up their pens to describe their journeys. But if you and I are consistent in our logic, we ought to conclude that the sacred, a journey outside time, is deprived of beginning and end. When does the sacred moment begin? No one really knows. One feels it coming on. And when does it end? With exhaustion, which is not an end. It is not original in nature, and it is up to the myth to articulate the two or three universal formulas repeated in all cultures: "At the beginning of time," At the beginning of the world," "In the beginning was . . . "

Now, myth is a linguistic object structured by a complex logic. It does not speak the truth about the origin, it simply speaks. My dear Lévi-Strauss—yes, him again—demonstrates throughout *Mythologiques* that myth has no other reality than the logic of thought concealed behind the narrative. For example, analyzing the myth he chose for his starting point, he breaks down the role of the macaw feather in Bororo society. The blue feather belongs exclusively to the ornamentation of men's belts, and, if someone finds it attached to a woman's belt, it can be deduced with the naked eye that somebody's been screwing around in secret. Granted. Then, the subsequent myths set in motion a logic as secret as the furtive prohibited coitus in the forest, and the process is never ending. Beyond it, religious extrapolation. And, sometimes, danger.

Until proof to the contrary, in fact, the search for the origin at the collective level has always produced the same effects: radicalism, racism, rejection of the cross-pollination of populations and the migratory flows that constitute the history of peoples. The examples are so numerous that one has to be selective. The myth of the original Aryan in Nazism found a following, alas. It proliferated in all forms of fundamentalism, whether Muslim, Jewish, or Hindu, in an immutable form: "We claim the origin of origins, the first territory, the lost race, the pure religion distorted by time." So Muslim slums are burned down in Bombay in the name of the purity, the "originality," of Hinduism, and a country, Palestine, claimed in the name of priority, is torn apart. In the valley of Band-i-Amir, the Talibans of Afghanistan want to blow up the giant statues of the Alexandrine Buddhas, older than the Revelation of the Prophet, on the grounds that they represent divine images contrary to Koranic instructions. The destructive effects of that tension between the purity of origin and the impurity of history are far from over. Let me take an example I see close at hand. Many Africans won't rest until they have demonstrated that humanity originated in Africa. And one of the most illustrious intellectuals of Senegal, Sheikh Anta Diop, wanted to prove that all Africans were descended from the Egyptians, who were black. Why Egypt? Because. The mother of civilizations. Granted, but then what? What does that prove? That the Egyptologists were Western whites who, for white men's reasons, dissimulated the Africanness of the Egyptians. Good, but so what? Oh! But all white man's thinking is antiblack, don't you see! No argument is made; because there was colonization by whites, the Africans are ancient Egyptians, so there! And now racism has resumed in reverse, on a question of origin. The quest for origins, what rubbish! Look at the legal battle between the holders of "blood" rights and the holders of land rights. The former are on the side of the origin and become racist without even realizing it. The latter cling to the only sacred element in the idea of the Republic, the one that stirs in both of us at the sound of *La Marseillaise*.

Let's talk about that feminine image, Marianne. The strange idea of erecting into an icon a woman who is doing battle while holding a bloody flag. . . . You'll tell me that, since the Revolution and the Empire, Marianne has been Bardot-ized, Deneuve-ized, Marceau-ized. Grave error! Marianne is a notion of the mother available to all her children, and a soldier for their freedom. Marianne must not be embodied in the features of a real woman, however representative her beauty may be at a given time. Marianne is not destined to be embodied, since she is the abstract concept of a mother protecting countless children. There is no origin in that. Marianne has no birthplace, age, face, or skin color.

I am the godmother of a little girl baptized in accordance with the republican rite, that is, I signed in writing a commitment to take care of her if need be. The republican sacred is registered on a paper that endures and is inscribed in law, which applies to everyone without discrimination on the basis of origin. Granted, the republican sacred has seen some deviations; it produced the Reign of Terror. But precisely! It became murderous only after it was transformed into a religion of the Supreme Being. Ritual, ceremony—and persecutions. A new origin is defined and "the past is wiped clean." Stalin, Pol Pot, Mao, Hitler, Kim Il Sung, your choice. They wipe clean or return, impose a clean and proper origin. Clean and proper, the opposite of dirty. And, you admit, the sacred requires disorder, even a kind of dirtiness.

Few ideas are as productive as the need for disorder, an old, very old idea that never wears out, and that demonstrates its political viability from time to time: I'm thinking of an excellent book by Jean-Luc Mélenchon on the mastery of chaos. Disorder, the moment of revelation that makes your head ache or makes you sweat blood. Disorder, the unexpected perception of the vacuity of the desert, of the immensity of the mountains, of the scope of the storm. Disorder, the process of artistic creation described by Anton Ehrenzweig in *The Hidden Order of Art*. As for myself, I do not see any disadvantage to folding a part of the process of art back onto that of the sacred.

Ehrenzweig describes the stages a bit laboriously, as a psychoanalytical drudge. First, he points to a brutal disruption of the elements, a disturbance in the order of life. Then, in a second moment, a "scanning," that is, a rapid sweeping away, a recomposition of the elements into an order about to give birth, a yet unknown lying-in. The third moment is a collapse into depression followed by profound disgust. Finally the work—that is, the acknowledged advent of a different order—springs forth. Let's leave the work of art to the artist; what interests me in all this is the first moments: agitation, scanning, depression. The totality of the process described by Anton Ehrenzweig makes me think of the "baby blues" experienced by new mothers in the hours following childbirth. The enormous agitation of the body is followed by the birth of the new, a moment of depression for the woman, and of joy.

"Baby blues" would be a fairly good characterization of the sacred, applicable to any act of creation, whether it is truly maternal or metaphorically so. That's enough to irritate Sollers. . . . Hasn't he sufficiently denounced the "baby" as currency in contemporary sexual commerce! Nonetheless, Sollers, come on. . . . The "baby" of baby blues is not emotional blackmail, since he is already born. He has already fallen from the body accompanied by his placenta wrapping, which, in so many regions, is buried under a tree or the house, out of fear that the double of the soul that has just been incarnated will be lost. That "baby" already has its own life, whereas the mother's baby blues designates the effect of vacuity; the belly is devoid of its burden, like the mind in Buddhism. "Baby blues" expresses the mother's psychological state in the aftermath, the pure feeling of having been the site of a passing, and the feeling that now it's over. Strangely, the image of a ferret comes to mind, that little furtive rodent Lacan uses to represent the signifier: it has come this way, it will return that way. . . . One generation follows another.

I understand the "baby"; the "blues" remain. Why, after the birth, is a musical term bestowed on the "baby"? The blues, the music of deported slaves, originated in songs about the land cultivated for the masters, a land that will never again be that of "Mother Africa" (I put the term in quotation marks to invoke the last two words of Senegal's national anthem, lyrics by Léopold Sédar Senghor, "Hail, Mother Africa"). Well, did you know that deported African slaves in Brazil committed suicide by eating dirt? I never understood the true meaning of that strange death until I was in Dakar, working with my students from Sheikh Anta Diop University—oh yes!—on the transitional object according to Winnicott. In Western Africa, the transitional object does not take the form of a diaper or a stuffed bear, but might very well be made of dirt, which the child joyfully swallows under the compassionate eye of the married women in the family. The custom is not only accepted, it is prescribed: to grow up, you have to eat dirt. In exile, die from dirt that is not your own. "Eat your *Dasein*," said Lacan, quoting Heidegger. It must be understood that, in Africa, the *Dasein* is "of" the earth. The "blues" came from it, just as the breath of song comes from the muscles of the belly.

I'm trying to connect disorder with your plumb line. And I think of the singers in India. Whatever their sex, their style, and the instruments accompanying them, they all have the same body posture, the same hand gestures. The body is seated, legs crossed, perfectly balanced. As for the hands, one is on the ear to ensure the proper resonance of the chord, and the other flutters about, up and down or side to side. The hand of the singer, whether male or female, cuts through space, horizontally when a note is held, vertically for an ascending scale. The voice never rises or falls without an accompanying gesture that traces the motif. The musical equilibrium is clearly traced in space, especially given the fact that the notes of Indian music are marked in half- and quarter-tones. Watching it all, the listener rises and descends the sound scale.

Among the Maulawiyah, the whirling dervishes in Turkey, the equilibrium of the spinning body is also ensured by the arms, one up, the other down. But one hand is turned palm up toward the sky, and the other down toward the earth, so that the whole body is a vertical vector between the two. A plumb line. Choreographers will tell you: dancing relies on a relation between the earth and verticality. I remember hearing Karine Saporta mention rural dances, dances of "the land," the foundation of which remains invariable: flamenco, shamanistic dances, the very slow dances of the *shite* in Japanese No drama. And it is from that vertical docking that the feeling of weightlessness arises, in music as in dance. Lightness.

Lightness. That's a word that Kierkegaard and Nietzsche resort to when they move beyond gravity. Both outline three dance steps, inviting women to their metaphysics. For Kierkegaard, they are, in Mozart's operas, the fleeting partners of Cherubino, Papageno, and Don Giovanni, in whom the philosopher perceives the three ages of manhood. "No so piu cosa son, cosa facio": a Cherubino aria, adolescent love. "Pa-pa-pa": a Papageno aria, procreative love. The "Champagne" aria for Don Giovanni: dispersed love. For Nietzsche, it is unnatural powers, Carmen in Bizet's opera, the small-eared Ariane. It is thus in "becoming" girls that the philosophers accede to the metaphysical lightness of music. What nonsense! As if music were not a heavy weight to bear. Have you ever seen a singer or a conductor as they come offstage? They are gasping for breath. After the famous aria at the end of act 1 of Mozart's *Don Giovanni,* the singer is prostrate, choking for several long minutes, struggling to catch his breath. At the end of the concert, the conductor has lost a few ounces of weight, and his uniform—black tie and tails—is soaked with sweat. Yet his baton is light; but, he says, the effort of carrying the orchestra on the end of his arm is terribly tiring. That's a different matter from Nietzsche and Kierkegaard! The price of lightness is always a huge physical weight. The result has to do with the sacredness of the stage; when the performance is over, the artist falls into a fatigue-induced blues. Hence the necessity for him, after the end of the show, to prolong the night, obliterate his effort and bring the body back to society's norm, which was left behind for the duration of the exercise. The cost of weightlessness is paid in sweat.

But, if you yourself have ever danced—I'm talking about so-called recreational dances—you must be familiar with these sensations:

after a long waltz, an interminable tango, any mbalax at all, you're "emptied out." Recent studies on fatigue have demonstrated what we already knew intuitively: during exercise, you don't feel fatigue, to the point that it drives you to rapture. And dance, when it is recreation, even has the purpose of tiring the body to achieve a lightness of consciousness. It ends, you breathe, you are empty, you are "fine." Ready for anything, for oneself, for the other, for nothing. That happy fatigue seems to me to verge on the sacred. Which means, in all cases, that it is necessary to "leave" the body. Nothing says you can't do it in the right mood.

Music, the "supreme mystery of the human sciences" that drives Lévi-Strauss to despair at the end of the introduction of *Mythologiques,* sets to the task. What Lévi-Strauss says about it, however, is not negligible. Music takes hold of its listener via the slow movements of the internal organs. It draws its effects from visceral time. A simple example: the binary rhythm of techno music, in sync with the rhythm of the heartbeat. More complex is the broken 3/2 tempo and the syncopes, which play on the stumbling, the swaying of time; something like the heart stopping, then starting right up again, let's call it a heart palpitation. But, as for accounting for the exact nature of the music . . .

For example, the musicologists have been at one another's throats on the subject of the effects of percussion on the trance: is it the percussive hammering on the drum that unleashes the trance, or is the percussion only the coded signal of the trance? You cannot imagine what pitched battles this little problem of drums was able to elicit! In the first case, the trance is of physical origin. In the second, it starts in the symbolic. And there is nothing that makes it possible to decide. Lévi-Strauss is right: music, material and ideal, physical and spiritual, remains an unassailable roadblock for the sciences. So much the worse for an understanding of the sacred. Or so much the better.

Music, unanalyzable, unthinkable, is the medium of the sacred. What I like about the myths on the origin of music is their cruelty. The invention of the lyre by Apollo was the result of the sacrilegious massacre of divine herds. His flute is inseparable from the flaying of his rival Marsyas. Then there's the story of Orpheus, who, in return for pacifying wild animals with music, has his head cut off by the bacchantes. There's the imagery of Shiva, god of life, death, music, and dance, marking out the expiration of the soul with his minuscule tambourine, and dancing on the exquisite corpses. We can make out the origin of the taut skin of drums, the dried guts of strings; we can discern the horror of the man chopped to bits. In fact, although the sound box may be a gourd, for sound proper there is nothing like the texture of a living being. At the time of the Hussite wars in the fifteenth century, the large rallying drum of Jan Zizka the Calixtine was, it is said, covered with human skin. . . . And, in Japanese myths, only the body of a consenting virgin who throws herself into the molten metal makes it possible for the founder to obtain the purity desired. These legendary acts of barbarism anchor music in an imaginary sacred, a bit like in *The Rite of Spring,* in fact, when the virgin is sacrificed. Chabrier, from whom Lévi-Strauss borrows the epigraph for *Mythologiques,* addressed this beautiful invocation to music: "Mother of memory and nurse of dreams." Maternal and soothing music. It is conceivable that something human was sacrificed to it. It is possible that music was then consoled by singing. Despite the excesses that it might elicit, it remains the best, the most sublime, cradle for journeying through the salubrious nostalgia for the sacred.

It is dark. My own gulls have gone to sleep, the river is emptied of their wings; a vague, sleepy squawking signals that, on the opposite bank, the herons are dreaming in their nests. The starry sky dear to Immanuel Kant is above my head, and I hope that moral law is within me, as simple reason requires. I imagine it is not by chance that, after beginning in Africa and America, we are ending our correspondence in France near the water, you on your island of Ré and I in my Loire, so close to each other and yet so far away. At a good distance for thought and epistles—about a hundred kilometers as the gull flies—a constant interval between worlds, which has allowed us to digress comfortably.

Have we digressed? Certainly. I claim the indefeasible right to digression, and, in the case of the sacred, the right to sacrilege. It does not seem to me that we have abused it, since we have sought the proper use of a minimal, indefeasible, and demanding sacred, like any true atheism. A digression draws to an end in the wait for dawn. It is three o'clock, it will not be long now. As a good philosopher owl, I'm going to take off my glasses and close my owl eyes.

Catherine

Dear Catherine,

WE WERE RETURNING from La Baleine Bleue, the port of Saint-Martin was swaying to the rhythm of the jazz festival, and now I receive your fax, which subsumes the sacred under music and dance! It could not have come at a better time.

Another point on which we agree: the cult of the "origin" is the religious aftereffect that feeds modern political fundamentalism on all sides. Nevertheless, who could criticize that fundamentalist illusion of a "foundation" to be restored, without recognizing that it is rooted in a sound intuition: namely, that there are other forms of logic that are, if not deeper, then at least *heterogeneous* to the well-policed and policing surface of rational and rationalist communication? The logic of the unconscious, the rhythms and polyphonies of the music underlying the verbal utterances and verbiage: the "infrasensical," as one speaks of the infrasonic.

Some believe they have exhausted the religious by demonstrating that secular thinking concerns itself just as much, if not more, with the "other" than does the charity of men of faith. But, so long as we have not recognized another *other*—which is not the other person, my neighbor, my brother, but *the other logic in me,* my strangeness, my heterogeneity, the musical scales that dwell within me under the standardized surface of users of technology—then the cult of the "origin," of the inaccessible foundation, of the unnameable paradise will embrace its "return of the repressed" in the form of a "faith" or, more brutally, in the form of fratricidal wars that claim to reconstitute the lost foundation.

Your letter is already tying things up as far as our exchange is concerned, and we could stop here: stay on the sidelines, the question unresolved, barely skimming the surface of the abyss of the "sacred." You must have noticed how topical we are: Catholic World Youth Day has turned all of France upside down, and has obliged the media stars to announce the existence of a "divine instinct" (of life, of death, or of a third nature?), enough to send Voltaire and Nietzsche back to their cherished studies if not to propel them into madness. And these same media stars have hailed a younger generation that is finally responsible.

There's a sense of relief, things got hot in May 1968, precisely because of jazz, abortion, if anyone still dares say the word, not to mention Picasso, Breton, Artaud, Bacon, Burroughs, and a few others . . .

I have already annoyed you enough with "my" Virgin Mary and the women saints of Catholicism; so I feel there's no danger of my lacking respect toward that religion, which is now showing a "demonstration of strength" (as I read in the press), or of my underestimating its subtleties as far as knowledge of the human soul—women's included—is concerned. It is simply that, deep down, in my analytical complicity with believers, I am surprised that people are surprised. Do not human beings, young and not so young, have an imperious need for love? And is not the presence of a Father who loves them the illusion par excellence, which has its whole life in front of it? Finally, it is unquestionably more reasonable that, if the world must kneel, it should kneel before a loving Father, preaching respect for the other, rather than before an ayatollah who calls for people's heads to be cut off.

Nevertheless, one question has disappeared from this World Youth Day, and from the media: are we still capable of freedom? I hold to the version formulated a long time ago, by a Catholic, in fact, though one who was condemned, Meister Eckehart (1260–1327): "I ask God to leave me free of God." If we take him and proceed to the philosophical questioning of Freud and Heidegger, another road remains open to us poor humans who need love: a branch of the alternative road, which does not lead simply to the authorization of condoms.

Take Freud: his subject is the religious man, who is not his enemy in any way. Psychoanalysis explores the anxieties and psychosomatics of that man, precisely—the man who, from the totem to the taboo, consecrates the father, love, and prohibitions. And psychoanalysis, in unveiling that man's desires to him, does not suppress his hopes: it restores them to him, but in lucidity. A morality and a sacredness now appear possible, finally disengaged from the need to hallucinate a maternal or paternal appearance, as Saint Theresa of Lisieux did, in the guise of "primal" thought, to borrow your word. You see, I feel just as far removed from the infantile need to restore the loving father as a way to unite the faithful around him, however sincere and the generous they may be, as I do from those who commonly deny that need. Indeed, freedom, in the name of which many crimes have been committed, nevertheless remains the most precious of legacies, as Kant magnificently said. When I see the grip that the spectacle and faith— the spectacle of faith—exert on the lawn at Longchamp, I grasp the ex-

traordinary level of courage it took for some men and women, beginning millennia ago, to free themselves from that magic. Pure heroism!
The metamorphoses of that freedom also have to do with the debates
internal to Catholic thought, and, as a reader of Hegel, I am persuaded that it is by traversing Christianity that the free subjectivity of men
and women flourishes. By traversing, that is, by knowing and analyzing: not by becoming imprisoned within it.

The discussion we have opened can only end arbitrarily. I would
like to leave the last word to you, if you're willing, but not before raising a few questions that, in the light of that "Catholic Pride" Day, open
on other continents of the religious and the sacred, which we have not
adequately tackled here, and which the twenty-first century, with the
awakening of women under way, will have to confront. Will these continents allow themselves to be assimilated by Catholicism or by another religion with universalistic ambitions? Will they coexist peacefully?
Will they do battle? I am persuaded that it is from the philosophical
tradition we have called "atheistic" that that diagonal, capable of fed-
erating a humanity that wants to be "free of God" without losing the
meaning of the labor of meaning, will emerge.

As I think over all these months of correspondence, it appears to
me that we are avoiding a question that has continued to preoccupy us
nonetheless, and that, even recently, we mentioned only briefly on the
phone. What about Islam in this journey through the sacred? Islam,
whose fundamentalist version horrifies the modern world, to the point
that nonspecialists—like you and me—have no desire to make subtle
distinctions between the "foundation" and the "excesses," because the
abomination of the carnage displayed on the front pages of newspapers
this weekend, though eclipsed by the death of Diana, defies reason to
such a degree. What can be expressed other than indignation, an un-
qualified condemnation?

In black Africa and in India, you are confronted with a different
Islam, and God knows how polymorphous Islam is. I would have liked
you to tell me about its strange and multiple faces. For myself, I am left
with the impression of horror. One of my friends, a journalist, is back
from Algeria: she visited the hospitals, interviewed the women who
had survived having their throats slit, some buried under a hundred
victims whose throats had been cut by Islamists in the name of Allah.
Sabrina is of Algerian origin, and, in France, she is fighting for the
emancipation of women. She belongs to an aid organization for Algerian women and did not have the words to comment on her report:

nothing but a core of anger and screams. For my friend, there is nothing sacred about religion, that religion: it sentences women to the
"wall" of the head scarf; it fates them to submission; it coldly kills all
those who do not share extremist dogma. Naturally, Sabrina can "understand" how it has reached this point: the corruption of the military
regime, the hardening of the dogmatism that dwells within all religion,
and whose anorectic and lethal impasses I distilled for you in a previous letter—less barbaric, all things considered, than this cold slaughter.
Then there is the economic crisis, the rivalry among the Western democratic powers, which leave their former protégés to sort things out,
not without stirring up hatred between the various factions in a fratricidal war. But it is religion itself that Sabrina abhors, and I must say
that my atheism is not impermeable to her anger. Yet I try to calm her.

Imagine me, if you please, in the role of a defender of the Koran! I
remember an excellent lecture that was given in my seminar in Jussieu,
already several years ago, before the Iranian crisis and Maghrebian fundamentalism, by the remarkable Eva de Vitray-Meyerovitch, a special-
ist in Islamic mysticism. She spoke to us about Koranic time: it is *vertical,* she said, comprehended within the Absolute, and imposes a
mirror image connecting the microcosm and the macrocosm, but it is
also atomized, shattered into autonomous, singular instants, respect-
ing the sensorial tonality of every element, whether cosmic or human.
The term *hal* conveys that modulation of the senses, whereas, in music,
the term *maqam* expresses the modes and degrees of its realization. Islamic mysticism is rich in these singularities, calculated and constructed into algorithms, into an algebra—rather than into a geometry, as in
our Greek tradition.

I like that Islamic idea of a poetics of beings in the time of their absoluteness, and I really want to believe that the whirling dervishes
(among other mystical currents), whose genius was Rumi, and whom
Eva Meyerovitch has studied, represent a pinnacle of that poetic subjectivity. Composed of dance, of sound, of meaning—both exalted in
the magic of a passion and mastered, purified, bleached out like the
gleam of the mirror reflecting a place beyond. Granted.

All the same, I am worried that so little space is reserved for a woman in that sublime sublimation. Hence, even in the mystical and very
aristocratic brotherhoods of Sama, which produce scholars, calligra-
phers, and musicians, and are democratic in the sense that they go into
the villages and have the peasants participate, women, as it happens,
are an integral part of the sessions of Koranic recitation—which is

extraordinary!—but they don't dance. The women's confraternities, which Maxime Rodinson has also studied, are not destined for a spiritual journey, as are the men's *tariqa:* for women, there is only the *zar*—a letting off of steam of sorts, without religious value. They cry, tell stories, play out a kind of psychodrama, console each other with a form of voodoo—but without achieving a discourse recognized, communicable, or, even less, valued, outside that cathartic community.

So why was I so relentless in seducing my dear Sabrina by asking her to seek out Islam's "good sides"? First, because the little I know about it tells me they exist, even though with less benefit for women than elsewhere: but I hope you will tell me more about that. And, above all, because I distrust the horror elicited in turn by the blind rejection of that tradition.

I am resolutely against communitarianism: I do not think France should follow the Anglo-Saxon model and become immobilized in closed communities that "respect"—quote unquote—the customs of the different ethnic groups and religions, only to better separate them in reality, and expose itself to their mutual ostracism and ignorance. I think that the "French model"—in fact, Montesquieu's model of the "general spirit"—is to be cultivated come hell or high water, but not any which way, not by ignoring the particularities of others. On the contrary: by deciphering them, or even by restoring them if need be. In this instance, by reconciling Sabrina with her Islamic memory—with the complexity and richness of that memory. So that she is able, not to imprison herself within the sullen defense of "her community," as some of her coreligionists do, or to condemn it purely and simply, as she does today, in shock at the horror and in the name of "scientific" thought, as she says (the pill, contraception, the right to work, and so on, of course, but then what?). But so that complex individuals with diverse traditions can live together . . .

We're far wide of the mark, I grant you that. Let's begin all the same, and let's begin by taking the heat off. I don't say by forgetting, or even forgiving—one forgives only those who ask for it, and even then, they must first reach an understanding of what they did. Hannah Arendt had essential things to say about that: personally, I think *interpretation* is the only path to for-giving. But who asks for an interpretation? Surely not an extremist . . .

In short, when you are suffocating under the strained passions of monotheism, when you see them stuck in their intransigent logics, you want the void, writing on silk, ducks dreaming in rice fields, and

Chinese women, who may have inspired "the art of the boudoir." Was not Scheherazade, the mother of the novel, an Islamic woman, you'll say. Of course, down with the chador, and long live the Scheherazades, wherever they may come from! In the meantime, I have a hunger for Chinese sacredness, composed of sexual duality, of the absence of action, and of an efficacity that draws its strength from the void. Am I dreaming?

I tried to learn Chinese once in an attempt to accede to that sacred, I even managed to earn my bachelor's degree in it: a waste of time, a bachelor's in Chinese is nothing in the face of the ocean of ideograms and wisdom that are so different from our traditions. I am still trying. I like that taste, bland perhaps but very subtle, of the sacred: so far removed from that other so-called sacred that cuts the throats of men and women as if they were sheep.

"Shun was surely one who knew how to govern through inaction. How did he do it? He simply sat enthroned, facing south, that's all, in point of fact." That's what the *Lunyu* (*Confucian Analects*) tells us. You read it right: "That's all, in point of fact." Perhaps, but how does one reach that "point," where one has only to face south to govern through inaction? It entails not forcing nature and history, not wanting to be heroic like Heracles, making water flow only "where it does not cause any trouble," deciphering not signs but precursors, the not-yet-visible, the *wei* (that is, the infinitesimal), and so on—as my friend, the sinologist François Jullien will explain to us.

I admit that, in the long history of "sacreds," I allow myself to be seduced first and foremost by the flavors of the Tao, which, as everyone knows, suits a sage reconciled with the mother and with nature, "the one who alone is nourished by the mother," and who has nothing to defy or to demonstrate or to prove. . . . Nevertheless, I see the tendencies that favor laziness, that leave history to other people, and I see its opportunism, which gains access to history only to capitalize on it effectively. We know only too well, in fact, that this gentle Chinese "inaction" has often allowed itself to be shattered by a political history that advanced by a series of crises, no less—and perhaps more—violent and barbaric than those whose techniques we learned from monotheism. . . . Granted, granted! To each its faults, to each its advantages. But today I am in the mood to praise the ecological cosmism of the Chinese sage, of the one who abandons heights and displays a *humilitas* in the etymological sense of the word: at the level of humus, ground level, the level of mother earth. You want him to define Spirit for you? Nothing is more accessible: "The most delicate and the most remarkable grass is called Spirit," says Liu Shao (second to third century). What about the Feat, while we're at it? Again, nothing is more commonplace: "The quadruped that distinguishes itself from its herd is called Feat." This is a sage who "thinks," in effect, who thinks at a basic level, the level of the daisies, with the grass and the quadrupeds, but in order to diffuse the human into it, and, at the same time, to extract the human from it. Chinese writers call that logic "little resemblance/difference." The great Joseph Needham, whom I had the opportunity to know at Cambridge, as I told you, enumerated the figures of that logic in his authoritative *Science and Civilisation in China*. Small resemblance/difference between nature and culture, between man and woman, and so on.

Their time is not vertical, it is cyclical: it is a time-space. These people inhabit. They have the serenity of a thinking habitat, of thought living in the world, from which they separate themselves only to better inhabit it. That living edge to edge, that silk shimmering under paintbrushes, that quivering of ducks dozing on the surface of the water, appear sacrément feminine to me.

Yin/yang. Everyone wants some: might it not be a new promised land, bisexuality stripped of guilt? But what does that mean? The texts emphasize, in the first place, the war between the sexes: Fu Xian (217–278) writes: "They [Man and woman], who were at first like the form and the shadow, are now as far apart as the Chinese and the Huns. And even the Chinese and the Huns meet sometimes, whereas the husband and the wife are as distinct as Lucifer and Orion."

A single Uniqueness is accepted by that dual world: conception. That's right, neither you nor me, but coitus, with, as a bonus, procreation and the jouissance of the two partners together. As far as unities are concerned, there have been simpler ones! "On the incarnation of the Tao, the true uniqueness [that is, conception] is difficult to represent [in effect!]. After that transmutation, the couple separates and each stands again on its own side" (*Alchemical Taoist Treatise: The Pact of the Triple Equation*). This has nothing to do with the tantric resorption of the other sex into oneself: "What need do I have of another woman? I have an internal woman within myself," boasts the tantric sage. In complete contrast, our Chinese, at grass level and as the friend of quadrupeds, absorbs nothing definitively. He lets himself be permeated by all currents, is not unaware of the war with the other, and recognizes a single unity: the couple, and only when it is coupling. What if that manner of thought, which so closely espouses the biology of man, which curls up so tightly within the destiny of the species and finds the meaning of the human adventure in it, were the condition for the detachment, the peace we are so sorely lacking?

You know I was seduced by the serene maturity of Chinese women when I brought back my book *About Chinese Women* from my trip to China, with Philippe and the Tel Quel group. I was seduced by them, and disappointed by the national Communism that was challenging the Stalinist model but still followed it intrinsically. My own history became mixed up in all that, and I turned my back on politics. Hence psychoanalysis, the novel, and the rest. But today, when the still totalitarian China is trying to modernize itself, when it does it at its own pace, apparently less brutal than what was observed in Eastern Europe, I return to my Taoist loves, I revisit old Confucius, the "woman eater," and I try to understand my female Chinese students who come to Jussieu from Shanghai to read Proust and Duras. They have slipped on jeans and T-shirts, have put on makeup, but they still have the gestures of ageless refinement that I admired among the serpentine woman basketball players in a stadium in Beijing. These athletes had beaten the Iranians, not as if they were playing a game, but as if they were performing a demonstration of acrobatics—as silent, androgynous tightrope walkers . . .

I'm not sure my students from China read what I read in Proust and Duras, and that may be all for the good. Sometimes, I have the impression that, for the moment, they are content to repeat to me, to repeat to us. But that's not my problem. My problem is to connect my thinking and my dreams to that universe of "little differences/resemblances," to that suppleness that the words *void* and *inaction* capture very poorly, because our words are not calligraphed and do not sing. That is what I was telling you the other day: the sacred lies in the mode of saying, and Chinese women "say" . . . *body-and-soul*: coupled. That is an image I propose to you, necessarily stemming from our history and not from theirs, but which tries to domesticate that other assemblage of limits, differences, and prohibitions that form their sacred as Chinese people, and that form it differently than among us. Naturally, my Greek or Judeo-Christian passions have not let go of me: I quickly find these charming Asians very superficial, altogether ready to let themselves be caught within the world of images and calculators. How greedily they swallow the media! Even on the couch, they talk to me through the intermediary of films rather than through personal associations . . .

Can we catch a glimpse of a synthesis of these diverse worlds? A new syncretism? We have not yet reached that point. It falls to us now to be amazed by the differences. What if that were the heart of the sacred? Here and now, diversities.

Julia

◆ ◆

Paris
SEPTEMBER 7, 1997

Dear Catherine,

DECIDEDLY, OUR CORRESPONDENCE does not want to end, a true accordion swelling with the blast of recent events. Now the Diana phenomenon is buffeting the planet (apart from the Chinese, as you may have guessed after my last missive!) and has carried away the admirable Mother Teresa in its wake.

The third millennium is therefore beginning with a new "saint": Diana Spencer, unhappy wife, perfect mother, manipulated manipulator of the media. Indeed, it is truly a *woman* that these new faithful, men and women, many women, but men as well, come to mourn, bowing down before that femininity, their own. Head bowed before her humanitarian virtues, but, first and foremost, before the distress of a woman and her battle for a little personal happiness. The suffering party in the "ménage à trois" that her royal spouse served up to her might have extricated herself through a "ménage à quatre": I know it well, it works marvelously. But no, the princess had to get depressed, she had to try to save her "ego," appearances, humanity—all very sacred, obviously! Family first, and you know how set I am on that! In the end, misfortune and accidental death added their touch of magic. The former dimwit, the deceived wife and betrayed seductress, became the most uniting religious leader at century's end. She brought together more followers than the pope, without church and without subsidies. A shattered woman, capable of conquering depression with the help of the society of the spectacle and the drugs of the jet set, is she in the process of creating a new religion?

One might think so. Like you, I smile at such hysterical naïveté: have not three apparitions of the deceased already been reported? I recognize, however, the spark of the sacred that that lady, a cross between a supermodel and one of Charcot's patients, sends out to the whole earth, which has finally been brought together. Her big-name humanitarian efforts are forgotten, her bulimia obliterated: the loneliness of a mother in search of love remains, and the intelligence of the tenderness she offered, which transforms her symptoms into an ideal. The pilgrims on TV, massed along English roads and highways, are not hailing a Father above who loves us. The society of the spectacle mourns a woman who died from a lack of communication. True or false, such is the event onto which humanity projects itself: men and women, we are all an unloved Diana. We play with the absence of truth to bring our suffering to heel. We waste our time loving. And there is only the spectacle to console us, but not all that much. Of all that worthy misery, which no one has dared say very much about but everyone has experienced, she is the living proof, and, even better, the dead proof, the Rose of England.

The cult of Diana is rooted in the melancholia of a humanity of orphaned children, children of divorce, abandoned children, as we all are. The courage to live with that psychic discomfort is truly the sacred little flower under the accumulation of losses and gains produced by the society of the spectacle. A sort of sorrowful feminism, but one proud of its struggles, is now replacing the militant feminism of a short while ago. The stoic faith of Mother Teresa, who also brought all the religions of India and elsewhere together, appears superhuman in the face of that vulnerability confessed in the spotlight, vanquished thanks to it . . . and by it.

In a world that now knows it is irremediably in crisis, the sacred Diana-style is a beautiful image—provided it can administer to wounds. Is it the ultimate triumph of the spectacle, which puts death itself in a dummy account? What if, on the contrary, the virtual universe were splitting under the rush of tangible time, of feminine timelessness? That would be a sacré ruse of the sacred.

Julia

Dear Julia,

WHAT A LETTER burning with devotion! So, just like that, you're a Dianomaniac? To say that some people were calling for canonization in due form. . . . Since when does popular support determine canonization? The sacred can suffice, for the love of Pete! And now people are calling Diana "Evita on the Thames"! Blonde, elegant, beautiful; died young . . . like Evita, so what then?

Her blondness is important; Eva was born a brunette and dyed her hair blond once she became the First Lady. Her elegance is important; Eva offered it to the poor. Her beauty is important: ugly women collect no dividends in secular religions. But the Rose of England was an aristocrat of more noble birth than the royal family, a rich woman who never had anything but disappointment in love. So, it was a beautiful ceremony? Of course. I watched it as well, like an opera. A successful performance. Soloists, choir, very good. Tears of emotion. As for me, I believe "id" is what people starving for Being have come to seek: tears. As for her, as you can tell, she doesn't touch me. Too much posing. I also watched the funeral of Mother Teresa, which barely affected the West. Tears of collective emotion rarely fall twice in one week in the world of images. And, since Mother Teresa died in Calcutta, let's just pull out every cliché! Calcutta, City of Joy—even though "City of Joy" is the name of a slum where the Holy Mother did not do her charity work, but where François Mitterrand stayed before he became president of the Republic. Nothing on the true nature of that city, a jewel of music, painting, and letters. With the refrain, "Calcutta-the-affliction, but-God-be-praised, Mother-Teresa-is-there."

When I saw her for the first time, I found Mother Teresa cantankerous, with a dull stare. But later on! Her large hands, which brought babies back to life with vigorous massage, said more about her saintliness than the popular fervor. That said, I also have not forgotten the backwardness of her women's psychiatric unit, where patients with shaved heads are confined to straitjackets in a dormitory, in a daze brought on by tranquilizers. On the questions of medication, treatment, and abortion, Mother remained reactionary. That does not eradicate the impression of the saintliness of her hands working on dying babies. The sacred was there, in her fingers during the massage. The astonishing thing in my view is that the Indian government had her body parade by on the cannon mount used for Gandhi and Nehru. On the scale of India, that is the equivalent of our republican sacred. Even Indira Gandhi did not have that honor. Finally, it is the very first time that a foreigner has had a national funeral that did not culminate in cremation. By some remote chance, the greatest man in Calcutta, the Bengali Rajah Man Mohan Roy, a reformist aristocrat and polyglot, who died during a mission to England in the mid-nineteenth century, was buried at . . . Westminster.

The fervor that manifested itself in Calcutta at the time of Mother Teresa's death is part of the Indian tradition called, since the twelfth century, *Bhakti*—devotion. The charming god Krishna was selected as the object of a cult, celebrated en masse by the women, with the help of trances. Indian immigrants, even before Britons, were the first to bring flowers for Diana to the residence in Kensington. What I have retained from your letter is that the devotional fire has broken out around the "Diana" feminine: a feminine whose depressive component is known to everyone. But depression did not appear in the spectacle in question—I mean the ceremony of mourning—whose purpose is to make people cry without harm, far from the abyss.

That stopgap is not our concern. Let's return to hysteria, where our correspondence began, with an African outdoor mass. Perhaps by connecting the two, depression and hysteria, we will find a key—or rather, a fall. Women, as exploited minorities, have the right to trances—or to hysterical attacks, depending on the vocabulary. But what is true in Africa is true of all situations of distress: magic, group worship, trance. And when you are exploited, you have the right to the depressive condition, that seems undeniably obvious. In fact, if I understand you properly, depression comes from an undervalued position, which can be called a "minority" position in comparison to that of the others, the normal people. Whatever the cause, it touches a weakness, enlarges a flaw. The real is no longer bearable when "the others" are capable of facing it and you are not. The depressive, necessarily different from the norm, is forced to retreat. The fact that it is a healthy ordeal changes nothing in its starting point; and the fact that rebirth follows gives food for thought.

That may mean that minorities know how to rebel—with the body. The good news is not so new as it seems, since Freud already announced it when analyzing the Viennese hysterics in the late nineteenth century. At the time, their symptoms coincided with a libertarian push among middle-class married women, who were "fed up" with the familial system based on the mama and the whore, the virtuous woman and the tart—a real movement of women's emancipation. So the singer got a sore throat, the good girl felt short of breath, had pins and needles, un-precedented paralysis, an arsenal of repressed expressions that leaked out, causing disturbances from one woman to the next, as one identified with another. Then came our own, contemporary symptom: depression. Social mobility, technological advances, women's emancipation, and the breakdown of the sacred. And, if we consider the sequence of events in Austria, we are obliged to observe that, at a given point, Hitler knew how to use the breakdown of the sacred in the Enlightenment Europe where he was born.

So? So it is not impossible that, at this very moment, by the de-pressive means women are so fond of, they are perceiving without knowing it the scandal of our time, that which is evacuated by ogling the poor of Calcutta filmed at the other end of the world. I mean the wealth gap between the rich countries and the "Southern" countries (as we know, ill-fed North Korea is one of them). It is not impossible that the stranger in you, in perceiving the sacred in Dianidolatry, sensed the secret revolt of immigrants in England, planted like a blurry flag be-hind the images of the dead Rose. It is not impossible that each of us, with our particular histories, sought in the sacred the juncture between depression and hysteria, the plumb line and disorder, as the genesis of a new, less inequitable world. It is certain that we want it. It is not cer-tain that we are right. That is what you call the fissure of the virtual universe under the rush of feminine timelessness. It is your hope, your guiding thread. In reality, I'm not sure that we see it, you and I.

They're going to snicker, our men. The dear souls, they'll say. The poor things. Those naive women. What about globalization? What about cynicism, violence, sex, despair? Of course, it would be more "trendy" to emphasize the dark side of depression, in short, modern comfort. Not a chance, we prefer gourmands to anorectics, the rebel-lious to the desperate, hysterics and saints to drug addicts, come on, even Diana, if you please. And we are both attached to motherhood, that's not insignificant. That's all we needed!

We got to know each other when we were thirty, nearly thirty years ago. At the time, rebellion was de rigueur, and, on that point, we have not completely changed. Life has been hard on us, and we won't say anything about that. It did a good job, we've gotten used to the blows. You are better at speaking of revolt than I am, since you theorize it. In the poor country where I am now residing, I can attest to it. They are right to revolt, it's barely begun. And I see that revolt in the "least de-veloped" countries of the world happens any way it can, in the sacred when it must. It is not reserved for women, but women in the poor countries know how to walk the paths of the sacred woods, which are so necessary. At least, the sacred woods are ancient. They are healing. In a sense, they limit the risk. But not always.

That's the other side of the sacred. Behind the sacred woods, massacre is always possible. Men, propelled by a strange absence, take up arms toward and against everything, and "everything" means the other in the house next door. For us in the rich countries, we wage a clean war, economic or military, which causes starvation or drops bombs. A precise, surgical war, like the "strikes" in the Gulf War, 250,000 dead in Iraq. But Boutros-Ghali was right to say there are rich people's wars and the other kind, poor people's wars, with weapons that are not clean but also kill, in quantity. It seems to me that quantity counts in this matter. And it is when revolt becomes the majority position that it takes to killing.

The sacred, if it is carefully monitored, can serve a good revolt. What must be monitored? Its extension. The sacred belongs to the private sphere, from which the rite stems, even if it is collective. Initiation, ritual, healing, love itself have to do with individuals. When the revolt contained within the sacred leaves the sphere of the private, it can become murderous. One must know how to remain a minority, I believe. Notice that, for both of us, the risk is very limited; our weapons as intellectuals are by definition in the minority. So much the better. It is night again, the hour of thought. A rendez-vous, in reality, for other minority revolts, which I would like, in remembrance, to call revolutions, albeit minuscule ones.

Catherine

✦ ✦

Toronto
OCTOBER 16, 1997

Dear Catherine,

NO, I AM NOT burning with devotion or with Dianomania: I am simply trying to decipher what is happening outside my own circle and outside France. Decidedly, you always need to attack the subject aggressively, an approach that is barely softened by humor! And that is all to the good: your verve has been the impatient and excited (I'm quoting you) note of our correspondence; as for myself, I have tried to reflect slowly in the background.

In a chapel of Victoria University (Northrop Frye's university, you remember?), Lord Chancellor Sang Chul Lee, a doctor in theology, who looks like a Mandarin straight off a Ming vase, blesses us in Latin with an irresistible Chinese accent, smiling very particularly at the women—an indispensable mark of the new openness of mind in North America, as everyone knows. Toronto is an increasingly Chinese city, Christianity is dispersed within an ocean of customs, with the Taoist and Confucian seemingly the most numerous; conversely, the Asian religions adopt only a veneer of the Western mentality. The third millennium is arriving here within a mosaic of human bodies that sometimes clash at night in the rough neighborhoods, as they do at home, but that nevertheless appear more flexible, with a more generous mutual tolerance. Was not this country a country of immigrants from its beginnings?

We decided to end our correspondence without coming to a conclusion, and I have nothing to add to your last letter except this rather surrealistic touch of Latin-American-Chinese-men-women cross-mixing, which seems to me to sum up the essence of our journey, its worries, its mixes, its promise.

Of course, nothing is complete in the rough sketches conveyed by fax and e-mail. I am left with the impression of a Brownian motion in them; we seem to have come across all sorts of memories and just as many spaces, in a state of emotion—rather than analysis—in gestation. We will continue, I'm sure of it, by other means, in other books, other activities. But you are right, let's let this complicity that has united us for a year come to rest at this point, after several years of parallel and friendly, somewhat distant, trajectories. This correspondence, in making each of us confront the resistance and limits of the other, has helped us to better meditate, in our own reflections or desires, on these continents we have not wanted to define, and that we have gradually allowed to take on form and meaning. The "feminine" and the "sacred." I would like readers to join us in the same frankness and questioning spirit that was proper to us, without affectation and without certainty. Therein lies the principal motivation that, in my view, justifies the publication of our letters. Publication appeared problematic to us at the beginning of this exchange, but the idea of it became clearer over the course of the year, and Monique Nemer's attentive reading finally persuaded us to undertake it.

The sacred is, of course, experienced in private; it even seemed to us to be what gives meaning to the most intimate of singularities, at the intersection of the body and thought, biology and memory, life and meaning—among men and women. Women, *perhaps,* stand at that intersection in a more dramatic, more symptomatic manner, in a more unknown manner in the future that is upon us. I say "perhaps," because there is always the surprise—and often even a happy surprise—of the "feminine" in men as well. A "private" sacred, therefore, since, as soon as it claims to become public, it totalizes and turns into totalitarian horror, as you say so well in your last letter, in a nod to the various "revolutions" and forms of fundamentalism. Nevertheless, it is in the sharing of it that the sacred unveils its risks as much as its vitality. And that men and women today are aspiring for new connections permeable to the sacred, as a continuation or a counterpoint to ancestral religions.

Our exchange has been a mere punctuation of that aspiration. We have been fussy, personal, rough, quick-tempered, incomplete, inexact as a result of abridgments and cursory glances. We tried to stick close to our particular truths and not mislead regarding our areas of ignorance or our choices. Perhaps the reader will hold on to the imperative for permanent questioning as the principal note of our approach to both the sacred and the feminine.

Julia

♦ ♦

ACT DULY NOTED. *Act* will therefore be the last word.

Catherine

Index

Abjection, 37–38, 91, 94

About Chinese Women (Kristeva), 170

Abraham, 98

Absence, 50–51

Adam, 96

Aditi, 54

Aesthetics, 78–79

Afghanistan, 131

Africa, 5–10, 18, 21, 157, 174

African American women, 11–12, 17, 19, 50

African myths, 51–52

Agave, 70–71

Agnes (analysand), 122, 135, 138, 140–42

Alchemical Taoist Treatise: The Pact of the Triple Equation, 169

Alexander VI, 45

Algeria, 165–66

Alone of All Her Sex: The Myth and the Cult of the Virgin Mary (Warner), 43

Althusser, Louis, 69

Amboception, 121–22

American culture, 137–38

André of Clairvaux, 63

Angela of Foligno, 35, 36–37, 52

Animal worship, 32–33

Animism, 6, 7

Anne, Saint, 61, 74

Anorexia, 23, 104, 105, 114–19, 124, 135, 139

Antigone, 53

Antony, Saint, 32

Aquinas, Thomas, 117

Arendt, Hannah, 13, 167

Aristotle, 78

Artaud, Antonin, 37

Arts, 62, 73, 78, 114, 120, 122, 158

Asceticism, 79, 108–10, 125

Ashes of Immortality (Weinberger-Thomas), 125

Athaliah, 99

Atharva-Veda, 93

Atheism, 24–26, 113, 165; female, 60, 64; mysticism and, 37, 154; *see also* Secularism

Attachment, 82

Augustine, Saint, 61–62, 89, 131

Baby blues, 158–59

Bacchantes, 70–71, 112

Bahia, 7, 19

Balzac, Honoré de, 19–20

Bardot, Brigitte, 32–33

Barthes, Roland, 13

Bataille, Georges, 24, 154

Bathsheba, 99–100

Baudelaire, Charles-Pierre, 16

Beauvoir, Simone de, 43, 60–61

Beginnings, 72–73

Being, 52–53, 56–57, 76–77, 173

Belief, 26, 37, 46

Bellière du Tronchay, Mlle. de, *see* Louisa of the Nothingness

Bellini, Giovanni, 77

Benincasa, Giacomo, 119

Bernard of Clairvaux, Saint, 37, 62–63, 74

Besterman, Theodore, 44

Bhakti, 174

Binary oppositions, 27, 58–59, 92–94

Binding, 7–8

Biography, 13–14

Bisexuality, 18, 21, 35, 50, 59; being and, 52–53; divinity and, 85–86; mysticism and, 30–32; other and, 57–58; psychic, 58, 63–64; as transitional space, 62; twinship, 51–52, 55; yin/yang, 169; *see also* Sexuality

Blanche of Castile, 79

Blondel, Marc, 149

Blood, 89, 91–92, 94–96, 96; separation and, 109–10

Boaz, 101–2

Body, 15, 36, 53; denial of, 123–26; hysteria and, 37–38; leaving/ flight, 132–33, 136–37, 161; love and, 104–5; as porous, 7, 9, 11, 14, 20

Bond, James, 72

Book of Visions, The (Angela of Foligno), 36–37

Borderlines, 129, 133; of language, 14–15; waste and, 92–94; woman as, 15–16

Boredom, 21–22

Borel, Adrian, 21

Bororo society, 156

Bossuet, Jacques-Bénigne, 138, 146, 147

Boutros-Ghali, Boutros, 176

Brahma, 89–90, 107

Brahmans, 86

Brazil, 7

Brazilian Indians, 111

Breast, 32–33, 62–63, 77, 88–89, 114, 118

Breton women, 8–9

Bucchini, Martine, 26

Buddhism, 55, 108, 125; Hinduism and, 68–69; nothingness and, 65, 67–68, 81; temples, 66–67; West and, 67–68

Bulgakov, Sergey, 74

Caelius Sedulius, 75

Calcutta, 19

Callas, Maria, 132, 136

Cambodia, 68

Cambridge, 42

candomblé, 7, 19

Carmelites, 34

Caste system, 7–9, 67, 89–90, 93–94, 107

Castration, 48, 99

Catherine of Siena, 117–19, 122, 126, 135, 145; imaginary and, 138–41

Catholicism, 7, 19, 24, 30, 64, 74, 141; *see also* Virgin Mary

Catholic World Youth Day, 163–65

Certeau, Michel de, 30

Chabrier, Emmanuel, 162

Chaos, 158–59

Child, 56–57, 60, 77–78

Chinese women, 167–71

Christ, 61–62, 105–6, 155

Christianity, 15; Catholicism, 7, 19, 24, 30, 74, 141, 163–65, 164; Eastern (Orthodox) Church, 61, 74, 77; Holy Trinity, 78, 106; Indian converts, 107; Protestantism, 19, 75, 131; *see also* Virgin Mary

Civilization and Its Discontents (Freud), 20

Clara (analysand), 24–25

Classification, 92

Class issues, 8–9, 50

Cleared-outs, 121–22

Clement of Alexandria, 61

Communication, 27, 28

Communism, 25–26, 47, 170

Communitarianism, 167

Community, 30, 60, 80, 108; Islam and, 30, 167; Virgin Mary and, 75–76, 80

Connections, 137, 140

Consciousness, 27, 35, 65–66

Contraception, 13

Cooking imagery, 108–13

Cosmologies, 88–90

Council of Mâcon, 63, 64

Counter-Reformation, 78

Countertransference, 114–15

Courtly love, 90, 104

Cows, sacred, 28, 63

Cow's Skull with Calico Roses (O'Keefe), 39, *41*

Creation, 50, 151–52, 158

Critique of Judgment (Kant), 30

Critique of Practical Reason (Kant), 121–22

Crucifixion, 88, 106

Dancing, 55; dervishes, 146–47, 160, 166; Indian dancing girls, 71, 86–88, 91, 95, 108–9; lightness, 160–61

Dante, 62, 136, 140, 144

Daughter, 24, 35, 37, 59, 77, 114–18

David, 102–3

Death, 47–49, 71, 119–20, 134; culture of, 81–82

Deborah, 99

Decency, 121–22

De l'angoisse à l'extase (Janet), 122–23

Dependence, 24–25

Depression, 59, 140, 142, 147; motherhood and, 59–60, 76, 115–16, 158–59; Princess Diana and, 171, 172, 174; *see also* Melancholia

Depths, 22–23, 140

Dervishes, 146–47, 160, 166

Descartes, 78

Desire, 38, 88

Detachment, 60, 67, 169–70

Deuteronomy, 97

Dialogue of Divine Providence (Catherine of Sienna), 117

Diana, Princess of Wales, 165, 171–72, 173, 174–75

Dictionnaire philosophique, 44

Diderot, Denis, 43

Diola of Casamance, 110

Dionysus, 70–71

Diop, Sheikh Anta, 157

Disbelief, 37, 46

Discontinuity, 47–48

Diversity, 167

Divine Comedy, The (Dante), 62

Divinity, 23–24, 30, 37, 85–86

Dogon myth, 51–52

Doing, 52, 56, 76–77

Dominicans, 131, 144

Dostoyevsky, Fyodor, 49

Double bind, 117

Douglas, Mary, 94

Duarte, Eva, 126

Duby, Georges, 90

Duns Scotus, 62, 74, 135

Duras, Marguerite, 83, 84

Durga, 127–28

Duty, 115–17, 138–40

East, 70–71, 131; *see also* India

Eastern (Orthodox) Church, 61, 74, 77

Eckehart, Meister, 72–73, 119, 164

Economy, 9–10, 135–36

Ecstasy, 31–32, 52, 55, 108, 129, 148, 151, 155

Egypt, 28, 157

Ehrenzweig, Anton, 158

Eleazar, Rabbi, 100

Elimelech, 101

Endogamy, 94

English academic ritual, 42–43, 46, 65, 69, 72

Epilepsy, 36, 156

Eroticism, 27, 56–57, 59, 81; motherhood and, 16, 56–57

Estates General, 90

Esther, 99

Ethiopians, 21

Ethnocentrism, 135

Eve, 61, 96

Evil, 95–96

Exodus, 97

Exogamy, 94

Extralinguistic figures, 78

Faith, 45, 47, 163, 164

Father, 70, 84–85, 116, 164; daughter and, 24–25, 35, 37; as omnipotent, 24, 85; sacrifice and, 106, 110

Feminine, 5, 73; being and, 52, 56–57; detachment, 60, 67; in male, 54, 62, 64, 178; Virgin Mary and, 75–76

Feminine principle, 51–54

Feminism, 75, 172

Ferry, Luc, 32

Fire, 108–9, 110

First Amendment, 145

Flame of the Sabbath, The, 110

Flaubert, Gustave, 32

Flight/leaving body, 132–33, 136–37, 161

Flowers of Evil, The (Baudelaire), 16

Forgiveness, 96, 167

France, 11, 22, 157–58, 163

Francis of Assisi, Saint, 78, 117

Freedom, 164–65

Freemasonry, 148–49

French culture, 138

French model, 167

French philosophers, 19

French Revolution, 2, 66, 90

Freud, Sigmund, 5, 21, 38, 73, 91, 164; *Civilization and Its Discontents,* 20; *On Female Sexuality,* 59; *The Future of an Illusion,* 26; meaning and, 151; motherhood, view of, 57; regression, view of, 154–55; religion, view of, 106; sublimation, view of, 122; on superego, 116

Fundamentalism, 19, 121, 156–57, 163, 165–66, 178

Future of an Illusion, The (Freud), 26

Fu Xian, 169

Gandhi, Indira, 54, 126–29, 144, 174

Gandhi, Rajiv, 128, 130

Gaze, 114

Generations, 70–71

Genesis, 64, 96, 98–100

Genetic code, 26, 58

Genies, 110

Gentileschi, Artemisia, 98–99

Giotto, 136, 144

Girl-Crazy-About-Honey, 111, 112

Globalization, 121

Goblins, 130

God, 23–24, 31–32, 85–86, 96, 152, 174

Gods/goddesses, 31, 50, 87, 92, 107, 110, 161–62

Goethe, Johann Wolfgang von, 137

Golden Fleece, 71

Goliath, 102

Gospels, 61, 74, 88

Great Schism, 119

Greeks, 44–45, 70–71

Green, André, 8

Gregory of Tours, 63

Gregory XIII, 34

Griaule, Marcel, 21

Guilt, 95–96, 114

Guizot, François-Pierre-Guillaume, 63, 64

Hair, 68, 91–92, 99, 100, 107; of dancing girls, 71, 86–88, 91, 95, 108–9

Hallaj, Sufi al-, 31–32, 50

Hallucinogens, 132, 133

"Hannah Arendt and the Concept of Life" (Kristeva), 12

Hasidism, 85, 134

Hathor, 28

Hatred, 129–30

Healers, 18, 20, 117, 130, 131

Hegel, G. W., 52–53, 60, 113, 165

Heidegger, Martin, 52, 56, 77, 134, 159, 164

Heroines, 28–29, 98–100

Hesychast monks, 77, 89

Hidden Order of Art, The (Ehrenzweig), 158

Hildegard of Bingen, 35–36

Hinduism: Buddhism and, 68–69; polytheism, 54, 62; sacred cows, 28, 63; separation and, 93–94; social system, 7–8; suttee, 124–25, 129; see also India

Historia Francorum (Gregory of Tours), 63

History of the sacred, 12–13, 91

Hitler, Adolf, 136, 144, 152

Hobson, Marian, 42–43

Holocaust, 68

Hombeline, 63

Homosexuality, 44–45, 52, 55, 77

Hroswitha of Gandersheim, 61

Humanism, 32

Humility, 26, 29, 33–34, 48

Husserl, Edmund, 16

Hysteria, 5–10, 11, 12, 37–38, 174–75; acrobatics, 8–9

Id, 27, 28, 32, 60, 71, 151, 153, 173; mother and, 50–51

Idealization, 24–26

Ignatius of Loyola, 88

Illusions, 38

Imaginary, 116–17, 137–41

Impermanence, 65

Impressions of Africa (Roussel), 21

Inaction, 168, 170

Incest, 45, 97, 98, 117

Incompleteness, 26–27

India, 28–31, 49–50, 159; bisexuality and, 30–31, 50; caste system, 7–9, 67, 89–90, 93–94, 107; cosmology, 89–90, 92–93; fatherhood, 84;

lunar system, 53–54; middle
class, 50; Mother Teresa and,
173–74; sacred dancing girls,
71, 86–88, 91, 95, 108–9; yoga,
145–46; *see also* Hinduism
Indifference, 66–68, 81
Individual, 66, 95, 103
Infanticide, 70–71, 77, 83
Inquisition, 130–31, 144
Intellectuals, 37, 47, 176
Interior Castle (Saint Teresa), 34
Intermediary role, 73–74, 77,
102–3
Iran, 131
Irony, 60, 64, 108
Isaac, 98
Islam, 6, 17, 30, 50, 54, 67, 88,
107, 165–67
Israel-Palestine conference, 150

Jacob, 85
Jacopone da Todi, 62
Jael, 99
Janet, Pierre, 122–23
Jason, 71
Jealousy, 83, 84
Jesuits, 62, 78
Jews, 68, 69, 75, 133–34, 144
Jezebel, 99
Joachim, Saint, 61, 74
Joan of Arc, 28–29
Job, 95
John 2:4, 64
John Chrysostom, Saint, 61
John of the Cross, Saint, 34
Jouissance, 15, 23–24, 38, 120,
169
Judaism, 15, 68, 80, 91, 98, 104;
monotheism, 54–55, 88
Judith, 28, 98–99

Judith and Holofernes (Artemisia
Gentileschi), 98–99
Juliana, Saint, 47, 48
Juliana of Lazarevskoy, 74

Kabala, 98
Kakar, Sudhir, 38
Kali, 31, 110
Kant, Immanuel, 30, 121–22, 155,
162, 164
Kant with Sade (Lacan), 121–22
Khatami, 131
Khmer Rouge, 68
Kierkegaard, Soren, 155, 160
Klein, Melanie, 76
Koran, 54, 55, 86, 88, 107, 166
Krishna, 174

Laban, 98
La Bruyère, Jean de, 138
Lacan, Jacques, 29, 88, 121–22,
123, 133, 151, 159
Language, 95, 135–36, 138;
borderlines of, 14–15; of
negotiation, 149–50;
nothingness of, 35–37
Lares, 130
Leah, 85, 98
Lébou women, 18–19
Leibnitz, Gottfried Wilhelm, 66
Leiris, Michel, 21
Lévi-Strauss, Claude, 31, 65–68,
87; "The Apotheosis of
Augustus," 32; *Mythologiques*,
108, 111, 156, 161–62; *Tristes
Tropiques*, 66–68
Leviticus, 88, 89, 95–97, 133
Libération (Duras), 83
Life, 12–14, 81–82
Lightness, 160–61

Liu Shao, 169

Logic, 35, 156, 163

Louisa of the Nothingness, 37, 50

Love, 44, 57, 82, 91, 94, 103–5, 135, 143, 164; courtly love, 90, 104; denial of body and, 123–26; as lethal, 123–24; social and, 126–29

Lunar system, 53–54

Lunyu (Confucian Analects), 168

Macumba, 19

Madeleine (analysand), 122–23

Madonna, 136, 144

Madwoman and the Saint, The (Clément), 38

Maids, 9–10

Malibran, Maria, 148

Malleus Maleficarum (Institoris and Sprenger), 130–31, 132

Management, 13

Manhood (Borel), 21

Mannassi, 99

Marabouts, 17

Marianne, 157

Marianne (analysand), 23–24

Marriage, 64, 76, 94, 108

Marx, Karl, 8

Mary, *see* Virgin Mary

Mary Magdalene, 22

Masculine principle, 51–54, 62, 64

Masochism, *see* Sadomasochism

Meaning, 13, 59, 84, 151–54

Medea, 70, 71, 83

Meditation, 108, 139

Meir, Rabbi, 100

Mejnûn and Laylà, 124

Melancholia, 12, 14, 77, 147, 172; *see also* Depression

Mélenchon, Jean-Luc, 158

Memory, 69–70, 71, 81, 151, 167; regression and, 154–55

Menses, 53, 95, 97; *see also* Blood

Michelet, Jules, 130

Minoan-Mycenaean civilization, 59, 60

Minority status, 10, 174

Miriam, 85

Mirror image, 166

Mitterand, François, 173

Monotheism, 54–55, 62, 74, 89, 91, 107, 167–68

Montesquieu, 44, 167

Monteverdi, Claudio, 62

Moses, 85

Moses and Monotheism (Freud), 106

Motherhood, 64–65; animal worship and, 32–33; baby blues and, 158–59; being and, 56–57, 76–77; coexcitation, 76–77; dependence and, 24–25; depression and, 22, 58–60, 76, 115–16, 158–59; as destiny, 13; eroticism and, 16, 56–57; as good, 28; id and, 50–51; idealization of, 24–26; infanticide, 70, 71, 83; male child and, 77–78; potential and, 50–51; as sacred, 137, 145; separation and, 116; as vocation, 102; waste and, 95; *see also* Virgin Mary

Mourning, 12

Muhammad, 155

Music, 19, 131–33, 136, 148; myths of origin, 161–62; Virgin Mary and, 62, 78; weightlessness and, 159–61

Mysteries, 38–39

Mysticism, 98, 112, 166; atheistic, 37, 154; bisexuality and, 30–32

Myth, 51–52, 87–88, 156, 161–62

Mythologiques (Lévi-Strauss), 108, 111, 156, 161–62

Naomi, 101, 102

Narcissism, 26, 29, 57, 76–79

N'Doeup ceremony, 18–19, 20, 21, 30, 110

Needham, Joseph, 42, 169

Negotiation, 52, 149–50

Neither-nor, 65, 66, 68

Nemer, Monique, 178

Nesting ritual, 84

Nietzsche, Friedrich, 155, 160

Nobility, 88–90

Nostalgia, 142, 162

Notat, Nicole, 149

Nothingness, 35–38, 39, 48–50, 119; Buddhism and, 65, 67–68, 81

Object, 50–51, 56–57, 156

Oedipus complex, 24, 59, 87

Oedipus myth, 87–88

O'Keefe, Georgia, 38–39, *40, 41*

Omnipotence, 24–26, 82, 85

On Female Sexuality (Freud), 59

Opera, 132, 143, 148, 160

Opisthotonos, 8–9

Orality, 118–19

Order, 112–13, 114, 158

Origen, 61

Origins, 154–58, 163; of music, 161–62

Orpah, 101, 102

Orpheus, 161

Other, 56–58, 60, 116, 163

Oyster women, 14

Paganism, 74, 86, 97, 130–32

Papin sisters, 10

Paris, 154

Parity, 27, 33, 39, 55, 64

Parmenides, 92

Parthenos, 72

Parvati, 87

Pascal, Blaise, 155

Pelléas et Mélisande (Maeterlinck), 88

Perfume, 16, 20, 22

Peron, Eva, 126–30, 132, 133, 136, 143–44, 173

Peron, Juan Domingo, 143–44

Perpendicular (plumb line), 139–41, 148, 149, 159–60, 175

Peter of Alacantra, Saint, 34

Phallus, 58–59, 61, 110

Phenomenology of Spirit, The (Hegel), 53

Philosophy in the Boudoir (Sade), 121–22

Piacenti, Lapa, 117–19

Pico della Mirandola, 45

Piero della Francesca, Giovanni, 61, 79

Pius XII, 75

Plato, 131, 132, 155

Plumb line (perpendicular), 139–41, 148, 149, 159–60, 175

Plutarch, 44–45

Political correctness, 12

Politics, 136, 143, 170

Pollution, 92–93

Polygamy, 17

Polytheism, 54, 62, 97, 109

Popes, 34, 45, 77, 119

Porousness, 7, 9, 11, 14, 20

Possession, 21, 22

Possessions (Kristeva), 22

Powers of Horror: An Essay on Abjection (Kristeva), 91

Pride, 29, 49

Priestesses, 110

Priests, 64

Primitive thought, 66

Private sphere, 129, 176, 178

Prohibitions, 15–16, 91–94, 135, 143, 152–53; alimentary, 95–97

Protestantism, 19, 75, 131

Proust, Marcel, 22, 35, 49

Providence, 137–38, 145

Psychoanalysis, 27, 38, 116, 135, 164; depths and, 22–23; French view of, 138; secrecy in, 142

Punishment, 118

Queens, 99–100

Rabelais, François, 138

Rabhia, 55

Rachel, 54, 85

Racine, Jean, 99

Racism, 157

Ram, 109

Ramadan, 54

Ramakrishna, 31, 32

Rationality, 78

Raymond of Capua, 117, 138–39, 145

Reason, 121–22, 154

Rebekah, 98

Rectitude, 140–41

Regression, 133, 151, 154–55

Religion, 26–27, 106–7, 136; impoverished, 115, 145; mother and, 24–25; as organization of worship, 30, 145; origins and, 155–57; sacred as predating,

29–30; sects, 30, 45–46, 106, 145, 152; United States, 136–37

Remembrance of Things Past (Proust), 22

Representation, 15–16, 34–35, 78, 152, 157

Reproduction, 13

Republic, The (Plato), 131, 132

Republicanism, 145, 157–58

Resistance, 53, 55, 174–75

Returns, 50, 154, 158, 163

Revelation, 155–56

Revolution, 175–76, 178

Rights of man, 65–66

Rigidity, 116, 148

Rimbaud, Arthur, 72, 73

Rite of Spring, The (Stravinsky), 162

Rites, 19, 69–70, 102, 129, 152; ceremonial, 42–44; depression as, 147; English academic ritual, 42–43, 46, 65, 69, 72; initiation, 32, 84, 125–26, 148–49, 154; nesting ritual, 84; origins and, 155–57; waste and, 91–93

Rodinson, Maxine, 167

Romans, 156

Roof image, 27, 28, 30, 36, 39

Roussel, Raymond, 21

Roy, Rajah Man Mohan, 174

Rublyov, Andrey, 73

Rumi, 166

Ruth the Moabite, 100–103

Sabbath, 133–34

Sacred: as backward, 132–33; incompleteness and, 26–27; life as, 12–14; motherhood as, 137, 145; as predating religion,

29–30; rejection of, 152–53; as sexual, 20; territory of, 121–23

Sacrifice, 15–16, 20, 21, 106, 110, 135, 143, 152, 162

Sade, Marquis de, 15, 121–22, 123

Sadomasochism, 15, 23, 26, 29

Sainte-Anne Hospital, 8–9

Saints, 30, 50, 74

Salic law, 79

Sama brotherhoods, 166

Sang Chul Lee, 177

Saporta, Karine, 160

Sarai/Sarah, 98

Sartre, Jean-Paul, 153

Scheherazade, 168

Science and the Civilisation of China (Needham), 169

Screen memory, 154–55

Secrecy, 140–42, 148–50, 151

Secretions, 20, 28, 55, 111; *see also* Blood; Waste

Sects, 30, 45–46, 106, 145, 152

Secularism, 60, 136; *see also* Atheism

Sefirot, 98

Self-assurance, 11–12, 15–16, 50

Sémiotikè (Kristeva), 69

Senegalese women, 5–10, 11, 16, 17–18

Separation, 106, 116; from God, 85–86, 96, 152; Hindu system, 93–94; of sexes, 31, 85–86, 91; waste and, 92–93

Serer women, 7, 8, 9–10

Series I, No. 1 (O'Keefe), 39, 40

Sexuality, 20, 132, 137–38, 169; boredom and, 21–22; homosexuality, 44–45, 52, 55, 77; repression of in Virgin

Mary, 61, 72, 73, 76, 78; *see also* Bisexuality

Shabbat, 110

Shabbetai Tzevi, 100

Shakti, 54

Shechinah, 54–55, 85

Shiva, 31, 50, 87, 107, 110, 161–62

Signification, 151

Signifier, 137, 151–52, 159

Sikhism, 107–8

Sin, 95–96

Sisera, 99

Slavery, 7, 19

Social, 60; love and, 126–29

Socrates, 92

Sollers, Philippe, 71, 78, 148, 158

Solomon, 83, 90, 103

Solovyov, Vladimir, 74

Song of Songs, 62–63, 81, 98, 103–5

Sophia, cult of, 74

Soul, 34–35, 63–64, 137

Spectacle, 27, 172

Spencer, Diana. *See* Diana, Princess of Wales

Spirit of Laws (Montesquieu), 44

Spouses, divine, 54

Stoicism, 66

Strangeness, 26, 59–60, 64, 100, 139, 154

Stranger to Ourselves (Kristeva), 102

Stravinsky, Igor, 162

Sublime, 30, 35, 122, 155

Suffering, 23, 65, 72–74, 77

Sufis, 55, 85, 146–47

Suicide, 159

Superego, 116, 139

Supernatural, 113

Susanna, 99

EUROPEAN PERSPECTIVES
Series in Social Thought and Cultural Criticism
Lawrence D. Kritzman, Editor

Julia Kristeva — *Strangers to Ourselves*

Theodor W. Adorno — *Notes to Literature*, vols. 1 and 2

Richard Wolin, editor — *The Heidegger Controversy*

Antonio Gramsci — *Prison Notebooks*, vols. 1 and 2

Jacques LeGoff — *History and Memory*

Alain Finkielkraut — *Remembering in Vain: The Klaus Barbie Trial and Crimes Against Humanity*

Julia Kristeva — *Nations Without Nationalism*

Pierre Bourdieu — *The Field of Cultural Production*

Pierre Vidal-Naquet — *Assassins of Memory: Essays on the Denial of the Holocaust*

Hugo Ball — *Critique of the German Intelligentsia*

Gilles Deleuze and Félix Guattari — *What Is Philosophy?*

Karl Heinz Bohrer — *Suddenness: On the Moment of Aesthetic Appearance*

Julia Kristeva — *Time and Sense*

Alain Finkielkraut — *The Defeat of the Mind*

Julia Kristeva — *New Maladies of the Soul*

Elisabeth Badinter — *XY: On Masculine Identity*

Karl Löwith — *Martin Heidegger and European Nihilism*

Gilles Deleuze — *Negotiations, 1972–1990*

Pierre Vidal-Naquet — *The Jews: History, Memory, and the Present*

Norbert Elias — *The Germans*

Louis Althusser — *Writings on Psychoanalysis: Freud and Lacan*

Elisabeth Roudinesco — *Jacques Lacan: His Life and Work*

Ross Guberman — *Julia Kristeva Interviews*

Kelly Oliver — *The Portable Kristeva*

Pierra Nora — *Realms of Memory: The Construction of the French Past*, vol. 1: *Conflicts and Divisions*, vol. 2: *Traditions*, vol. 3: *Symbols*

Claudine Fabre-Vassas — *The Singular Beast: Jews, Christians, and the Pig*

Paul Ricoeur   *Critique and Conviction: Conversations with*
                François Azouvi and Marc de Launay

Theodor W. Adorno   *Critical Models: Interventions and Catchwords*

Alain Corbin   *Village Bells: Sound and Meaning in the*
                Nineteenth-Century French Countryside

Zygmunt Bauman   *Globalization: The Human Consequences*

Jean-Louis Flandrin   *Food: A Culinary History*
& Massimo Montanari

Alain Finkielkraut   *In the Name of Humanity: Reflections on the*
                      Twentieth Century

Julia Kristeva   *The Sense and Non-Sense of Revolt: The Powers*
                  and Limits of Psychoanalysis

Régis Debray   *Transmitting Culture*

Sylviane Agacinski   *The Politics of the Sexes*